French Encounters wit Ottomans, 1510–1560

Focusing on early Renaissance Franco-Ottoman relations, this book fills a gap in studies of Ottoman representations by early modern European powers by addressing the Franco-Ottoman bond. In *French Encounters with the Ottomans*, Pascale Barthe examines the birth of the Franco-Ottoman rapprochement and the enthusiasm with which, before the age of absolutism, French kings and their subjects pursued exchanges – real or imagined – with those they referred to as the 'Turks.' Barthe calls into question the existence of an Orientalist discourse in the Renaissance, and examines early cross-cultural relations through the lenses of sixteenth-century French literary and cultural production.

Informed by insights from historians, literary scholars, and art historians from around the world, this study underscores and challenges long-standing dichotomies (Christians vs. Muslims, West vs. East) as well as reductive periodizations (Middle Ages vs. Renaissance) and compartmentalization of disciplines. Grounded in close readings, it includes discussions of cultural production, specifically visual representations of space and customs. Barthe showcases diplomatic envoys, courtly poets, 'bourgeois,' prominent fiction writers, and chroniclers, who all engaged eagerly with the 'Turks' and developed a multiplicity of responses to the Ottomans before the latter became both fashionable and neutralized, and their representation fixed.

Pascale Barthe is Associate Professor of French at the University of North Carolina Wilmington, USA. She received her Ph.D in French Language and Literature from the University of Virginia. Her areas of research focus on early modern France, Orientalism, and the Mediterranean world.

Transculturalisms, 1400–1700

Series Editors:
Mihoko Suzuki, University of Miami, USA,
Ann Rosalind Jones, Smith College, USA, and
Jyotsna Singh, Michigan State University, USA

This series presents studies of the early modern contacts and exchanges among the states, polities and entrepreneurial organizations of Europe; Asia, including the Levant and East India/Indies; Africa; and the Americas. Books will investigate travelers, merchants and cultural inventors, including explorers, mapmakers, artists and writers, as they operated in political, mercantile, sexual and linguistic economies. We encourage authors to reflect on their own methodologies in relation to issues and theories relevant to the study of transculturism/translation and transnationalism. We are particularly interested in work on and from the perspective of the Asians, Africans, and Americans involved in these interactions, and on such topics as:

- Material exchanges, including textiles, paper and printing, and technologies of knowledge
- Movements of bodies: embassies, voyagers, piracy, enslavement
- Travel writing: its purposes, practices, forms and effects on writing in other genres
- Belief systems: religions, philosophies, sciences
- Translations: verbal, artistic, philosophical
- Forms of transnational violence and its representations.

Also in this series:

Early Modern Exchanges
Dialogues Between Nations and Cultures, 1550–1750
Edited by Helen Hackett

The Chinese Impact upon English Renaissance Literature
A Globalization and Liberal Cosmopolitan Approach to Donne and Milton
Mingjun Lu

***Commedia dell' Arte* and the Mediterranean**
Charting Journeys and Mapping 'Others'
Erith Jaffe-Berg

Early Modern Catholics, Royalists, and Cosmopolitans
English Transnationalism and the Christian Commonwealth
Brian C. Lockey

French Encounters with the Ottomans, 1510–1560

Pascale Barthe

Routledge
Taylor & Francis Group

LONDON AND NEW YORK

First published 2016 by Routledge

2 Park Square, Milton Park, Abingdon, Oxfordshire OX14 4RN
52 Vanderbilt Avenue, New York, NY 10017

Routledge is an imprint of the Taylor & Francis Group, an informa business

First issued in paperback 2018

British Library Cataloguing in Publication Data
A catalogue record for this book is available from the British Library

Library of Congress Cataloging-in-Publication Data
Names: Barthe, Pascale, author.
Title: French encounters with the Ottomans, 1510–1560 / by Pascale Barthe.
Description: Burlington, VT: Ashgate, 2016. | Series: Transculturalisms,
    1400–1700 | Includes bibliographical references and index.
Identifiers: LCCN 2015039196 | ISBN 9781472420428 (hardcover: alk. paper) |
    ISBN 9781472420435 (ebook) | ISBN 9781472420442 (epub)
Subjects: LCSH: French literature–16th century–History and criticism. |
    Turks in literature. | Literature and history–France–History–16th century. |
    Literature and transnationalism–France. | Turks–France. | French–Turkey.
Classification: LCC PQ239 .B36 2016 | DDC 840.9/003—dc23
LC record available at http://lccn.loc.gov/2015039196

ISBN: 978-1-4724-2042-8 (hbk)
ISBN: 978-0-367-17578-8 (pbk)

Typeset in Times New Roman
by Apex CoVantage, LLC

To my home birds, all very well-traveled—hoopoe, red sparrow, bird of paradise

Contents

Illustrations

Acknowledgements

This book owes a great deal to scholars and friends. Some critiqued early drafts while others helped polish the argument. Much inspiration came from specialists in other disciplines and from individuals who are not academics, but who exercise their right to think and to express themselves freely and daringly. Their individual and professional determination and accomplishments, their perspicacious analyses, their curiosity and depth, and their lightness of being were highly invigorating at vital junctures of this project.

I am especially thankful to Mary McKinley, a most generous mentor and model. The group of *seiziémistes* she trained at the University of Virginia and the scholars who gravitate around her are a constant source of knowledge, support, and good humor. To name a few, in no particular order: Hope Glidden, George Hoffmann, Jeff Persels, Kendall Tarte, and Marcus Keller. Scott Juall and Olga Trokhimenko, my *sarcelles* colleagues at the University of North Carolina Wilmington, provided intellectual stimulation, encouragement, and laughs. Further away geographically but always present and constant in her friendship as in her feedback, Cara Welch has been instrumental to this project. So has Winnie Chan, for a brutal push and sudden vanishing that proved determining to the completion of this work.

I am grateful for the Cahill award and the research semester the University of North Carolina Wilmington granted me to work on this project, as well as the extraordinary opportunities for thought-provoking discussions offered by a Folger Seminar led by Palmira Brummett on "Constantinople/Istanbul: Destination, Way-Station, City of Renegades" and a National Endowment for the Humanities Institute on "Empires and Interactions" co-directed by Charles Parker and Ahmet Karamustafa. My gratitude goes to the Special Collections staff at the University of Virginia and to those working at the Archives Départementales du Tarn and at the Médiathèque Pierre-Amalric d'Albi. Last but not least, Monsieur Charles-Henri de Noblet d'Anglure opened his doors to me unconditionally; without his generosity, an important part of this project would have never been possible.

Both my immediate and extended families, located on two continents, have been unknowingly crucial to the fruition of this project: the Barthes in Europe, especially my parents Jean-Simon and Yvette, my grand-parents François and

Lucie, Jacques and Mireille, Françoise, and Jean-Marie, the patriarch; and the Sukheras in Asia, in particular Rabiah, Rani, Sadia, Fozail, ammiji, and abbuji, whose premature passing could not rob us of his presence. For their inquisitiveness, their unconditional support, their wit, and the peace they afforded me at important times, I am forever indebted.

Introduction

The French Are All Ottomans

Ils voyagèrent des années par monts, vallées, déserts et plaines. Leur vie s'en fut à cheminer. Comment conter leurs aventures ? Je n'ai pas la plume qu'il faut! Fais donc le voyage, lecteur, et tu découvriras toi-même les tours et détours du chemin. Tu sauras tout de ces oiseaux, de leurs peines, de leur courage.

They travelled on for years; a lifetime passed
Before the longed-for goal was reached at last.
What happened as they flew I cannot say,
But if you journey on that narrow Way,
Then you will act as they once did and know
The miseries they had to undergo.
———Farid-ud-Din' Attar, *La conférence des oiseaux*[1]

Like the birds in Farid-ud-Din' Attar's allegory, sixteenth-century Frenchmen embarked on a long and strenuous journey when they chose to comment on their neighbors, the Ottomans. Notwithstanding the difficulty, the Islamic East attracted many more souls than the Atlantic lure, and scriptorial journeys often complemented a physical voyage which not only took explorers across vast territories and seas, but also followed well-travelled literary and geographical paths in and around the Mediterranean and the Levant. These explorations gave the French plenty of opportunities for religious, commercial, artistic, and political discovery. The result of pragmatism, chance, curiosity, and renewed experiences, these rich and complex encounters are a window into early modern *mentalités*. This book captures the long moment of the alliance between Francis I and Sultan Süleyman. It tells the story of Frenchmen who, from the 1510s to the 1560s, dared to bring the Ottomans to the forefront of the French literary scene, as well as the political and religious scenes. More specifically, it uncovers how chroniclers, poets, and diplomats expressed their hesitation, fears, and excitement while discussing the possibility and, from the mid-1530s, the reality of a Franco-Ottoman alliance. This book thus interrogates the birth of the Franco-Ottoman rapprochement and the enthusiasm with which, before the age of absolutism, French kings and their subjects pursued exchanges—real or imagined—with those they referred to as the 'Turks'.[2] Diplomatic envoys, courtly poets, "bourgeois," prominent fiction writers, and kings all engaged eagerly with the Ottomans. Their reasons for doing so were many, and their aim was rarely to discover any mystical truth as it was for Attar's feathery companions. Sometimes, early modern Frenchmen were fulfilling their responsibilities and dutifully reporting back their discoveries to their patrons, relying on literary traditions and ideologies. On other occasions, they borrowed liberally from fellow traveler-scholars taking part in the humanist transformation by adopting earlier texts while adding personal or anecdotal evidence and sometimes ethnographic analysis. Often, by observing and questioning the Ottomans, they attempted to respond to particular challenges at home—personal or collective—and to shape their own society. In all cases, the French embarked on rich and at times complicated cross-cultural interactions.

In their writings, early sixteenth-century Frenchmen reacted passionately and sometimes paradoxically to their eastern neighbours. Before encountering themselves in the mirror of the Americas, then, the French first met with foils closer to home: the Ottomans.[3] This encounter happened at a time of profound changes. Not only was a new continent discovered, but old ones were further explored geographically as well as intellectually with the rediscovery of ancient texts. In addition, the first half of the sixteenth century witnessed an unprecedented level of religious contestation in the form of Shia Islam in Safavid Persia and Protestantism in Western Europe. Advances in the "sciences" and technology—such as printing, botany, surgery, astronomy, and weaponry—were backed by an accelerated flow of goods, slaves, as well as diseases. Europe's population grew as empire-building in Habsburg Spain as well as in Ottoman, Safavid, and Mughal lands led to a centralization of state bureaucracy across Eurasia. Last but not least, a new individual emerged as a communal age was gradually replaced by new forms of polities such as the absolutist state and, centuries later, its heir, the modern nation-state.[4] These changes were received by some with eagerness and by others with alarm. In France, they were seen mainly through the prism of the Ottomans who provided the French with a significant amount of original material and, perhaps more importantly, a time for pause and reflection. Franco-Ottoman "creative encounters" and their "generating properties"[5] thus deserve to be examined because they tell us about how the French viewed themselves and other "nations," what they were aspiring to be in the early modern era and why, who they eventually became, and perhaps even something about who they are today. The texts that resulted from these encounters demonstrate that no religious or political group lived in isolation in the early modern period and that the sixteenth century in particular was characterized by close inter-religious contacts around the Mediterranean. If only because these encounters call for an unwavering dose of curiosity, a time for reflection, a diversity of opinions, and the (power and) enjoyment of a good story, they are worth paying attention to.

The 'Turks,' of course, did not arrive on the French scene in a vacuum. The 'Saracens' and the 'Moors' are historical and literary predecessors in both French territory and imagination. As loosely defined as the 'Turks,' the 'Moors' recall today's 'Arabs,' another all-encompassing and unsatisfactory label to designate (pejoratively) all those in France—immigrants and French citizens alike— who are identified as sharing a North-African heritage perceived (wrongfully) as solely Islamic. Although not the biological inheritors of the 'Turks,' these 'Arabs' regularly bear the brunt of discrimination in modern France and are easy, regular, and undifferentiated targets for current right-wing and extreme-right-wing political parties. In all historical periods, the challenges and contributions of Muslims to French culture have been complex and varied. Critics—and the media—have long focused on challenges. Recently, however, some have underscored the positive impact of Muslims and Orientals in France.[6] This study pursues this long-awaited turn and reveals that early sixteenth-century France's responses to the Ottomans were exceptionally diverse; they denoted much wider possibilities for questioning, interpreting, and playing than what is too often offered today in our post-colonial era, dominated as we are by a monolithic filter deriving from the acceleration of time and the exponential growth of information.[7] Indeed, for a short moment during the sixteenth century, the French were all Ottomans.[8]

This claim could appear bold, especially since the popular as well as the scholarly collective imagination continues to portray the Franco-Ottoman alliance as a marriage *contre-nature*. Certainly, a prejudiced attitude toward the 'Turks' was present since the first days of Franco-Ottoman relations in the late fifteenth and early sixteenth centuries. Moreover, the idea of a despotic Orient was undoubtedly in place in France by the second half of the sixteenth century, long before Montesquieu, as it was in Venice.[9] In France, the tyrannical 'Turk' was slow to emerge but was definitely sealed by the publication in 1575 of a polemical pamphlet that vehemently expressed the perceived denaturation of Catholic France into 'Turquie'.[10] Before the ossification of the Franco-Ottoman couple, however, alternative representations of the 'Turks' were available in France. This study details some of them. The following chapters present a canonical text of the period—François Rabelais' *Pantagruel* (1532)—alongside lesser-known authors and writings that warrant being brought to light not only in the context of sixteenth-century Orientalism but also more generally. Covering a variety of genres, these texts unveil reactions of the elite to the Ottoman *Other* without ignoring the impact of courtly culture on commoners. This book looks into works of fiction as well as historiographical documents and artistic production in order to grasp the breadth and multiplicity of French responses while attempting to distinguish between official and less formal or conventional reactions towards Ottomans and Islam. In brief, it recreates crossed and connected histories[11] that show that, between 1510 and 1560, there was first an opening and then a closing of the French mind towards the Ottomans.[12] That a plurality of (sometimes dissonant) voices is audible in French documents of the period—up to the 1530s at least—is hardly surprising. As France itself, befriending the Ottomans, moved from crusade to absolutism, nation-state, and empire, a common culture was shared in Eurasia and across the Mediterranean world, despite the deep religious and political changes occurring at the time.

In his magisterial *La Méditerranée et le monde méditerranéen à l'époque de Philippe II*, Fernand Braudel was the first to note similarities between early modern Mediterranean and Eurasian societies.[13] More recently, Andrew Walters and Mehmet Kalpaklı have shown the affinities between Ottoman and European literary traditions in *The Age of Beloveds*, while Molly Greene has established economic and cultural ties in *A Shared World* and Sanjay Subrahmanyam has convincingly argued for a shared courtly culture in Eurasia.[14] Moreover, ideas of universalism and millenarism were common to both sides.[15] In other words, without falling into the trap of collapsing two societies which were, in many ways, very different indeed, we can safely argue that, for French authors of the early sixteenth century, there was enough continuity between the large Islamic and Christian Mediterranean worlds to make compromises and negotiations possible.[16] Whether economically oriented or politically motivated, exchanges going beyond or bypassing religion were taking place. The crusade, while remaining a theoretical option, did not preclude interactions and formal agreements such as Capitulations,[17] making the period studied in this book particularly rich in unexpected combinations between France and the Ottoman Empire.

A Brief History of Criticism on the Franco-Ottoman Bond

Relations between the early modern Ottoman Empire and Venice have been the subject of recent important studies that have highlighted communities of expatriates, the exchange of commodities, and artistic collaborations between the Sublime Porte and the Serenissime.[18] Similarly, Nabil Matar has studied early modern Britain's views of Islam.[19] The Franco-Ottoman bond, though, has not yet received the full attention it deserves. In the nineteenth and early twentieth century, scholars, and particularly historians, began to examine the Ottomans in France; leading Orientalists include Victor-Louis Bourrilly, J. Ursu, and Ernest Charrière.[20] Clarence Rouillard was the first to focus on representations of the Ottomans.[21] His work remains an excellent source of bibliographical, literary, and historical references. After a hiatus of several decades, scholars took on the 'Turks' again in the late twentieth century. In their studies, they responded, directly or indirectly, to Edward Said's theory of Orientalism, according to which the East, as it was depicted by nineteenth-century French and British travelers and scholars, was a creation aimed at justifying France and Britain's colonial enterprises in Africa and Asia, most particularly in the Islamic world.[22] This representation of the East was based on hegemony and power relations and fed into notions of cultural supremacy. In short, French and British scholars, themselves subjects of their nations, helped to subjugate foreign Muslims. Following Said's approach, Michèle Longino demonstrates that colonial France was already at work in the seventeenth century. In *Orientalism in French Classical Drama*, she shows that the 'Turks' became extremely popular theatrical figures under Louis XIV as they were generously used as devices to assert the French king's superiority over other peoples and to support his attempts at dominating the world, both economically and culturally.[23] Nicholas Dew complements Longino's analysis in *Orientalism in Louis XIV's France* by focusing on the scholars of the Republic of Letters.[24] Read in conjunction, the work of these critics demonstrates that canonical authors such as Corneille, Racine, and Molière depict the 'Turks' as easily tamed while Barthélemy d'Herbelot's and Melchisédech Thévenot's engagement with eastern cultures shows a form of proto-orientalism that Dew calls "baroque Orientalism."[25]

In *L'écriture du Levant à la Renaissance*, Frédéric Tinguely is the first to study an earlier timeframe, part of the one chosen for this study.[26] Focusing on French scholars who gravitated around Ambassador Gabriel d'Aramon in Constantinople between 1547 and 1553, the scholar argues that the sixteenth-century discourse about the Orient is constructed on and oscillates between *imitatio* and *mimesis*. The texts Tinguely analyzes so beautifully are the products of humanists who traveled to or through Constantinople, where they benefited from d'Aramon's hospitality and largesse. These travelogues are representative of the ethnographic turn in fifteenth- and sixteenth-century writings about the 'Turks.'[27] In the present book, I broaden the historical period, the genres studied, and the theoretical scope in order to create a resonating chamber that allows us to better grasp French discourses of the Orient at a time of profound change.[28]

Why take such a step? Longino and Dew argue in favor of proto-Orientalism in the seventeenth century, while Tinguely alludes to it more indirectly. Two important conclusions transpiring from these studies need to be addressed. The first is that in the seventeenth century and perhaps even 100 years earlier—in other words, long before the nineteenth century's colonial empires—there was one dominant discourse about the Orient. The second is the idea that East and West are resolutely and fundamentally dissimilar and thereby competing with one another, the West having the upper hand, politically, economically, and culturally. Pertinent as they are, these analyses give a somewhat unidimensional perspective on East-West relations in the early modern period, hinting at an early stage of imbalance and conflict that might result in a clash of civilizations.[29] In this book I propose an alternative in which literary criticism meets history; I suggest that when fiction meets historiography the realm of possibilities remains wide open.

Recent publications by historians on both sides of the Atlantic have begun to rectify a certain *oubli* that has characterized the Franco-Ottoman alliance and the oversimplification attached to it. Édith Garnier gives what she calls the impious alliance a serious and factual look, whereas Christine Isom-Verhaaren draws from Ottoman sources to fill the historiographic void regarding this important moment in international relations and to reassess preconceived notions stemming from modern predicaments.[30] Both works shed important light on Francis I's alliance with the Ottomans and offer a more nuanced and accurate picture of the complex reasons behind the relationship. This book seeks to continue the trajectory proposed by these two scholars, while providing additional historical examples infused with more literary and artistic illustrations of the encounter. Simply put, military conflicts meet literary fantasies in this cross-generic tale of encounters.

This study, therefore, merges early and recent discussions by historians and literary critics and offers a more capacious look by way of a cross-disciplinary analysis. It takes on the idea of Orientalism first defined by Edward Said and later explicitly or implicitly examined by scholars like Longino, Dew, and Tinguely, and the subsequent responses by historians Garnier and Isom-Verhaaren; it also looks at an assortment of French discourses on the Orient between 1510 and 1560. The following questions resonate throughout this book. Was there one dominant discourse about the Islamic East and particularly the Ottomans in the sixteenth century? Can one talk about a Renaissance or humanist Orientalism? Were East and West perceived as radically different? If so, in what ways? Were cross-cultural exchanges desirable and possible nevertheless? To what extent? How transformative were these interactions? What was an Ottoman for a Frenchman of the Renaissance? Was the Ottoman Empire geographically circumscribable? To what ends were the French willing or able to associate with the Ottomans socially, politically, or by way of the imagination? Was religious difference insignificant and surmountable?

To begin our foray, it is necessary to emphasize what scholars like Isom-Verhaaren are finally reminding us, the fact that in the sixteenth century the Empire was Ottoman. Michel de Montaigne only stated the obvious—often forgotten by critics, past and above all present—when he declared that "Le plus fort Estat qui paroisse pour le present au monde, est celuy des Turcs"[31] (It appears that the strongest state in the world today is that of the Turks). Under Sultan Süleyman (r. 1520–1566), the Ottomans were an international power and as such they mattered not only to their immediate Muslim neighbours like the Safavids and the Mamlūks, but also to western rulers in Rome, Spain, Portugal, Venice, Austria, Burgundy, and France. Dominating the Mediterranean thanks to their commanding fleet, they controlled the economies of Eurasia, and even if they did not engage actively in the conquest of the Americas, they were aware of Christopher Columbus's discovery. Their own scholars gathered and processed new information, discussed the New World, and engaged in 'scientific' projects.[32] While the Spanish Empire was burgeoning, the Ottomans had solidly established their presence on vast areas of land in Eurasia. France, in the meantime, was far from being the colonial power it would become in the nineteenth century. Even though some sixteenth-century scholars endorsed the idea of a *translatio imperii*—the transferring of political power from the Greeks to the Romans, and finally to the French—the kingdom was hardly emerging from its locked and relatively insignificant political base. Squeezed between Charles V's territories and dwarfed by the Ottoman Empire, Francis's realm was politically inconsequential. It continues to be argued that the French-Ottoman alliance was motivated mainly by political insecurity, and this is certainly one compelling reason;[33] yet I would like to suggest that intellectual curiosity mixed with opportunities and a sense of adventure were also causes for French individuals and collective groups to turn outward and befriend the Ottomans.

Not only was Empire Ottoman in the sixteenth century, but there was no formal Republic of Letters in France. What would become the *Collège royal de France* was of course created by Francis I in 1530, but this was a small-scale project characterized by lack of a proper location and irregular salaries for the eminent scholars the new institution did manage to hire. The *lecteurs royaux* taught Hebrew and Greek first, and later Latin, mathematics, rhetoric, medicine, and philosophy, as well as Arabic. Guillaume Postel was the first to hold the chair of Arabic. He and his colleagues like Pierre Danès were certainly well-traveled, well-connected—so were their patrons—and trained in the new humanist approach.[34] Mobility characterized these scholars; however, one cannot speak of the kind of structured and centralized environment that allowed for a systematic exchange of information with a precise religious or political goal in mind, as would be the case several decades later with the Jesuits and Louis XIV.[35] In fact, as Pierre Belon remarks, the court still seemed to provide the strongest intellectual setting in the sixteenth century.[36] As a result, the knowledge of Oriental languages in sixteenth-century Europe was limited. The Qur'ān, first translated into French in the twelfth century, was printed for the first time by Theodor Bibliander in 1543; Postel published his Arabic grammar in 1540. Yet very few individuals could read and speak Farsi, Ottoman Turkish, or Arabic until a much later period.[37]

A last fundamental difference between modern and early modern France concerns religious inclination. Sixteenth-century France was a Christian society that relied heavily on concepts such as the crusade that it reinvented to adapt to current political situations. As orthodoxy was questioned by Islam as well as Evangelical and Reformed movements, religious identities were constantly negotiated. Still, the French king remained a "roi treschrétien" (very Christian king) with divine powers and even though the concept of religion became ethnographic in the fifteenth and sixteenth centuries,[38] only during the French Revolution did a much more secular France appear.

Taking into consideration the particular historical context in which sixteenth-century Frenchmen wrote, the close readings that follow highlight the divergent responses French commentators gave to the Ottomans and show a gradual reduction of what were initially diverse representations of the 'Turks.' Often echoing or refuting one another, their commentaries are testimony to a profound societal transformation as France's goal shifted from universal religion to state imperialism. Sixteenth-century encounters with the Ottomans might explain a paradox, that modern France as a country prides itself on its inalienable (and universal) *droits de l'homme*, but was once a powerful empire (and feels a lingering nostalgia for that status). Even now, France is a country that generates inveterate and ever-curious travelers who continue to view themselves as human rights leaders even though they are occasionally grasped by resurgent discourses of extremism or national identity. Although not formulated in these precise terms at the time, the question "Colonized or colonizer?" was very much at the crux of early sixteenth-century France as the kingdom was "situated in the murky middle ground between barbarism and civilization".[39] The following chapters underscore the delicate balance between Catholics, Muslims, and Protestants; religion, commerce, and politics in sixteenth-century France.

Chapter 1 reviews the French kingdom's ambiguous position in the larger context of sixteenth-century politics. Chapter 2 focuses on two inheritors of the crusade tradition, Jean Lemaire de Belges and Jean Thenaud. In the *Traicté de la différence des schismes et des conciles de l'Église* (1511) and *Voyage d'outre-mer*, published between 1525 and 1530, Lemaire and Thenaud look into competitors to the Ottomans: the Safavids and the Mamlūks. Addressing political agreements concluded between Louis XII and Qānsūh al-Ghawrī in 1511, both authors attempt to give a fresh and complex description of the Islamic world. In his allegory, Lemaire compares Shah Isma'il, the Safavid leader, to a peace-bringing dove, while the head of the Catholic Church is presented as a black raven. Thenaud, on the other hand, chooses to narrate the intricacy and the economic opportunities of the eastern world through a reinvented pilgrimage that takes the *cordelier*, physically and imaginatively, to the Holy Land as well as to Egypt, Persia, and Mecca. Gallicanism and burgeoning capitalism replace Jean Molinet's and André de La Vigne's apocalyptic tales of doom. Writing positively about Muslim leaders and positioning themselves comfortably within Islamic cultures, both Lemaire and Thenaud open the door to later relations between French and Ottomans.

Jacques de Bourbon's chronicle of the fall of Rhodes in 1522 is the subject of Chapter 3. It reaffirms the significance of Lemaire and Thenaud's Mediterranean world by focusing not on pilgrims or on religious polemics like Bourbon's predecessors, but on the Knights of St. John of Jerusalem. Acknowledging his and his companions' crusading vows, Bourbon warns of dissensions among Christians while evoking a united and powerful Ottoman rule. The Knight's *Oppugnation* (1525) does stress religious differences between Muslims and Christians, but more importantly it posits the Sultan as a model to emulate in order to tackle the internal divisions that plague both the Order of St. John and Christianity as a whole. Rather than viewing a Franco-Ottoman alliance as a creative political option for a kingdom of France squeezed by Charles V's Empire, Bourbon suggests that a close look at the 'Turks' may help recover an endangered Christian ethos. Simultaneously, the chronicler also questions the possibility of a crusade in an increasingly global world. Echoing both Lemaire and Thenaud, and reinforcing their proposition by directly taking an Ottoman sultan as model, Bourbon anticipates the officialization of the Franco-Ottoman alliance.

In Chapter 4, I read François Rabelais's fictitious grappling with the Ottomans in Chapters 14 and 32 of *Pantagruel* (1532). In contrast to pilgrimages, religious polemics, and historiography, these two chapters offer a playful meditation on the Ottomans, the former recounting Panurge's captivity in comical detail, the latter engulfing the narrator in the mouth of the giant. In his fantastic tales, Rabelais conflates three territories—Ottoman, French, and American—into a phantasmagorical space. While still relying on negative clichés and preconceptions, Rabelais succeeds in crafting a most tolerant image of the 'Turks' through laughter and language while acknowledging that the Reformation is beginning to change the French religious landscape. Under Rabelais's playful pen, fictional characters merge into one another and form the backdrop for the first significant cross-cultural encounters between French and Ottomans.

The crusade becomes an imaginary game, the universal monarchy a dangerous alternative, and the community a utopia.

Chapters 5 and 6 demonstrate the settling of the Ottomans in French culture. As individuals affirm and reinvent themselves opportunistically, the kingdom of France enters into open competition with other European powers and turns an envious eye to foreign lands in order to establish its own version of empire. Chapter 5 depicts Bertrand de La Borderie's poetic rendition of a friendly military enterprise turned sour between French and Ottomans in 1537. In *Le discours du voyage de constantinoble* (1542), literature and history converge to show the capital of the Ottoman Empire as a contested space and a focal point of reflection on culture, otherness, and power. While justifying the Franco-Ottoman alliance of the 1530s, the poem nevertheless includes strong elements of Ottomanism and points firmly to a limited and increasingly limiting perception of the 'Turks' while positing the French as heir to the Trojans and to Empire. Chapter 6 analyzes Jean Yversen's diplomatic missions to Constantinople in the 1550s and their subsequent manifestations in the 1580s. Mediating between two cultures, the envoy physically brings the West to the Ottoman Empire while, in his correspondence, he translates the East to the French. Having returned to his hometown in southern France at the onset of the wars of religion, Yversen is faced with yet another mighty opponent, the Protestants. For the seasoned diplomat, the religious troubles in Gaillac become an occasion for storytelling and self-aggrandizement as Protestants take the place of the Ottomans. In Yversen's 'travel journal' and in a sculpted panel decorating his fireplace, the Frenchman's status rises from special envoy to ambassador and, simultaneously, to Catholic activist.

Highlighting a 1575 pamphlet entitled *La France-Turquie*, the conclusion illustrates the end of France's Ottoman polyphony.

Notes

1 Farid ud-Din Attar, *The Conference of the Birds*, transl. Afkham Darbandi and Dick Davis (Harmondsworth, UK: Penguin Books, 1984), 214.
2 This is the term used in French and other European literatures of the period to describe the Ottomans. I use it here and in what follows to describe the imagined Ottomans as opposed to their historical counterparts.
3 Almut Höfert makes this important point, arguing that the 'Turk' gave rise to modern occidental anthropology. See Almut Höfert, "The Order of Things and the Discourse of the Turkish Threat: The Conceptualization of Islam in the Rise of Occidental Anthropology in the Fifteenth and Sixteenth Centuries," in *Between Europe and Islam: Shaping Modernity in a Transcultural Space*, ed. Almut Höfert and Armando Salvatore (Brussels: P.I.E. Peter Lang, 2000): 39–69, here 67.
4 In *The Gargantuan Polity: On the Individual and the Community in the French Renaissance* (Toronto: University of Toronto Press, 2008), Michael Randall describes the contractual agreements linking late medieval and early modern individuals and tempering the princes' outbursts of power. Randall's perceptive study suggests that modern polities reduced the subjects by depriving them of their collective meaning. In other words, the liberation of the self occurred at the expense of the collectivity and of the plurality of opinions previously voiced.

5 "Rencontres créatrices" and "propriétés émergentes" are terms used by physicist Hubert Reeves during his presentation on "Cosmos et créativité" (lecture, École des Mines, Albi, December 1, 2010).

6 Pascal Blanchard et al., *La France arabo-orientale: Treize siècles de présences du Maghreb, de la Turquie, d'Égypte, du Moyen-Orient et du Proche-Orient* (Paris: La Découverte, 2013) is a case in point. See also Jonathan Laurence and Justin Vaïsse, *Integrating Islam: Political and Religious Challenges in Contemporary France* (Washington, DC: Brookings Institution Press, 2006), and Françoise Gaspard and Farhad Khosrokhavar, "The Headscarf and the Republic," in *Beyond French Feminisms: Debates on Women, Politics, and Culture in France, 1989–2001*, ed. Roger Célestin, Eliane DalMolin, and Isabelle de Courtivron (New York: Palgrave Macmillan, 2003): 61–68. *La haine* (1995) directed by Mathieu Kassovitz and *La marche* (2013) directed by Nabil Ben Yadir are examples of cinematographic musings on the topic. The latter recounts "La marche pour l'égalité et contre le racisme," also called "La Marche des Beurs," a peaceful walk from Lyon to Paris in 1983.

7 See Paul Virilio, *Le grand accélérateur* (Paris: Galilée, 2010) for a serious look at our post-modern world.

8 This is a nod at Anouar Majid, *We Are All Moors: Ending Centuries of Crusades against Muslims and Other Minorities* (Minneapolis: University of Minnesota Press, 2009), which argues that the treatment of the Moors in the medieval period is equivalent to that of the Hispanics in today's United States of America, or of the Arabs in contemporary France. Ultimately, the author suggests, every ethnic group, every one of us, shares the same path of exclusion or repulsion when faced with emigration. Despite the calque I use, my borrowing is less intellectual than linguistic as my work considers a smaller geographical and historical period and points to specific sixteenth-century conditions that allowed for a more heterogeneous reaction on the part of French spectators and actors.

9 Studying sixteenth- and seventeenth-century reports from Venetian ambassadors, Lucette Valensi notices a shift in perception in the 1570s whence the Ottomans are viewed more systematically as tyrants. She explains the change by a new climate of uncertainty in Venetian politics. See Lucette Valensi, *Venise et la Sublime Porte* (Paris: Hachette, 1987). In the case of France, the equation of despotism with the Ottomans was firmly in place in the seventeenth century; see Alain Grosrichard, *Structure du Sérail* (Paris: Seuil, 1979).

10 I discuss this text in the conclusion.

11 Sanjay Subrahmanyam calls for the latter in "Connected Histories: Notes towards a Reconfiguration of Early Modern Eurasia," *Modern Asian History* 31, no. 3 (1997): 735–62. Michael Werner and Bénédicte Zimmermann are proponents of crossed history/ies. See their "Penser l'histoire croisée: Entre empirie et réflexivité," *Annales. Histoire, Sciences Sociales* 58, no. 1 (2003): 7–36.

12 My analysis, therefore, nuances the findings of Andrei Pippidi, who posits three stages in the European assessment of the Ottomans—shock, mobilization, and balance—and those of James Harper, according to whom the 'Turks' were perceived first as invincible, then as vincible, and finally as innocuous. See Andrei Pippidi, *Visions of the Ottoman Empire in Renaissance Europe* (New York: Columbia University Press, 2012), 3; James G. Harper, ed. *The Turk and Islam in the Western Eye, 1450–1750: Visual Imagery before Orientalism* (Farnham, UK: Ashgate, 2011), 8.

13 Fernand Braudel, *La Méditerranée et le monde méditerranéen à l'époque de Philippe II* (1949; rev. ed., Paris: Armand Colin, 1966).

14 Walter G. Andrews and Mehmet Kalpaklı, *The Age of Beloveds: Love and the Beloved in Early-Modern Ottoman and European Culture and Society* (Durham: Duke University Press, 2005); Molly Greene, *A Shared World: Christians and Muslims in the Early Modern Mediterranean* (Princeton, NJ: Princeton University Press, 2000); Sanjay Subrahmanyam, *Courtly Encounters: Translating Courtliness and Violence in Early Modern Eurasia* (Cambridge, MA: Harvard University Press, 2012). See also Lisa

Jardine, *Worldly Goods: A New History of the Renaissance* (New York: Nan A. Talese, 1996) and Gerald MacLean's edited volume, *Re-Orienting the Renaissance: Cultural Exchanges with the East* (Basingstoke: Palgrave Macmillan, 2005), especially the introduction, 1–28.

15 For apocalyptic prophecies in the Ottoman world and Islamic millenarism, see Cornell Fleischer, "The Lawgiver as Messiah: The Making of the Imperial Image in the Reign of Süleymân" in *Soliman le Magnifique et son temps: Actes du Colloque de Paris, galeries nationales du Grand Palais, 7–10 mars 1990*, ed. Gilles Veinstein (Paris: Documentation française, 1992), 160–74; and "Shadows of Shadows: Prophecy in Politics in 1530s Istanbul," *International Journal of Turkish Studies* 13 (2007): 51–62. Marya Green-Mercado analyzes similar topics in the Morisco population in "The Mahdī in Valencia: Messianism, Apocalypticism, and Morisco Rebellions in Late Sixteenth-Century Spain," *Medieval Encounters* 19 (2013): 193–220.

16 Richard Bulliet has argued for an Islamo-Christian civilization. See Richard W. Bulliet, *The Case for Islamo-Christian Civilization* (New York: Columbia University Press, 2004).

17 See Chapter 1.

18 Eric Dursteler, *Venetians in Constantinople: Nation, Identity, and Coexistence in the Early Modern Mediterranean* (Baltimore: Johns Hopkins University Press, 2006); Jerry Brotton, *The Renaissance Bazaar: From the Silk Road to Michelangelo* (Oxford: Oxford University Press, 2002); Deborah Howard, *Venice and the East: The Impact of the Islamic World on Venetian Architecture, 1100–1500* (New Haven, CT: Yale University Press, 2000).

19 Nabil Matar, *Islam in Britain, 1558–1685* (Cambridge: Cambridge University Press, 1998); *Turks, Moors, and Englishmen in the Age of Discovery* (New York: Columbia University Press, 1999); *Britain and Barbary, 1589–1689* (Gainesville: University Press of Florida, 2005).

20 In the following chapters, I will refer specifically to several of Bourrilly's articles dealing with Franco-Ottoman relations in the 1530s. For a first appraisal of Francis I's policy of *ouverture* towards his eastern neighbors, see J. Ursu, *La politique orientale de François Ier (1515–1547)* (Paris: Champion, 1908). Ernest Charrière's collection of primary sources is invaluable. See his *Négociations de la France dans le Levant* (New York: B. Franklin, 1964).

21 Clarence Rouillard, *The Turk in French History, Thought, and Literature (1520–1660)* (New York: AMS Press, 1973).

22 Edward Said, *Orientalism* (New York: Vintage Books, 1978).

23 Michèle Longino, *Orientalism in French Classical Drama* (Cambridge: Cambridge University Press, 2002).

24 Nicholas Dew, *Orientalism in Louis XIV's France* (Oxford: Oxford University Press, 2009).

25 Ina Baghdiantz McCabe pursues a similar line of thought, focusing in Chapter 2 on Guillaume Postel whom she posits as the first Orientalist. See Ina Baghdiantz McCabe, *Orientalism in Early Modern France: Eurasian Trade, Exoticism, and the* Ancien *Régime* (Oxford: Berg, 2008). Urs App expands Dew's and McCabe's analyses by examining French commentaries on non-Muslim Asia in the eighteenth century. See Urs App, *The Birth of Orientalism* (Philadelphia, PA: University of Pennsylvania Press, 2010).

26 Frédéric Tinguely, *L'écriture du Levant à la Renaissance: Enquête sur les voyageurs français dans l'empire de Soliman le Magnifique* (Geneva: Droz, 2000).

27 Höfert, "The Order of Things."

28 Marcus Keller and others continue the discussion on early modern Orientalism in France in a recent special issue of *L'Esprit Créateur* on "The Turk of Early Modern France". See *L'Esprit Créateur* 53, no. 4 (2013).

29 The "clash of civilization" thesis was put forth by Samuel Huntington in "The Clash of Civilization?" *Foreign Affairs* 72, no. 3 (1993): 22–49.

30 Édith Garnier, *L'Alliance impie: François Ier et Soliman le Magnifique contre Charles Quint (1529–1547)* (Paris: Le Félin, 2008); and Christine Isom-Verhaaren, *Allies with the Infidel: The Ottoman and French Alliance in the Sixteenth Century* (New York: I. B. Tauris, 2011) respectively. One can only regret that despite the important steps both scholars take to address facts and historical balance, the titles of their works suggest an enduring fascination with the idea of the Ottomans as unnatural friends. See also Claude Postel, *La France-Turquie: La Turquie vue de France au XVIe siècle* (Paris: Les Belles lettres, 2013).

31 Michel de Montaigne, *Les essais*, ed. Pierre Villey, 3 vols, 2nd ed. (Paris: Presses universitaires de France, 1992), here "Du pédantisme," 1: 143.

32 Giancarlo Casale makes the case for the Ottomans' knowledge of and engagement in the New World discoveries in *The Ottoman Age of Exploration* (Oxford: Oxford University Press, 2010). See also Avner Ben-Zaken, *Cross-Cultural Scientific Exchanges in the Eastern Mediterranean, 1560–1660* (Baltimore: Johns Hopkins University Press, 2010).

33 Isom-Verhaaren, *Allies with the Infidel*.

34 On Danès, see Chapter 1.

35 The Jesuits were the first to conceive of and to put in place a network of informants and correspondents. See Steven J. Harris, "Mapping Jesuit Science: The Role of Travel in the Geography of Knowledge" in *The Jesuits: Cultures, Sciences, and the Arts, 1540–1773*, ed. John W. O'Malley et al. (Toronto: University of Toronto Press, 1999), 212–40.

36 Refering to Francis I's entourage, Belon states: "Sa cour semblait quelque belle Académie ou ancienne école de philosophie, en laquelle était montrée la théorie et la pratique de toute vertu" (His court resembled a beautiful Academy or some ancient school of philosophy in which the theory and practice of virtue was shown). Pierre Belon, *Voyage au Levant (1553): Les observations de Pierre Belon du Mans de plusieurs singularités & choses mémorables trouvées en Grèce, Turquie, Judée, Égypte, Arabie, et autres pays étranges* (1553), ed. Alexandra Merle (Paris: Chandeigne, 2001), 52.

37 On the limited European knowledge of Ottoman Turkish, see Stéphane Yérasimos, "Le turc en Occident: La connaissance de la langue turque en Europe (XVe–XVIIe siècles)" in *L'inscription des langues dans les relations de voyage (XVIe–XVIIIe siècles)*: Actes du Colloque de Décembre 1988 (Fontenay: E.N.S. Fontenay/Saint-Cloud, 1992), 191–210.

38 Almut Höfert, " 'Europe' and 'Religion' in the Framework of Sixteenth-Century Relations between Christian Powers and the Ottoman Empire," in *Reflections on Europe: Defining a Political Order in Time and Space*, eds. Hans-Ake Persson and Bo Strath (Brussels: P.I.E. Peter Lang, 2007), 211–30, particularly 229.

39 Sara Melzer, *Colonizer or Colonized? The Hidden Stories of Early Modern French Culture* (Philadelphia: University of Pennsylvania Press, 2012), 18.

1 All Birds Assembled

> Voici donc assemblés tous les oiseaux du monde, ceux des proches
> contrées et des pays lointains.
>
> The world's birds gathered for their conference.
> —Farid-ud-Din' Attar, *La conférence des oiseaux*[1]

The Crusade Tradition and Its French Response

In the late fifteenth century and early sixteenth century the ideal of the crusade
was alive[2] and very much aimed at the Ottomans. On September 25, 1396, they
had severely crushed the crusaders at Nicopolis, and in 1453 they captured Constantinople, making their presence ever more unavoidable in Christian Europe.
As woodcuts portraying monstrosities perpetrated by the Ottomans inundated the
German market,[3] French courtiers authored poems that carried an obvious crusading element and consequently were virulently opposed to the 'Turks.' Jean
Molinet (ca. 1435–1507) and André de La Vigne (1470–1527?) wrote vitriolic
examples of this ambient Ottomanophobia that was as strikingly visual as it was
long-lasting.

In the "Complainte de Grèce," a poem alternating prose and verse that he
wrote in early 1464, Molinet sets out to describe three allegorical queens: England, France, and "la povre Gresse oppressee des Turcz infidelles" (poor Greece
oppressed by the Turkish infidels).[4] The poet describes Greece's aggressor either
as a wolf, a snake, or an abominable seven-headed dragon whistling of content-
ment and opening its mouth to swallow her.[5] Directly inspired by biblical prophecies, the apocalyptic beast is identified with the 'Turks' by the Queen of France:

> *O Grece, ma chiere amie, qui sera celle horrible beste venant des parties
> d'Orient? N'est ce mie ce tres furieux dragon, le Turc infidelle, le prince des
> tenebres, le patron de tirannie, le pere des mescreans sathalites, le filz de per-
> dition, le disciple de Mahommet, le messagier de Antechrist, l'espantaille des
> povres brebisettes, le flaÿau des Crestïens, le rieu d'enfer et la dure verge de
> Dieu poindant et criminelle de qui tu es persecutee?* (lines 45–53, pp. 17–18)

Greece, my dear friend, who will this terrible beast coming from the East be? Is it not this furious dragon, the infidel Turk, the prince of darkness, the patron of tyranny, the father of unbelieving torturers, the disciple of Muhammad, the messenger of the Antichrist, the one that frightens the poor lambs, the scourge of Christians, the announcer of hell and the hard curse of God by whom you are persecuted?

Answering the French queen's hopelessness, the poet suggests that, were England to dispatch George to kill the new dragon, she could be Greece's savior. Or else France or Bourgogne could produce a second Charlemagne. The end of the poem builds on the last suggestion and shows the Duke of Burgundy, Philip the Good, as the western lion that will save his eastern neighbor:

> *O Grece [. . .] as tu veu en tes forests orientelles lyon pareil a cestuy revestu de la couleur du ciel, ton reparateur rugissant en Occident, le tres victorieux duc de Bourgongne, qui, par raison et comme renommé par le siecle univers, est appelé le puissant lyon?* (lines 99–105, p. 19)
>
> Oh, Greece, . . . have you seen in your oriental forests a lion such as the one dressed in azure, your savior roaring in the West, the powerful Duke of Burgundy who, with reason, is known as the great lion of our time?

In the final section of the poem, *acteur* and England complete the casting of Philip the Good as crusader by adding a "prophetie de Merlin" to earlier biblical apocalyptic references.

One could view the "Complainte de Grèce" as a particularly effective *poème de circonstance* written by a poet entirely devoted to his patrons at the court of Burgundy: by flaunting war against Islam, the *rhétoriqueur* uses an argument to which Philip the Good could not be indifferent since his father, John the Fearless, had been defeated by the Ottomans in the battle of Nicopolis in 1396. This would be a hasty judgment, however. Jean Devaux has shown that Molinet, while aptly and consistently legitimizing the politics of the Dukes of Bourgogne—including their crusading agenda—was also able to criticize the results of their political decisions.[6] More than a docile historiographer focused on Burgundy, Molinet looked far beyond his court and was not blindly serving a dynasty. Deeply influenced by conduct literature, the *rhétoriqueur*'s entire literary production served to empower his ruler while expecting accountability from him. This is particularly visible in the "Complainte de Grèce" where the poet, *indiciaire* and *literatus*, calls for a crusade at the same time as he speaks in favor of union among Christian princes.[7] In other words, in Molinet's poetry, a belligerent *topos* overlaps with what Devaux calls a pacifist discourse. As Michael Randall states, "Molinet's poems are turned outward."[8] From the individual, the *rhétoriqueur* seeks out the collective; from Burgundy, he observes and engages with France, England, and Greece, as well as the Ottoman Empire.

Thirty years after Molinet's "Complainte de Grèce," André de La Vigne penned a *Ressource de la chrestienté*, a poem rallying against the 'Turks' and geared toward a position at court which the poet obtained soon afterwards.[9] The poem, which was most likely written between February and May 1494, closely reflects and offers a justification to the political ambitions of Charles VIII in Italy, Naples more specifically.[10] The chief rationalization for an Italian invasion by a French king was a crusade against the Ottomans, one that, according to popular prophecies, would eventually lead to the Holy Land. Indeed, a "prenosticacion du roy Charles huytieme de ce nom compillée par l'une des sibiles," claims that a French prince named Charles would conquer Florence and Rome, become king of Greece, annihilate the 'Turks,' and die in Jerusalem.[11] This prophecy, in Latin, was included in one version of the *Ressource*.

In La Vigne's poem, *Dame Crestienté*,[12] persecuted by "Les Turcs maulditz, desloyaulx chiens mastins" (v. 136) (the damned Turks, these treacherous dogs), is rescued by *Dame Noblesse* and *Magesté Royalle*, the latter being identified in several acrostics as Charles de Valois. The most intriguing part of the *Ressource* is the interchange that takes place in the second half of the poem between *Je ne sçay qui* and *Bon Conseil*. Opposing war against the Ottomans, *Je ne sçay qui* cautions against the possible death of the French monarch whose life should be protected and not endangered by travel outside of the kingdom that could shorten his life. The anonymous character warns against a courageous opponent and suggests that the French king should fight back if he is attacked on his territory; war, however, should not be waged unprovoked for it might bring death among the French population at large. Therefore, according to the war skeptic, it is better to adopt a *laissez-faire* attitude and to wait for God to act.[13] The pope can go ahead if he wants, *Je ne sçay qui* adds, but the French should be wary about war spilling onto their territory. In short, the French should not "aller a Napples pour faire du Rolant" (v. 1163) (go to Naples and be a martyr like Roland).

Bon Conseil counters *Je ne sçay qui*'s arguments by accusing his debater of lying and serving his own interests.[14] *Bon Conseil* then encourages everyone to consider the honor that the French and Christian warriors, and potential martyrs, would receive for centuries to come. Like Charlemagne's exploits, their heroic actions would be sung and remembered while the legendary valor and reputation of the French would remain intact. *Bon Conseil*'s advice ultimately prevails and the poem ends with *Magesté Royalle* calling on the French soldiers to gather their arms and rally to *Dame Crestienté*'s defense.

In the late fifteenth century, however, the crusade might have been an excuse more than a motivation and a goal in itself. Isom-Verhaaren claims that the crusade was not the main motive for Burgundian and French rulers who were more interested in territorial expansion than costly campaigns to Jerusalem.[15] Furthermore, what is striking in Molinet's and La Vigne's poems is not only the pretext that the crusade conveniently offers to the French kings who have their eye on Italy, but also the fact that crusading has become a princely duty. Popes may agree to a crusade, but princes decide to conduct them. Still, objections like the ones voiced by *Je ne sçay qui* are publicly heard and acknowledged, before being debunked.[16]

The rhetoric of the crusade is undeniably present in Molinet and La Vigne's poems, but the crusade itself is singularly absent, both poets seeking to exalt the expansionist agendas of either a Burgundian duke or one of two French kings,

Charles VIII (r. 1483–1498) and Louis XII (r. 1498–1515), rather than rallying Christian princes and peoples behind a war against Islam. The crusade had
become more a façade than a reality by the late fifteenth century. It did not entirely
hide political preoccupations in Italy, but the crusade was used as a parade and a
deflector for the French; early modern readers of these two *rhétoriqueurs* would
have understood as much.[17]

Nevertheless, poets like Molinet and La Vigne—who were influential at court
and who responded to the court's political agenda, but who could not simply
have been opportunists—gave the Ottomans' significant territorial conquests and
military success at least considerable attention if not very real concern, and they
translated them into striking belligerent verses. The concern was all the more real
since the Ottomans neither started nor stopped at Byzantine Greece and Constantinople. Under Selim I (r. 1512–1520), they defeated the Mamlūks and conquered
Syria, Palestine, and Egypt within months (1516–1517), thereby becoming the
guardians of the two most sacred places of the Islamo-Christian civilization, Jerusalem and Mecca. The Ottomans took the island of Rhodes from the Knights of
St. John of Jerusalem in 1522[18] and controlled most of the Mediterranean in the
next decade thanks, in part, to the famed Khayr-ed-Din from Algiers, known in
the West as Barbarossa (ca.1478–1546). On land, they pushed deep into Europe,
conquering Belgrade in 1521, Mohács in Hungary in 1526, Buda in 1529, more
Hungarian territory in 1541, Transylvania in 1551–1552, and Cyprus in 1571.
Before laying siege to Malta in 1565, they had progressed into continental Europe
as far as Vienna, where they had been stopped in 1529. Most historians accept
that the Ottoman Empire was at its peak, territorially speaking, but also militarily,
politically, and artistically, during the reign of Sultan Süleyman between 1521 and
1566.[19] The Christian world of the sixteenth century agreed.

What was perceived as an inexorable march toward Rome prompted the papacy
to call on Christian princes to unite against Islam. After Julius II, Leo X tried
to jumpstart a crusade. Francis I (r. 1515–1547), who had impressed the pope
in Marignan in 1515, responded to this call in the affirmative, although rather
equivocally. Wishing to appear as Christianity's champion, the young king agreed
to embark on a crusading project with the papal state:

> *[je] me offre entrer et condescendre sincèrement, sans fraude, dol ne machi-*
> *nation en icelle paix, tresve ou fraternité, d'autant que sur toutes choses ay*
> *toujours désiré (comme si fais encores), ainsi que on a peu voir, paix, amour*
> *et union universelle en la chrestienté, afin que l'effusion du sang que longue-*
> *ment y a eu cours au grand détriment et affoiblissement d'icelle, cesse et*
> *soit rétorqué et converty contre les ennemis de nostre foy, et pour ce faire*
> *ay déliberé n'espargner ma personne ne mes biens, ainsi que par l'effect se*
> *pourra cognoistre.[20]*

> [I] propose to enter and accept sincerely, without fail nor calculation, this
> peace, this truce, this brotherly alliance, [for] above all things I have wished
> and still do, as one can see, peace, love, and universal union within Chris-
> tendom, so that the bloodshedding that has been happening for a long time

at the expense of Christianity stops and is converted and aimed at our faith's enemys, and in order to do so, I have decided to spare neither my person nor my wealth as it will be seen.

Concretely speaking, Francis agreed to give men, horses, artillery, and all his boats in the Mediterranean (p. 44). He ended his letter by saying:

> *Je loue Dieu de tout mon coeur de ce que voy le chemin préparé sur ce que ay tousjours tant souhaitté et désiré, qu'est de voir en la chrestienté paix univer-selle et faire la guerre et invader d'un bon et commun accord les ennemys de la foy chrestienne. Sy prie tant dévotement que m'est possible Votre Sainteté de persévérer et parachever ceste excellente et fructueuse délibération que avez si bien et vertueusement commencée.[21]*

I pray God with all my heart that I am able to see the path that I have always wished and desired, that is, universal peace in Christendom and war against the enemies of the Christian faith as it is agreed by all and for our own good. And so I pray as devoutly as possible that I may be able to persevere and to achieve this excellent and profitable goal that you, Your Holiness, have so well and so virtuously set.

The exaggerations and the insistence expressed by Francis I could be purely rhetorical, but they appear slightly sardonic and seem to denote the king's discomfort with his own crusading claim, thereby questioning the sincerity of his commitment. When the monarch asserts that peace is what he always wishes— "sur toutes choses [. . .] toujours désiré," "tousjours tant souhaitté"—and that, therefore he will participate in a crusade "sincèrement, sans fraude, dol ne machination," are we to believe him? Since the thirteenth century, the French king was known as the "roi treschrétien," an expression based on the notion of divine election; as such, the French king was deemed predestined to lead the crusade.[22] It was thus expected for Leo to call upon Francis and for the French king to respond positively. In his missive to the pope however, could Francis I be trying to masquerade as a crusader and to convince Pope Leo (and himself?) of the usefulness of the call while contemplating goals more political than religious for himself?[23] Indeed, once Charles V became Holy Roman Emperor in 1519, Francis would worry more about keeping his rival at a safe distance than investing his forces in a new crusade which was already unpopular among the French.[24] Allying with the strongest military partner who could not compete with him religiously speaking was strategically astute for Francis I. His capture by Charles V's imperial troops in Pavia in 1525 leading to his captivity in Madrid was a turning point in Franco-Ottoman relations. It prompted a series of secret embassies between French and Ottoman officials, Louise de Savoie attempting to convince Sultan Süleyman to help negotiate her son's release.[25] After two decades of covert rapprochement and tinkering around the edges, the Ottomans and the French agreed on Capitulations, formal economic and political covenants, in the mid-1530s.

"Puisque Tel est le Plaisir du Roi": The Franco-Ottoman Alliance

Sealed, if not signed, in 1536, the alliance between the French and the Ottomans gave religious and economic advantages to the former over other European powers by granting them the control of pilgrimage routes to and in the Levant and exclusive trade with the Ottoman Empire in the Mediterranean.[26] The Capitulations also provided Francis I with an indisputable political advantage vis-à-vis Charles V. Tightly squeezed between the territorial possessions of the Holy Roman Emperor to the south and the northeast, the French king found an escape route through the Mediterranean via the Ottomans.

The Franco-Ottoman alliance was the result of long-established contacts between the kingdom of France and Islamic powers in the Levant. Chapter 2 will give detailed examples of early interactions between France and the wide Islamic world before the 1536 agreements. Concretely, the burgeoning partnership manifested itself in the appearance of Ottomans on French soil. Honorat de Valbelle notes in his 'journal' that, on October 14, 1534, there arrived in Marseille

> *une équipe turque qui ramenait en France un ambassadeur qu'elle avait embarqué à Constantinople. On le logea dans la maison de Boniface et l'on proclama au nom du Roy qu'il était défendu d'offenser ces Turcs qui débarquèrent devant le Loge et ils allaient par la ville comme s'ils eussent été à Constantinople.*[27]

> a Turkish group bringing to France an ambassador who had boarded in Constantinople. He was housed in Boniface's home and it was declared that, in the name of the King, it was forbidden to offend those Turks who disembarked in front of the loggia and [who] were going about in the town as they would in Constantinople.

The embassy headed toward Châtellerault and then followed the king to Paris,[28] and the *bourgeois* from Provence felt compelled to add that this was "une chose bien nouvelle que de voir ici des Turcs, cela ne s'est jamais vu" (a very new thing to see Turks here, this has never happened before). Valbelle, in Marseille, was particularly well located to spot the Ottomans' presence on French territory. In 1538, four years after his first Ottoman sighting and two years after the Capitulations, he mentions three boats entering the port:

> *Certains disent que c'est notre Sénéchal qui les a appelées, d'autres que c'est d'elle-mêmes qu'elles y sont venues. Quoi qu'il en soit, cette arrivée ne me plaît pas, car ce sont de méchantes gens, hors de foi, mais puisque tel est le plaisir du Roi, il est bien forcé que cela nous plaise.* (319)

> Some say that it is our Seneschal who called them, others [claim] that they came of their own will. Whatever may be the case, I do not like this arrival for these are evil people, heretics; but since this is the King's wish, we are obliged to like it.

Willing or not, the French had to accept a more regular Ottoman presence on their own soil. Valbelle did not approve of it and expressed his opposition to the idea of a 'Turkish' diaspora in France, even such a temporary one. Regardless of his sentiment, he had to surrender to his king's wishes. Thus, in the 1530s, a bourgeois from Marseille could express his personal views and take issue with the king while resigning himself and accepting significant changes in the political landscape and the cultural makeup of his city and of France. Recognizing the primacy of the collective, the individual bowed to his king's desire, but not before stating his opinion first.

In addition to the more frequent spotting of Ottomans in the Mediterranean and in French ports, military agreements began to take form, which implied an even more continuous and more visible presence of 'Turks' in coastal cities and among the French population. In 1537, the French and the Ottomans planned to attack Italy conjointly. This episode forms the backbone of Bertrand de La Borderies's *Le discours du voyage de constantinoble* which will be the focus of Chapter 5. Similarly in 1543, the Ottomans were invited to spend the winter in Toulon after a joint attack on Nice and presumably in anticipation of another common military venture. Far from being the cause of tension that one might imagine, this first successful episode of substantial and sustained cohabitation between the 'Turks' and the French occurred without much commotion on the part of both Ottomans and Toulonnais.[29] In 1555 a second *hivernement* that was not agreed upon by Süleyman was proposed by Henri II.[30]

Diplomatic affairs accompanied military cooperation and a French ambassador was named in Constantinople in 1535, the first in a long series.[31] Circumventing if not entirely replacing the Venetians at the Sublime Porte, the French quickly established themselves as the Ottomans' privileged Christian interlocutors long before the English and the Dutch.[32] As a result, travels to the Ottoman Empire flourished. So did publications, the most significant of which—in size as much as in content—were Pierre Belon's *Observations* (1553), André Thevet's *Cosmographie de Levant* (1554), Guillaume Postel's *De la republique des Turcs* (1560), and Nicolas de Nicolay's *Navigations* (1567). Pierre Gilles also penned works in Latin on the Bosphorus and Constantinople while Jean Chesneau and Jérôme Maurand recounted their voyages. All sought to elucidate the Ottoman world and to convey an accurate image of it to their French readers.[33] These mid-sixteenth-century observers offered sophisticated commentaries on the Ottomans, some enthusiastic and rather devoid of prejudices, others more biased. Regardless, all contributed to the dissemination of Oriental knowledge in France and many supported the alliance during and after Francis I's reign.

A volume available at the Médiathèque Pierre-Amalric in Albi gathers a series of documents indicating the position several prominent Frenchmen took publicly in the early 1550s. Located in the Henry Pascal de Rochegude collection, the work is catalogued as having appeared in 1552 in Paris, but it comprises documents dated as late as 1554. It bears the title *Apologie, faicte par un serviteur du roy, contre les calomnies des imperiaulx: sur la descente du Turc* (Apology, made by a servant of the king, against the slanders of the Imperial army on the descent of the Turk).[34] In addition to the apology of the same name attributed to Pierre Danès, it includes Danès's second apology along with six additional pieces aiming at expressing public support for the French king and Franco-Ottoman cooperation.[35] These collected texts vary in length, style, and genres; however, they all seek to counter accusations that appeared at the beginning of Henri II's reign against France. Some focus on intra-European matters. "L'oraison de Seigneur Claude Tolommei ambassadeur de Siene: prononcee devant le Roy, A Compiegne, au mois de Decembre, l'an 1552," for example, attempts to justify Henri's wars against Charles V in Italy—particularly in Siena. It thanks Henri for having freed the Italian city from imperial domination and for not imposing taxes or heavy tribute on its inhabitants. In this *oraison*, the French king is portrayed as a disinterested party who only wished to alleviate the Sienese's lot:

> *L'ambition de dominer n'a oint meu vostre cueur, ny l'appetit de subiuguer pays d'aultruy, ny l'attente d'avoir plus grandes richesses, mais un beau & net desir de soulager les opprimez, de subvenir aux necessiteux, consoler les desolez, & sauluer les affligez.*
>
> The ambition to dominate did not move your heart; neither did the hunger to subjugate the country of another or the expectation to gain more riches. Instead, [you were moved by] a beautiful and strong desire to relieve the oppressed, to help the needy, to comfort the desolate, and to save the stricken.

Siena is now France's daughter, the short text concludes, and its fate is intertwined with that of its new ally. Henri did not come to the rescue of Italian Siena only; he also helped other European neighbors, particularly the Protestant princes living in the Emperor's lands. "Henry par la grace de Dieu Roy de France, a noz treschers & tresaymez Cousins, anciens allies & amys perpetuels, les Princes & Estats de Sainct Empire," dated February 26, 1552, makes it clear that France is ready to intervene further north in Europe because of the kingdom's sympathy for Germany, the cultural consanguinity of the two 'nations,' and the duty that France feels towards ancient allies. It incites Protestant princes to revolt against the Holy Roman Emperor who is described as a ruler who breaks treaties and uses traitors to win his battles instead of just war. Germany's sick body needs France's intervention; such is the conclusion of the final text entitled "response a une epistre." Echoing the signature of the Traité de Chambord on January 15, 1552, these two texts announce and rationalize the military confrontation that Henri would begin a month later in Germany and the Low Countries.

While giving a precise snapshot of the clashes occurring in continental Europe between Christian rulers in the early 1550s, the *Apologie* also focuses on situations involving the Ottomans in Hungary and the Mediterranean. The "Traicté de la guerre de Malte, & de l'issue d'icelle faulsemēt imputee aux Francois" (treatise on the war of Malta and on its outcome falsely attributed to the French) by Villegaignon denies any sort of French involvement in the Ottomans' attack and capture of Tripoli in 1551. Addressed to Charles of Spain, it exonerates Ambassador d'Aramon while blaming the Order of Malta's grand master, the Spaniard

Juan de Homedes, for the loss of the city. Similarly, the first *Apologie* demonstrates that the Ottomans decided to attack Transylvania in retaliation for the Holy Roman Emperor's offensive moves at the castle of Ionolk in Hungary and on two African posts held by Dragut Reis, the corsair. The text claims that, rather than accepting a French invitation to a joint military enterprise, the Ottomans responded to Charles's aggressive acts in kind.

In the *Apologie*, Jean du Bellay, François Olivier, and Africain de Mailly most unabashedly support the Franco-Ottoman alliance. They claim that pacts with non-Christians have always been common: the Bible, for example, shows David, Solomon, and Tobias dealing with the gentiles. Furthermore, the text underlines that other Christian nations and the Emperor himself have contracted such agreements. In addition to having precedents, the Franco-Ottoman alliance is not secretive and, by fostering commercial partnership, it aims at guaranteeing peace for the French king's subjects. Besides, the text concludes, the cooperation was requested by the Sultan and not by Francis, who did not have a choice but to oblige and agree to Süleyman's request. Du Bellay and his companions remind us that political affairs of the kingdom in the 1550s ran deep in the Mediterranean and that when the Franco-Ottoman alliance was concluded in the mid-1530s, it was not opposed by everyone; in fact, some major political figures approved of it publicly.

The documents contained in the Rochegude's volume accuse the pope of not protecting his own Farnese family in Parma and Plaisance, but focus forcefully on Charles V who is consistently depicted as overly and unreasonably powerful. Ambition and greediness have made the Holy Roman Emperor lose common sense and measure. He is a new Caesar who uses religion for own interests; his rule can only translate into servitude for the peoples he governs. On the contrary, the king of France only wishes to preserve his honor and reputation, as well as peace in Christendom—"paix & tranquillité en la Chrestienté." Henri is not fighting Charles for pleasure. However, he has the right to reclaim and take by force what has been unjustly taken away from him. His duty is to fight for his and his allies' possessions. The *Apologie* neglects to discuss religious differences between French and Ottomans; instead, it focuses on political matters. However slanted the remarks made about the Holy Roman Emperor might appear, the volume paints the Franco-Ottoman alliance as a sanctioned necessity and an unquestionable *fait accompli*.

The purpose of this book, then, is to recall that before it became an insult for France to be associated with an Islamic power, such an alliance was an option that was very much on the table, a desirable goal even—for some like du Bellay and Danès at least. I thus seek to challenge incommensurability and the stereotype of an inevitably and necessarily disastrous relation between France and an Islamo-Oriental society.[36] In other words, this book presents both faces of history's coin by looking at an age of conflicts that was also a time of exchange and collaboration between cultures. What is proposed in the following pages is a much more inclusive understanding—including an optimistic and even a utopian version—of a long-lasting, mutating, definitely challenging, but also incredibly enriching relationship between the French kingdom and the Ottoman world. This study unearths the basis of the Franco-Ottoman alliance and recounts its rapid evolution in the sixteenth century as French diplomats, literati, chroniclers, and poets saw it. It focuses on sixteenth-century travelers *au sens large* and, more specifically, on the *états d'âme* of these men who once embarked on the difficult question of the Ottomans.

As the 'Turks' literally invaded the French literary production two decades after the Capitulations in the mid-1530s, everyone mentioned the Ottomans: bourgeois like Valbelle, but also the king's own sister Marguerite de Navarre in her *Heptaméron*.[37] In his fourth edition of his *Histoire d'un voyage faict en la terre du Brésil*, Jean de Léry added a 16th chapter entirely devoted to the Ottomans, who become the pivotal point around which his New World narrative revolves.[38] Playwrights, poets, diplomats, scientists, but also painters and sculptors titillated the French mind with nuggets of 'Turquie'.[39] This proliferation of commentaries was not only the result of artists' fertile imaginations; it was also due to the now solidly documented physical presence of Ottomans on French soil in the sixteenth century and the early modern period.[40] Not only were Ottoman merchants, scholars, and emissaries regularly active in commercial, intellectual, and political negotiations in France, but enough evidence of individuals permanently settled in the kingdom has been collected to suggest an adaptation and an absorption of Muslim and in particular Ottoman subjects into early modern French society. The galleys stopping in Mediterranean and Atlantic ports brought their share of Ottomans with them. While stationed on French territory, the 'Turks' left traces of their presence and of their religious rites, which seem to have been tolerated to a certain extent as allowances made for Muslim captives in Christendom were expected to be reciprocated toward Christians enslaved elsewhere in the Mediterranean. We know that a wall of the Major church in Marseille was once decorated with an Arabic inscription similar to one on funeral steles.[41] Records of baptisms and *lettres de naturalité*, official documents issued by the king establishing that a foreign individual was henceforth a subject, prove that Muslim individuals lived in France. For example, two young females from Constantinople spent years of their lives as servants of Catherine de Médicis.[42] Through their daily lives and literary accounts, the Ottomans and the 'Turks,' by reflecting and simultaneously deflecting France's own image, stimulated French society and thought and began to shape it. While remaining quasi-invisible, Muslims—and particularly Ottomans—in early modern France found enough commonalities with French culture to try to integrate its society.

Notes

1 Farid ud-Din Attar, *The Conference of the Birds*, transl. Afkham Darbandi and Dick Davis (Harmondsworth, UK: Penguin Books, 1984), 32.
2 "The crusading ideal was alive in the sixteenth century" states Jonathan Riley-Smith in *The Crusades: A Short History* (New Haven, CT: Yale University Press, 1987), 249.

However it took new forms, some of which Géraud Poumarède examines in *Pour en finir avec la Croisade* (Paris: Presses universitaires de France, 2004) and others analyze in *Crusading in the Fifteenth Century: Message and Impact*, ed. Norman Housley (Basingstoke: Palgrave Macmillan, 2004).

3   In 1529–1530 for instance, the printmaker Erhard Schön produced woodcuts representing Ottoman atrocities, one of which is discussed in Chapter 4. See Larry Silver, "East is East: Images of the Turkish nemesis in the Habsburg world" in *The Turk and Islam in Western Eye, 1450–1750: Visual Imagery before Orientalism*, edited by James G. Harper (Farnham, UK: Ashgate, 2011), 185–211, here 198. For examples of Schön's and other German printers' woodcuts, see Max Geisberg, *The German Single-Leaf Woodcut, 1500–1550*, edited by Walter L. Strauss, 4 vols. (New York: Hacker Art Books, 1974). Volume 4 contains examples of Ottoman atrocities (G.1243), devilishness (G.1250), enslavement (G.1274), massacres (G.1593), and a combination of all of the above (G.1251–3).

4   *Les faictz et dictz de Jean Molinet*, ed. Noël Dupire (Paris: Société des anciens textes français, 1936–39), vol. 1, 9–26, here p. 11, lines 57–58. Unless otherwise indicated, translations are my own.

5   "*Ung tres horrible dragon ayant sept testes abhominables, qui, tout foursené, sifflant autour elle, beant la gheulle pour lengloutir*," ibid., p. 11, lines 50–53.

6   Molinet commented on the 1480 siege of Rhodes and authored an "Epître à la maison de Bourgogne sur la Croisade Turque projetée par Philippe le Bon." On Molinet as a successful court poet who succeeded in expressing his own personal views, see Jean Devaux, *Jean Molinet, indicidaire bourguignon* (Paris: Champion, 1996); pages 581–91 deal expressly with the *rhétoriqueur* and the crusade. See also Randall, *The Gargantuan Polity*, 120.

7   As does Jean Lemaire de Belges in his *Concorde du genre humain* and, to a lesser extent, in his *Traicté*. See Jean Lemaire de Belges, *Concorde du genre humain*, ed. Pierre Jodogne (Brussels: Palais des Académies, 1964) and Chapter 2.

8   Randall, *The Gargantuan Polity*, 84.

9   André de La Vigne, *La ressource de la chrestienté*, ed. Cynthia J. Brown (Montreal: CERES, 1989), 3.

10   André de La Vigne wrote several other poems supporting the political ambitions of Louis XII, Charles VIII's successor, against Venice, including *Les Ballades de Bruyt Commun* and *Le Libelle des cinq villes d'Ytallie contre Venise* (La Vigne, *La ressource*, 8).

11   La Vigne, *La ressource*, 20 and 157–80.

12   I keep the names of allegories and characters italicized as in La Vigne's text.

13   "*Actendre fault la volunté de Dieu,/Car ou il veult, il en donne la gloire*" (vv. 1059–60).

14   "*Homme qui parle encontre verité/Pour maintenir particularité/De syen proffit n'est pas digne de croire*" (vv. 1184–86).

15   Christine Isom-Verhaaren, *Allies with the Infidel*.

16   Similarly, Brown points out that opponents to a war with Italy were numerous and vocal, and belonged to various categories of society, clergy, nobles, and urban folks alike. See La Vigne, *La ressource*, 23.

17   This helps explain the seemingly paradoxical juxtaposition of works such as the "Complainte" and *La ressource* with La Broquère's *Le voyage d'Orient* and its much more sympathetic portrayals of Muslims. La Broquère's work was commissioned by Philip the Good. See Bertrandon de La Broquère, *Le voyage d'Orient*, ed. Hélène Basso and Jacques Paviot (Toulouse: Anacharsis, 2010).

18   I discuss the fall of Rhodes in Chapter 3.

19   For the Ottomans' architectural accomplishments under Süleyman, see Gülru Necipoğlu, *Architecture, Ceremonial, and Power: The Topkapi Palace in the Fifteenth and Sixteenth Centuries* (Cambridge, MA: MIT Press, 1991) and *The Age of Sinan: Architectural Culture in the Ottoman Empire* (Princeton, NJ: Princeton University

Press, 2005). Voices have recently been heard against the theory of the Ottoman Empire's decline after the reign of Süleyman, one of the most interesting ones being that of Baki Tezcan in *The Second Empire: Political and Social Transformation in the Early Modern World* (New York: Cambridge University Press, 2010). The reexamination of historical documents in order to get a better sense of the rise and fall of the empire, or the usefulness of these concepts, is well underway. I will not discuss these issues here.

20 Charrière, *Négociations*, 1: 42.

21 Ibid., 1: 46.

22 In *Naissance de la nation France* (Paris: Gallimard, 1985), Colette Beaune speaks of "chef prédestiné de toute croisade," 82.

23 Rouillard, *The Turk*, 36; Ursu, *Politique orientale de François Iᵉ*, 7–14.

24 Rouillard stresses that the money taxed for the crusade was interpreted as a way for the Church to accumulate more riches and to avoid reforms (*The Turk*, 35).

25 On early French embassies to Constantinople, see Rouillard, *The Turk*, 105–10, and Charrière, *Négociations*, 1: 112 and passim.

26 The text of the Capitulations is given in Charrière, *Négociations*, 1: 283–94. The term 'capitulations' comes from Latin *capitula*. It does not suggest a military defeat, but rather a agreement presented in the form of a list, an enumeration of terms. Drafted in the mid 1530s, they may not have been signed until 1569; see Robert Mantran, *Histoire de l'empire ottoman* (Paris: Fayard, 1989), 222. Signed or not, the agreements between the French and the Ottomans did lead to some very concrete actions such as the joint military offensive of 1537 discussed later in this chapter and in Chapter 5, and the 1543 Ottoman "hivernement" in Toulon, on which, see Christine Isom-Verhaaren, "'Barbarossa and His Army Who Came to Succor All of Us': Ottoman and French Views of Their Joint Campaign of 1543–1544," *French Historical Studies* 30, no. 3 (2007): 395–425.

27 Honorat de Valbelle, *Histoire journalière d'Honorat de Valbelle (1489–1539): Journal d'un bourgeois de Marseille au temps de Louis XII et de François Ier*, ed. Victor-Louis Bourrilly, trans. Lucien Gaillard, 2 vols. (Marseille: Laffitte, 1985), 1: 264.

28 *Journal d'un bourgeois de Paris sous le règne de François Premier (1515–1536)* (Paris: Renouard, 1954. New York: Johnson Reprint, 1965), 440. On this Turkish embassy, see V.-L. Bourrilly, "Un ambassadeur turc à Marseille en octobre 1534," *Revue Historique de Provence* 1 (1901): 463–69.

29 Rouillard, *The Turk*, 120–21; Charles de La Roncière, *Histoire de la marine française* (Paris: Plon, 1906), 386–87; André Clot, *Soliman le Magnifique* (Paris: Fayard, 1983), 189–96. The most detailed rendition of the encounter is given by Isom-Verhaaren who takes into consideration the Ottomans' view of the military collaboration. See her *Allies with the Infidel* and "'Barbarossa and His Army'."

30 See Chapter 6.

31 Jean de La Forest was ambassador to Constantinople between 1535 and 1538, Antoine Rincon from 1538 to 1541, Antoine Escalin des Eymars—also known as Capitaine Polin—between 1541 and 1547. Gabriel d'Aramon was named in the year 1547 and served until 1553; Michel de Codignac followed from 1553 to 1556; Jean de La Vigne replaced his predecessor from 1556 to 1559. Therefore, relations between French and Ottomans continued unaltered after Francis I's death in 1547.

32 The first English ambassador was named in 1579. As for the Dutch, they sent their first permanent envoy to Constantinople in 1612.

33 Pierre Belon, *Les observations de plusieurs singularitez et choses memorables, trouvées en Grece, Asie, Judée, Arabie, et autres pays estranges* (Paris: Guillaume Cavellat et Gilles Corrozet, 1553); Guillaume Postel, *De la Republique des Turcs* (Poitier: Enquibert de Marneff, 1560); Nicolas de Nicolay, *Les navigations, pérégrinations et voyages faicts en la Turquie* (Anvers: Guillaume Silvius, 1576); André Thevet,

Cosmographie de Levant (Lyon: Jean de Tournes et Guillaume Gazeau, 1554); Pierre Gilles, *Petri Gyllii de Bosporo Thracio libri III* (Lyon: Guillaume Rouillé, 1561). On these authors, see Tinguely, *L'écriture du Levant*.

34 *Apologie, faicte par un serviteur du roy, contre les calomnies des imperiaulx: sur la descente du Turc* (Paris: Charles Étienne, 1552) RES. ROCH. 00294.

35 Pierre Danès, born in Paris in 1497, studied philosophy in the *collège de Navarre*, was ordained a priest in the late 1510s and taught at the *collège de Lisieux* before being appointed *lecteur royal* in Greek at the *collège de France* in 1530. Between 1535 and 1539, he traveled to Italy and in 1546 was named ambassador by the king at the Council of Trent. *Précepteur* of the Dauphin in 1549, he became bishop of Lavaur, in southwestern France, in 1557. Briefly arrested by Huguenots, he could not prevent his library from being pillaged or Catholics from being massacred. He died on 23 April 1577 at Saint-Germain-des-Prés.

36 On questions of incommensurability, see Sanjay Subrahmanyam, "Par-delà l'incommensurabilité: Pour une histoire connectée des empires aux temps modernes," *Revue d'Histoire Moderne et Contemporaine* 54, no. 5 (2007): 34–53.

37 See Mary McKinley, "An Ottoman 'Fixer' in Marguerite de Navarre's *Heptaméron*," *L'Esprit Créateur* 53, no. 4 (2013): 9–20.

38 Scott Juall, " 'Beaucoup plus barbares que les Sauvages mesmes': Cannibalism, Savagery, and Religious Alterity in Jean de Léry's *Histoire d'un voyage fait en la terre du Brésil* (1599–1600)," *L'Esprit Créateur* 48, no. 1 (2008): 58–71.

39 One such playwright was Gabriel Bounin. See my "Oriens Theatralis: La France dans le miroir de *La Soltane* de Gabriel Bounin," *EMF: Studies in Early Modern France* 13 (2010): 107–20. The château de Cénevières in southwestern France contains a painted ceiling dating from the late sixteenth century representing Constantinople. This series of cityscapes has not been formally studied and calls for attention.

40 The examples that follow come from Jocelyne Dakhlia, "Musulmans en France et en Grande-Bretagne à l'époque moderne: Exemplaires et invisibles" in *Les musulmans dans l'histoire de l'Europe*, ed. Jocelyne Dakhlia and Bernard Vincent, vol.1 (Paris: Albin Michel, 2011), 231–413.

41 Dakhlia, "Musulmans en France," 244, quoting Casimir Bousquet, *La Major, cathédrale de Marseille* (Marseille: Marius Olive, 1857), 196.

42 Frédérick Hitzel, "Turcs et turqueries à la cour de Catherine de Médicis" in *Les musulmans dans l'histoire de l'Europe* 1: 33–54, in particular 44–54.

2 A Dove or a Crow?

Jean Lemaire de Belges and Jean Thenaud Open the Way to the Ottomans

In late August 1510, a skirmish between the Knights of St. John and Mamlūk sailors showed how volatile the Mediterranean could be in the early modern world. The scuffle happened in the gulf of Ayas on the far eastern side of the *mare nostrum*.[1] The Knights, seeking to demonstrate their power in the Mediterranean and more specifically their control over the wood trade, attacked and quickly overpowered two dozen Mamlūk ships carrying lumber. After killing many of the mixed Ottoman and Mamlūk crew, the Knights sailed back to Rhodes, taking the enemies' vessels with them. Qānsūh al-Ghawrī of Egypt, who had allied with Sultan Bayezid for this trade, reacted vehemently. Christian merchants in Egypt and Syria were arrested and imprisoned, and so were the guardians of the Holy Land's sacred sites. The crisis was eventually resolved after a serious diplomatic effort—or, some might say, a quite opportunistic involvement—on the part of the French.

Two different French documents relate this episode of Mediterranean warfare and the negotiations that ensued. The first is a polemical piece signed by Jean Lemaire de Belges (1473–1525). It includes, in its final section, the agreements that were subsequently signed between the French kingdom and the Mamlūks. The second is an account of a pilgrimage to the Holy Land written by Jean Thenaud (c.1480–1542), whose travel companion during his Mediterranean crossing was André Le Roy, the French envoy charged with brokering peace between the Knights of St. John and the Mamlūks. Studying these texts side by side allows us not only to gain a fuller picture of a particular incident that indicates the unpredictability of the Mediterranean in the early sixteenth century; it presents us with a complex set of players whose allegiances were constantly fluctuating and whose politics were profoundly shaping and being shaped by the French kingdom. Sharing a strong anti-papal stance, Lemaire and Thenaud's accounts provide competing images of the 'Turks' taking the reader to the wide Islamic East in very different ways—one via a virulent attack on popes, the other through a hodgepodge of commonplaces and unusual anecdotes. Both, however, offer a glimpse of concrete and imaginary connections between the kingdom of France and Muslim powers in the first decade of the sixteenth century. They show that France was deeply interested in and connected to the eastern Islamic Mediterranean in the first decade of the sixteenth century since despite the significant distance between the Gulf of Ayas and Europe, the incident involving the Knights of St. John and the Mamlūks with which this chapter began reverberated as far as the French kingdom and caused disruption all the way to the city of Angoulême, situated some one hundred kilometers inland from the vibrant cities of Bordeaux and La Rochelle on the Atlantic coast.

"Ung Corbeau et Ung Coulon": Jean Lemaire de Belges's Politics of Religion

At the opening of the sixteenth century, Europe found itself seriously troubled by newcomers on the international scene: the Ottoman Turks. Following the capture of Constantinople in 1453, the Ottomans' advance on Christian territories appeared threatening to European observers who began to discuss and devise means to stop the progression of Muslim armies and their faith. The presence of the Mamlūks in Egypt and of independent Muslim rulers on the Barbary Coast did not ease tensions. Representing a certain degree of political competition for Constantinople in the Levant, these Muslim powers shared much in common with the Ottomans, both religiously and economically, as the example mentioned above shows. The emergence of a new center of power within the Islamic world, however, provided temporary relief from the Ottoman threat, as well as food for thought for Western Europe. Founding the Safavid dynasty and establishing Shiism as the state religion in what is today Iran, Shah Isma'il (r. 1501–1524) challenged the Ottomans not only militarily, but also religiously.[2] Known as Sophy in the West, Shah Isma'il dominated the Ottomans' concerns from 1502 to 1524, thereby also attracting the attention of Christian leaders, Italian first and soon afterward French.

Jean Lemaire de Belges responded passionately to this unprecedented situation. In a 1511 polemical work in which he seemingly comments on events closer to home, the historiographer sets out to demonstrate a Manichean thesis by using a dichromatic palette. The popes, Lemaire claims, are responsible for all the dissension and schisms that have plagued Christianity since the beginning of times— they act like crows. The princes on the other hand, and in particular the French ones, must be credited for their unifying councils—they are doves. The title of Lemaire's work leaves no ambiguity: *Le traictié intitulé, de la difference des scismes et des concilles de l'eglise. Et de la preeminence et utilité des concilles de la saincte eglise gallicane* (The treatise entitled: On the difference between schisms and councils of the church and on the pre-eminence and usefulness of the councils of the Holy Gallican Church).[3] In order to demonstrate the superiority of the Gallican Church over Rome—and by extension the pre-eminence of Louis XII, to whom the *Traicté* is dedicated, over Pope Julius II—Lemaire adopts a simple strategy. Intertwining examples of peace-bringing councils with instances of devastating schisms, he offers a striking contrast similar to the one conveyed in the colors white and black.[4] Presented side by side, schisms and councils (and their respective negative and positive consequences for Christianity) are thus clearly exposed.

What is particularly intriguing in Lemaire's work is that the historiographer introduces two contemporary Muslim leaders to the readers. Shah Isma'il of Safavid Persia and Qānsūh al-Ghawrī, the Mamlūk Sultan, could appear as secondary characters in his denunciation of papal exactions and praise of gallicanism. Yet these essential political figures of the early sixteenth-century Mediterranean are also critical to Lemaire's treatise, the main antithetical pair formed by Louis XII and Julius II being echoed in and reinforced by that of Shah Isma'il and—more problematically—Qānsūh al-Ghawrī. In the following pages, I examine the roles of these non-Ottoman Muslim rulers in the context of early sixteenth-century religious politics before discussing their textual impact on the quasi-absent Ottomans. By analysing the overall structure of Lemaire's work and by focusing on the final sections of the *Traicté*, I underline an early portrayal of the Safavid shah as the "epitome of goodness"[5] and show its limitations. I further show how the active use of Muslim leaders in Lemaire's program of antipapalism and gallicanism might have had the unintended consequence of bringing the Ottomans into clearer focus in France.

A fine *rhétoriqueur* trained by Molinet, Lemaire is keenly aware of the dialectical structure of his treatise. Repeatedly in the *Traicté*, the first edition of which he closely supervised,[6] the historiographer emphasizes the specific arrangement that he has chosen for his ideas regarding schisms and councils, regularly summarizing some sections and announcing others. Repetitions, summaries, prolepses, and analepses give an oral quality to a text that has been carefully crafted and organized. Lemaire, for example, explains what he views as the ternary structure of his central section concerning schisms and councils. The first part, he states, lists the first seven schisms and the early councils and discusses how the church's wealth led to sins such as tyranny and pride. The second part focuses on French councils, while the third part enumerates schisms 8 through 23, as well as the impending 24th one. Lemaire's ternary structure is carried further and strengthened when he acknowledges and names three fifteenth-century authorities—Pope Pius II,[7] Robert Gaguin, and Platina—and gives three reasons for the fall of the universal church—ambition (which he calls the mother of avarice), the absence of general councils, and the interdiction on marriage for Latin priests (96).[8] The *Traicté* functions thus as a triptych: just as one panel echoes and enriches the others, each council responds to schisms. Occupying the central portion of the work, councils are crucial to Lemaire's argument but better understood when viewed with their side panels, schisms—as well as paratextual elements, as we shall see. In other words, each segment of the work can be viewed and interpreted independently as it stands on its own and forms a coherent whole. However, the overall meaning can be better grasped when all the distinct elements are assembled and examined together. More context and more examples build a better case.

Looking at the larger structural level of the *Traicté*, then, one notices the attention paid to its textual design. As already mentioned, the largest section of the *Traicté* reviews the 23 examples of schisms that have plagued Christianity since the Donation of Constantine while evoking in no uncertain terms the 24th one which is yet to come. The councils of princes are described to counterbalance the papacy-induced discords. Jennifer Britnell, who underlines the antipapalism in the *Traicté* and the prophetic sources used by Lemaire, has studied this section in detail.[9] What has not been analyzed by scholars thus far is the paratext. A profusion of introductory 'chapters' and three complementary pieces frame the bulky unit that deals explicitly with schisms and councils. The following outline gives a sense of the intricate structure of the entire work, including its copious introductory pieces. I list the complete titles of the sections or, if there is no heading given in Lemaire's text, the opening words of the segment, to which I add a summary in parenthesis. The number that follows the summary indicates the number of pages devoted to each section in Britnell's edition. Following the title page, the structure of the *Traicté* is thus as follows:

Intitulation de ceste presente euvre . . . (a dedication to Louis XII) (1)

Prologue sur toute l'euvre (a first prologue addressed to benevolent readers that includes a letter to the Venetians in Latin by Emperor Maximilian, along with its translation) (9)

Autre prologue de la matiere principale . . . (a second prologue focusing on both Louis XII and Maximilian) (2)

Commence la premiere partie de ce traictié (the announcement of the beginning of the first part of the *Traicté*) (3)

S'ensuyt ce qui sera contenu en chascun des trois parties de ce traictié (a summary of what is to come, including both content and structure) (2)

Comment sur trois auctoritez principales ce present traictié prent sa fundation (an acknowledgement of the main textual *autorités* used by Lemaire in his *Traicté*) (2)

Le temps du premier scisme . . . (the history of schisms and councils) (140)

Prologue de l'histoire moderne du prince Syach Ysmail, dit Sophy Arduelin (Lemaire's translation of Rota's *La Vita del Sophi* detailing Shah Isma'il's life and accomplishments) (25)

S'ensuit l'occasion et matiere du recent et nouveau saufconduit, donné de plain vouloir par le souldan aux subgectz du roy treschrestien, tant pour aler en pelerinaige au sainct sepulchre, comme trafficquer marchandement en ses terres et seignouries d'oultremer (the background and contents of the economic and religious agreement signed between Louis XII and the Mamlūk sultan in 1511) (10)

Le blason des armes des Venitiens (a satirical rendition of the lion, the symbol of the Venetians) (3)

Lemaire's abundant introduction occupies no less than 16 pages of Britnell's edition, slightly over 8% of the entire work. Lemaire's final pieces, those showcasing Muslim rulers and appearing topically unrelated to the discussion on schisms and councils, occupy roughly 19% of the *Traicté*. In all, the paratext counts for more than 25% of the entire work, a significant proportion that calls for further commentary.

Were it not for the numerical information gathered above, it might be tempting to dismiss such an accumulation of introductions as an example of unskillful poetics that distract the reader from the main text, only delaying the argument, the examples, and the punch line. It would be equally possible to view the last three pieces of the *Traicté* dealing with Muslims in the wide Mediterranean as only tangentially related to the topic at hand focused on Western Europe's Christianity. On the contrary, the paratext, and particularly the final segments that seem so far removed from the antipapal strike, are essential to Lemaire's argument, not only because they occupy such a significant portion of the work, but also because they support the polemicist's Manichean thesis regarding the superiority of the Gallican Church over papacy in a most unexpected and striking way. In addition to accusing Julius II of the Roman Church directly for wrongdoing, these sections highlight a geo-political situation that is opportune for the kingdom of France. Thus, by offering the boldest statement on Pope Julius II, the paratext forms the actual core of the *Traicté* and sets the tone for France's future political directions. Britnell claims that the *Traicté* was written for an unsophisticated audience with the purpose of rallying the masses behind Louis XII. While the seemingly simplistic dichotomy between white and black, councils and schisms may imply a rather uneducated readership, the attention Lemaire gives to the overall structure of the text and its final sections in particular suggests that he intended his work also for a sophisticated audience versed in both international politics and contemporary politico-religious controversies concerning Christianity and Islam. A detailed examination of the *Traicté* is in order.

Lemaire firmly establishes his dichromatic palette and his favorable disposition towards Shah Isma'il at the very beginning of his treatise. In his first prologue, the historiographer declares:

> *Or dit l'auctorité du Philosophe que les choses opposites et differentes se monstrent mieulx quand elles sont approuchées l'une de l'autre, si comme le blanc auprès du noir. Pourquoy n'est possible de mieulx monstrer le bien des concilles qu'en declairant le mal qui s'est ensuivy des scismes, ne de donner à cognoistre ung conservateur de paix, fors en designant par contraire l'infracteur et mutilateur de la ligue et union confederée entre les princes.*
>
> *Pareillement n'est-il possible de donner plus plainement à entendre lequel est digne de plusgrand louenge ou reprehension, ou le chrestien qui a prommis et juré solemnellement faire la guerre aux Turcz et mescreans, et ne le fait pas, ains garde les autres de le faire, et qui plus est trouble toute la Chrestienté, ou l'autre, qui n'a point de loy certaine, et neantmoins tasche à destruire les autres infideles à l'aventaige des chrestiens, ainsi que fait Sophy?* (83–84)

The Philosopher claims that opposite and different things are better revealed when they are shown side by side, like black and white. For this reason there is no better way to show the good aspects of the councils than by announcing the bad that followed schisms; and if one wants to show who keeps the peace, it is better to identify the opposite, the offender and breaker of the league and of the confederate union between princes.

Similarly, how can one show who is worth the highest praise or reproach: the Christian who promised and swore solemnly to fight the Turks and the infidels but keeps others from doing so, in addition to troubling the entire Christendom; or the other, who does not have a sure [religious] law and yet seeks to destroy the other infidels to the advantage of the Christians, as Sophy does?

A series of opposing pairs emerges from this passage: white and black; the good of the councils and the bad caused by schisms; the keeper of the peace and the offender and breaker of the league. Although no Christian ruler is identified by name at this point in the text, the polemicist refers to two of the three signees of the League de Cambrai. Signed in December 1508 between Louis XII, Emperor Maximilian, and Julius II, the League of Cambrai sought to unite Christians in order to launch a crusade against the 'Turks'.[10] Lemaire insists on French loyalty to the League, whereas the pope renounced the treaty in 1510 and planned an offensive against the French. Thus, in the quote, the "conservateur de paix" is the French king, and the "infracteur et mutilateur de la ligue et union confederée entre les princes," the pope.

The second paragraph of the quote offers a parallel structure introduced by "pareillement," leaving no ambiguity about the unexpected equation drawn between Louis XII and Sophy, the Safavid ruler. Hence, Julius II, "the offender and breaker of the league," is the "chrestien qui a prommis et juré solemnellement faire la guerre aux Turcz et mescreans, et ne le fait pas," now counterbalanced by the one who, according to the text, does not hesitate to wage war against the 'Turks,' that is to say the Safavid shah. Caught between Louis XII and Shah Isma'il, Pope Julius II is framed, both textually and politically. In the above quote, the French king and the Safavid shah are aligned thanks to an indirect reference to Louis XII and the naming of Sophy which surround two allusions to Julius II as if to contain and offset what Lemaire sees as the pope's regrettable decision to break the League. Using terms recalling this quote, the *rhétoriqueur* expresses his accusation against Julius II again in a second passage:

> *Après avoir monstré par le traictié precedent combien il y a de différence entre scismes et concilles, et que les scismes sonnent tousjours en mal et les concilles en bien et que le xxiiiie tresgrand scisme futur sera precurseur de la venue d'Anthecrist, selon la prommesse que nous avons faicte ou premier prologue de ceste euvre, nous monstrerons consequemment lequel est digne de plusgrand louenge ou reprehension, ou le chrestiien qui a prommis et juré solennellement faire la guerre aux Turcz et mescreans et n'en fait riens, ains garde les autres de ce faire, et qui plus est trouble et scandalise toute la Chrestienté, ou l'autre qui n'a point de loy et neantmoins tasche à destruire les autres infideles de la loy machometiste. Et qui plus est, ledit prince sans loy [. . .] enhorte par exemple de faict et s'efforce de admonester par embassades expresses les princes chrestiens à faire le semblable, là où celui qui se dit le chief de la religion chrestiienne monstre tout l'opposite.* (238–39)

In the preceding [section of the] treatise, we showed how major a difference there is between schisms and councils—the former always resounding
badly, and the latter positively—and discussed the impending twenty-fourth
schism that will precede the coming of the Antichrist. As promised in the first
prologue, we will now demonstrate who is deserving of praise or admonish-
ment: the Christian who has promised and solemnly sworn to fight the Turks
and the disbelievers but who does nothing save preventing others to act and
who, moreover, troubles and scandalizes the entire Christendom; or the other
who is without religious law and yet tries to destroy the other infidels of the
Muhammadan law. In addition, this lawless prince [. . .] rules by example
and, sending embassies to Christian princes, encourages them to do the same
whereas the one who calls himself head of the Christian religion shows all
the opposite.

Occuring 154 pages after the first quote, this passage serves as both the conclusion
to the section on schisms and councils and the opening of the "Histoire moderne
du prince Syach Ysmail." Expressly linking two ostensibly disparate sections of
his treatise together, the historiographer reminds readers of the opposition he sees
between the head of the Catholic Church in 1511 and the Safavid ruler while seg-
ueing into a detailed biography of the latter. Lemaire continues to accuse the pope
of wrongdoing until, in a logical conclusion to the "Histoire moderne du prince
Syach Ysmail," he compares Julius II to a crow while presenting the Safavid ruler
as a dove:

> *Si par l'autre traictié precedent nous avons monstré quelle difference il y a
> entre les scismes et les concilles, maintenant aussi avons-nous donné bonne
> et facile conjecture combien il y a adire entre ung corbeau et ung coulon:
> le coulon apporta en l'arche de Noé la branche d'olive, qui est signe de
> paix entre Dieu et les hommes, mais le corbeau demoura obstiné sur une
> charongne puante. Sophy cerche et tasche par tous moyens d'accorder les
> princes chrestiiens pour destruire les infideles, et le grand evesque de nostre
> loy n'y veult entendre.* (262–63)
>
> In the other [section of the] treatise we showed the difference between
> schisms and councils; we have now revealed in a fine and easy conjecture
> what there is to say between a crow and a dove. For the dove brought the
> olive branch to Noah's ark, a sign of peace between God and men, but the
> crow remained stuck on a stinking rotten carcass. While Sophy is attempting
> to unite Christian princes in order to destroy the infidels, the great bishop of
> our law wants to hear nothing about it.

In this passage, whereas Shah Isma'il is associated with the white bird that
announced the end of Noah's trial and commonly represents the Holy Spirit in
Christian iconography, Julius II is compared to a scavenging crow. This image of
crow and dove is directly inspired by Genesis 7 and 8, which do not simply mention the presence of pure and impure animals aboard Noah's ark, but specifically

single out a crow and a dove.[11] Lemaire's vivid imagery echoes a woodcut found in a fifteenth-century *Vie de Jésus-Christ* published in Lyon in which both dove and crow are depicted, the latter eating the carcass of a bovine, the former flying with an olive branch in its beak toward Noah and his wife in the ark.[12] The fact that Lemaire punctuates his narrative with visual and ideological contrasts located at important junctures and that his boldest attack against the papacy occurs not in the section dealing with schisms but at the conclusion of the "Histoire moderne du prince Syach Ysmail" demonstrates how crucial the final sections of the *Traicté* are to his main argument regarding the superiority of gallicanism—and by extension France—over Rome.

Lemaire's indictment of the papacy in general and of Julius II in particular is accompanied by a glorious, if not entirely unequivocal, portrayal of Shah Isma'il. The *rhétoriqueur* indicates that this section of the *Traicté* is a *histoire* that he translated "d'ytalien en françois" (257), and Pierre Jodogne has demonstrated that the polemicist's version of Shah Isma'il's story is a rather literal translation of Giovanni Rota's *La vita del Sophi*, published most probably in 1508 in Venice, where Lemaire may have acquired it.[13] The differences between *La vita del Sophi* and the *Traicté* are minimal, but they are not insignificant. As Peter Burke has shown, there was no simple act of translation in the Renaissance.[14] Here the historiographer, acting as cultural broker, translates an Italian text into French, occasionally adding his own commentaries to Rota and importing into French society new information on the Islamic East. Lemaire's translation project was not simply a scholarly exercise in linguistic dexterity; it also had a utilitarian dimension. The story of Shah Isma'il served as the perfect illustration for Lemaire's case in support of the Gallican Church and against the corruption and wickedness of popes.

In order for Lemaire to convince his readers that Shah Isma'il is the pope's foil, he distinguishes between the Safavid leader and the Ottomans. Lemaire notes that Shah Isma'il, a Shia, belongs to a group of Muslims whose ancestors go back to "Haly," Prophet Muhammad's cousin and son-in-law. According to the Shia tradition, Lemaire explains—closely following Rota—Ali should have been recognized as Muhammad's rightful successor but was not. Like his illustrious ancestor, Shah Isma'il was denied power: his father's untimely death forced him to spend his childhood in exile. Patient, just, generous, virtuous, the Safavid leader is depicted as an avid reader like his father, an erudite patron who justly appreciated the scholars who surrounded him. Furthermore, Shah Isma'il is oblivious to vanity and comes from "tresnoble et royalle lignée" (242) (very noble and royal lineage). He and his followers, (Rota and) Lemaire suggests, might belong to the one sect of Muslims that will access Paradise. Mixing *hadith* with the Christian understanding of Heaven, Lemaire thus encourages readers to fathom the Safavid leader as rightful leader in addition to generous patron. His abundant qualities match his numerous military victories, notably in Tabriz, Shiraz, and Herat, all of which Rota and, in turn, Lemaire described. As a consequence, Shah Isma'il is feared by the Ottomans, whom he abhors. His recent conquests, in fact, suggest that he might be a prophet ready for future and even more dramatic wars against no other than the 'Turks' and the Venetians.

Besides underlining Shah Isma'il's temperament and military successes, Lemaire also notes and comments on more mundane characteristics, such as his dietary habits. "Il boit du vin, mais secretement, et menge chair de porc, lesquelles choses sont deffendues en la loy machommetiste" (245) (He drinks wine, but secretly, and eats pork, both of which are forbidden by Muhammadan law), claims the historiographer, thereby suggesting that the Sunni Ottomans have a stricter understanding of dietary laws than Shia Safavids. Here, Lemaire translates Rota—"il boit du vin," "menge chair de porc"—while inserting his own commentary—"mais secretement"—on how Shah Isma'il transgresses Islamic rules concerning the consumption of alcohol and meat, "lesquelles choses sont deffendues en la loy machommetiste." While intensifying the gap between the Ottomans and the Safavids, uniformly represented as Sunnis and Shias respectively, the polemicist aligns Shah Isma'il further with Louis XII. He de-islamicizes and christianizes the Safavid shah who, according to Lemaire, is engaged in a crusade against his enemy, the Ottoman sultan (248).[15] A pseudo-Christian Shah Isma'il was not unheard of in the 1510s; in 1507 a *canard* claimed that the Safavid leader had been baptized.[16] Lemaire insists on the proximity between French and Safavid rulers and claims that because Shah Isma'il prefers Christians over Jews and Ottomans he is making friendly overtures to western powers:

> *Syach Ysmail het si tresparfondement les Juyfz que partout il en treuve il leur fait crever les yeulx et puis les laisse aler. Mais . . . il persecute encoires plus les Turcz. . . . Aux chrestiens il se monstre benivolent, car il laisse en son entier toutes leurs eglises et chappelles sans y toucher par violence, et maine avec lui le patriarche d'Armenie et pluiseurs prestres et religieux tenans nostre foy. Dont pour monstrer le grand desir qu'il a de destruire de rasse et de fons en comble la loy machommetiste, il s'est efforcé par pluiseurs foys de solliciter les princes chrestiens à ce qu'ilz esmeussent la guerre au Turc du costé d'Europe, et que de la part d'Asie il ne lui fauldroit pas. (258–59)*
>
> Shah Isma'il hates the Jews so deeply that whenever he meets them he puts their eyes out before letting them go. But . . . he persecutes the Turks even more. . . . He is benevolent to the Christians for he leaves their churches and chapels alone; he does not strike them violently but he brings with him the Armenian patriarch and several other priests and clergymen of our faith. And to show the great desire he has to destroy the Muhammadan faith in its entirety, he has tried on several occasions to solicit the Christian princes to fight the Turk in Europe while he attacks him in Asia.

Lemaire suggests that if Shah Isma'il is serious about fighting fellow Muslims and extending his hand to Christian princes to crush their common enemy, the Ottomans, then why not take advantage of this situation? Here the *rhétoriqueur* anchors his historiography in the present and shows an acute awareness of the delicate balance of power within the Islamo-Christian world of the early sixteenth century. He goes beyond the dichotomy of Islam and Christianity and breaks the barrier of incommensurability between the two religions by suggesting certain affinities between Louis XII and Shah Isma'il.

Nevertheless, Lemaire is cautious not to assimilate the French Catholic king to a Muslim ruler too directly. He mentions, for example, that when it comes to lust Shah Isma'il is "assez honneste selon la coustume du pays et selon ce que porte sa loy" (245) (rather honest according to his country's customs and what his law recommends) implying that, despite the Safavid ruler's sophistication and tolerance—if not quite inclination—toward Christianity, he is limited in his potential by his culture and his religion. These precautions seem to be in line with the fact that the sections of the *Traicté* depicting Muslim rulers come at the end of Lemaire's work. Regardless, while seemingly presented as accessory, these segments treating new and foreign elements regarding Shah Isma'il paradoxically form the crux of the *Traicté*.

In spite of a clear textual rapprochement between Louis XII and Shah Isma'il, and however sympathetic Lemaire may be toward Shah Isma'il, the historiographer reminds the reader that the ultimate goal, one that the pope is miserably failing to accomplish, is the eradication of all faiths other than Christianity. Lemaire specifically targets Islam, which he considers as a heresy that needs to be crushed. He adds his own strong-worded commentary to Rota's text—"Mahometh, seducteur, faux prophete" (Muhammad, the seducer, the false prophet), "leur loy, ou plustot superstition" (their [religious] law; or, rather, their superstition)—and thereby aligns himself with his predecessor and mentor, Jean Molinet who, in his "Complainte de Grèce," pleads—perhaps not so honestly—in favor of a crusade aimed at the Ottomans.[17] Lemaire himself had expressed his hope for unity among Christians following the demise of Cambrai in his *Concorde des deux languages* (1508). A similar optimism is stated in his *Illustrations de Gaule et singularités de Troie* (1511–13): "De tous lesquelz grandz peuples les princes et dominateurs qui auront prins origine de Troyens, après l'abolition de toutes vielles querelles et ennemistiez anciennes, s'armeront par concorde unanime contre les tyrans de Turquie" (Of all these great peoples, the princes and rulers who originate from Troy, after the abolition of old quarrels and oppositions, will arm themselves in unanimous agreement against the tyrants of Turkey).[18]

Although he firmly situates himself within the tradition of a universal Christian Church and the crusade, Lemaire advocates an alliance with an Islamic ruler. Still, his narrative makes clear that, despite Shah Isma'il's similarity with Louis XII, the Safavid ruler is neither the "epitome of goodness" as Britnell argues, nor Christianity's new ally. Rather, in Vihlo Harle's terms, he is a "worthy enemy."[19] According to Lemaire, for whom gray is never an option, the Persian shah will sooner or later turn into either a dove or a crow. The poet does not evoke how Shah Isma'il and his followers will eventually convert or be eradicated but, in translating Rota's work, the polemicist finds the occasion to openly accuse Julius II of incompetence while presenting striking and novel information about Islam to a French audience. In his *Traicté*, politics and religion remain inseparable entities. Nevertheless, a step has been taken toward the Islamic East.

We do not know Louis XII's reaction to Lemaire's proposal to establish ties with Shah Isma'il. However, Francis, who would succeed Louis XII in 1515, would consider such an option seriously. Before being crowned, he asked a Franciscan monk, Jean Thenaud, to gather information about Shah Isma'il. Once king, the young Francis responds to Pope Leo X's attempt to rally Christian kings for a new crusade in 1516–1517 as follows:

> *T[rès]. S[aint]. P[ère]. Vosdits déléguez ont aussi advise que seroit utile et profitable d'avoir intelligence au sophy ou autre prince infidelle pour mieux parvenir à confondre le Turc. Sy me semble leur advis ester bon, et mesmement car par ce moien leur sera osté le chemin d'eux joindre, et avec ce, par la communication et intelligence que pourrons avoir ensemble, se pourra faire, avec l'ayde de Dieu, qu'ils pourront réduire à la foy chrestienne; et, d'autre part, la fin et intention pourquoy on le faict est bonne, car ne consiste à les favoriser et augmenter, ains pour les réduire à la foy chrestienne et pour la conserver et augmenter et affoiblir nos ennemis par leurs mains.[20]*

Holy Father, your delegates have also advised that it would be useful and profitable to negotiate with Sophy or some other infidel prince in order to better confound the Turk. This seems to be good advice, especially because this way they will not be able to join forces and so it could be that, with our common communication and intelligence, they might, with God's help, convert to the Christian faith; and besides, the goal and reason why we are seeking such an alliance are good ones, for it is not in order to favor and augment their faith, but it is to reduce them to the Christian faith and to preserve and strengthen it as we weaken our enemies with their own hands.

Lemaire was never as explicit in his *Traicté*, but his suggestion to consider the Safavid ruler as a potential ally was neither outlandish—it made a lot of geopolitical sense—nor unique, the Italian humanists having alluded to such a possibility.[21] Thus, long before Jean Chardin and Jean-Baptiste Tavernier, a French observer emphasized the Safavids' cultural proximity with the French, and embodied a new *politique d'ouverture* towards the Islamic East, one that coincidentally was already in effect in 1511.

Indeed, agreements between Louis XII and Qānsūh al-Ghawrī were passed following the skirmish involving the Knights of St. John and the Mamlūks with which we began this chapter. Lemaire gives precious, if not unbiased, details about this episode, which is otherwise poorly documented. Off the coast of Ayas and Alexandretta, the Knights captured 24 or 25 Mamlūk ships in August 1510 and killed or took to Rhodes as captives 2,000 Muslims. The consequences for Christians in the Levant were immediate and dire: merchants in Egypt and Syria were imprisoned while clerics in Jerusalem and the Holy Land were arrested. To resolve the standoff, the Mamlūks chose to send an envoy to the king of France, whom they saw as a powerful interlocutor and possible intercessor with the Knights. Lemaire indicates that Qānsūh al-Ghawrī chose a Christian from Ragusa to represent him, a detail showing once again the political workings of religion at

the beginning of the sixteenth century, especially the capriciousness and the pragmatism that characterized the Islamo-Christian relationship. The idea of having
the French as mediators came from Philippe de Peretz, one of the countless early
modern go-betweens whom official history has forgotten. A Frenchman, de Peretz
was the consul for the French and the Catalans in Alexandria. He viewed himself
as the spokesperson for the entire Frankish community of merchants and as such
antagonized the Venetians, whose presence in Mamlūk Egypt was not neglige-
able. Lemaire describes de Peretz's rapport with Qānsūh al-Ghawrī as excellent.
Though de Peretz was arrested like all the other merchants, he nevertheless managed to contact the Mamlūk sultan to propose a way out of the impasse. The
French king will help solve the dispute, de Peretz suggested, putting Louis XII
himself in the position of an intermediary. A message offering Louis XII jurisdic-
tion over all holy sites in the Levant was soon carried by the envoy. The king
responded quickly, sending a messenger back to Qānsūh al-Ghawrī on a Rhodian
ship, proving therefore his authority over the Order. The agreement was passed:
Frankish merchants were released and the French became guardians of the sacred
places in the Levant.

What Lemaire's story does not tell is the Mamlūk's side. Were the captives,
now in Rhodes, freed or bought back? Were goods—wood, weapons—recovered?
These considerations are superfluous for Lemaire, who first praises the victory
of the noble and valiant Knights over the Mamlūks. This success was just, he
claims, since the Mamlūks, the Ottomans' political competitors in the southern
Mediterranean in the 1510s, had conveniently allied with them in order to attack
Rhodes, exactly as Christians had united under the League of Cambrai to wage
war against the 'Turks.' The fact the Knights had commandeered the Gulf of Ayas
directly caused Louis XII to gain the right to administer the sacred places in the
Levant and Christian travelers to gain safe conduct there, both of which privileges
gave "grand honneur et gloire" (263) to the French king. By indicating that the
agreement was announced publicly in Lyon and by giving it the semblance of a
faithful reproduction in his own text, Lemaire emphasizes the new and enviable
position of France in the Mediterranean and the Levant, obtained miraculously at
the expense of the Venetians, who were seen not only as economic rivals, but as
the papacy's and the Ottomans' allies:

> *Brief, ung chascun bon prince ne quiert aujourduy que paix, et a postposé*
> *toutes vielles ennimistiez et rancunes, excepté les Venitiens . . . lesquelz ont*
> *suborné le pape, et ne se monstrent estre autre chose synon les certains pro-*
> *cureurs et deffenseurs des Turcz, et ne se convertissent à bien pour mal ou*
> *infortune qui leur adviegne. Ilz mesprisent les signes du ciel, les prodiges,*
> *les comettes, les tremblementz de terre (qui sont admonitions divines) et sont*
> *obstinez, comme les Juyfz estoient du temps de leur grand ruyne faicte par*
> *Vespasian.* (272)

In short, each and every noble prince only desires peace nowadays and has
postponed all ancient quarrels and rancour, except for the Venetians . . . who
have subordinated the pope and show themselves to be nothing but the Turks'

advocates and defenders, and who do not convert to doing good regardless of the evil and misfortune that strike them. They ignore heavenly signs, prodigies, comets, earthquakes (that are all divine warnings) and are as obstinate as the Jews were when they were crushed by Vespasian.

The concluding *blason*, a scathing satirical rendition of the lion, symbol of the Republic of Venice, underlines the vanishing power of Venice in favor of Louis XII, the hedgehog that has domesticated both the Venetian lion and Rome's elephant. Lemaire concludes by inserting two short prophecies forecasting the demise of the Republic and referring to his other polemical piece targeting Venice, *La légende des Vénitiens* (1509).

While criticizing Christian Venice, Lemaire reiterates the superiority of a Muslim leader, Qānsūh al-Ghawrī, over Pope Julius II one last time:

> *Grandz merveilles differentes voyons-nous en nostre temps! Velà le souldan Abymazar Sarrasin, qui se monstre tant gracieux et tant benivole, et donne au roy treschrestiien le tiltre de la conservation du sainct sepulchre, et oultreplus saufconduit, seurté et grandz privilieges aux subgectz de la couronne de France. Et le pape au contraire les mauldit et excommunie à tort et par grand ingratitude.* (270–71)
>
> What great marvels do we see in our time! Here is the Sultan Abymazar Sarrasin who shows himself to be so gracious and helpful and gives to the most Christian king the right to oversee the Holy Sepulchre and to his subjects the rights of passage, safety, and privileges. And then there is the pope who curses and excommunicates wrongfully and thanklessly.

Lemaire's *Traicté* gives France a fresh and significant role in Mediterranean affairs by taking the idea of uniting with a Muslim leader seriously. Jean Thenaud would show its viability.

Decentering Pilgrimage:
Jean Thenaud's *Peregrinatio* as Prelude to the Ottomans

Barely two months after the publication of Lemaire's *Traicté*, a *cordelier* took advantage of the agreements concluded between Louis XII and Qānsūh al-Ghawrī. Jean Thenaud departed from Angoulême on July 2, 1511, to perform a pilgrimage to the Holy Land on behalf of Louise de Savoie. By late August, he was fulfilling her wishes:

> *Je fuz au couvent de Bethleem le vingt et uniesme d'aoust, environ unze heures au matin; auquel lieu premierement offriz en la saincte chapelle de la Nativité, or, myrrhe, et encens que avoye apporté et preparé selon le mandement et vouloir de la souveraine tresredoubtée et illustre dame, qui vouloit telles choses estre offertes audict lieu à son intention et de monseigneur à present notre Roy tresauguste et serenissime.* (89–90)[22]

I arrived at the convent in Bethlehem on August 21 at about 11 in the morning; there, at the holy Chapel of the Nativity, I first offered gold, myrth, and incense that I had brought and prepared according to the request and wishes of my illustrious lady, the queen, who wanted such presents to be offered there on her behalf and that of my present lord, our august Highness, the king.

Thenaud returned to France with some cotton saturated with oil that had oozed from Saint Catherine's bones, as well as pieces of candle and rock from the tomb where the saint was originally buried near Mount Sinai. These relics were then placed in the Angoulême and Cognac convents.[23] Thenaud's pilgrimage and its corresponding exchange of intentions and gifts had ended. However, in addition to displaying material proofs of and souvenirs from his trip that were intended to keep the memory of the saint and of the *cordelier*'s pilgrimage alive, Thenaud may also have delivered one or several oral accounts of his journey. More tangibly, he composed a narrative from which the quote above is excerpted, *Le voyage et itinaire* (sic) *de oultre mer faict par frere Jehan Thenaud, maistre es ars, docteur en theologie et gardien des freres mineurs d'Angoulesme*. The *Voyage* was published several years after the *cordelier*'s journey, well into the sixteenth century when pilgrimage narratives continued to be generated.[24] At first sight, Thenaud's account falls squarely within the tradition of medieval pilgrimages as described by Friedrich Wolfzettel in *Le discours du voyageur*.[25] Reiterative more than innovative, the pilgrim's account follows a structure that is both familiar and linear. Repeating or echoing previous narratives such as Felix Faber's and Bernard de Breydenbach's,[26] it relates a collective experience characterized by its atemporality and its telos, both geographical and spiritual. Jerusalem occupies a central position in the mind of the Christian pilgrim, as it did on medieval maps. The pilgrim-narrator follows ancient routes which he carves further for future travelers, detailing curiosities on the way to and in the Holy Land. He reproduces, in his physical itinerary, the spiritual voyage on which he has embarked. According to his account, Thenaud traveled from Angoulême to Cairo, where he visited Saint Catherine, before heading for Jerusalem. On the return trip, he describes numerous cities and islands on the Mediterranean—among which Rhodes occupies a special place—but, structurally, the core of the account remains the Holy Land which constitutes roughly the middle section of the narrative. His experience can, then, benefit "ceulx qui auront devotion à la Terre Saincte" (those who will come to pray for the Holy Land) since, thanks to Thenaud's report, they will be able to safely visit the Holy Land in spirit if not in body.[27]

Even though the *Voyage* fits well into the theoretical model delineated by Wolfzettel, Thenaud's account does not fit neatly the category of medieval pilgrimage narrative. Frédéric Tinguely has shown the changes occurring in sixteenth-century accounts of pilgrimage and judiciously underlined the uniqueness and the modernity of the *cordelier*'s work that, like Lemaire' *Traicté*, openly supports gallicanism.[28] Thus, in addition to reporting his religious travels to the Holy Land, the *cordelier* comments on the political situation in France. Thenaud's *Voyage* is the counterpoint and complement of Lemaire's polemical work, the latter bringing Islam into a seemingly exclusive Christian debate, the former discussing French matters during a trip through the Mediterranean and to the Levant. Thenaud's account delves into both the Islamic world and French realpolitic. Looking at centers and peripheries in the *Voyage* highlights the generic ambiguity and the richness of a work that deviates from established conventions.[29] I will consider the following four aspects of the work: the multiplication of named places outside of Jerusalem; the role of commerce in a pilgrimage account; the presence of the "I"; and the importance of the present within a supposed collective and self-effacing account. Even though Jerusalem is the goal of the traveler, several other *loci*—Egypt, Persia, Medina, and Mecca—populate the narrative in a major way, decentering the pilgrimage narrative. What happens, then, when the periphery becomes central? Similarly, although religion is the apparent engine of the narrative, politics and trade are obvious points of interest for Thenaud, who weaves them tightly into his account. Under these circumstances, what remains of the pilgrimage and of Christianity? And what to make of the narrator's presence in the text? Looking at specific anecdotes involving an interpreter and an Arab prince, I analyze the repercussions a strong narrative voice might have had on the reception of the *Voyage* in France. Finally, I probe the text's atemporality. Published more than a decade after Thenaud's travel, the pilgrimage narrative was impacted by events that shaped its composition; it might in turn have affected future political decisions in the French kingdom.

Mapping the Periphery: Cairo, Persia, Mecca

In the *Voyage*, Thenaud takes several stops and detours from his acknowledged destination—Jerusalem. The opening of the narration is explicit: this will be the story of several voyages, in the plural.

> *Recommendations et veux faictz ès glorieulx sainctz Ausonne et Cibart patrons de la cité et ville d'Angoulesme, partis dudict lieu le second jour de juillet, l'an mil cinq cens et unze pour faire les voyages d'oultremer, c'est assavoir Hierusalem, du mont Sinay et du Cayre.* (1–2)
>
> Having recommended myself and expressed my vows to the glorious Ausone et Cybard, patron saints of the city of Angoulême, I left from the said place on the second of July, in the year fifteen hundred and eleven, to go on travels to the Levant, that is to say to Jerusalem, Mount Sinai, and Cairo.

In the medieval period and still in the sixteenth century, Egypt, and particularly Cairo, was a typical passageway for pilgrims traveling to the Holy Land.[30] The *Voyage*, however, depicts the Egyptian city not simply as a mandatory or expected pause in a long trip, but as a goal in itself. From periphery, Cairo becomes center. Indeed, during parts of his journey, Thenaud joins the political delegation to Cairo headed by André Le Roy, whom Louis XII sent to Qānsūh al-Ghawrī to reestablish cordial relations between the Knights of Rhodes and Mamlūk Egypt—as well as to obtain the liberation of the Frankish merchants in the Levant and the reopening of the Levantine sacred sites. More specifically, Le Roy is in charge of

> ... *porter lettres au Souldan d'Egipte et de Babilloyne qui detenoit en prison le gardien et les religieux de Hierusalem, lesquelz avoit osté du Sainct Sepul-chre en le fermant à tous les Latins ; qui semblablement detenoit le consul des Françoys et Castellans, Phelippes de Peretz avecques plusieurs marchans et marchandises qui se trouverent en ses terres, païs et seigneuries, après ce que les nobles chevaliers de Rhodes (inconcussibles coulompnes de la foy) eurent deffaict son armée de mer, bruslé nefz, occis mammelus et capit-aines, au gouffre de la Iace, par le vouloir et mandement de treshonnorable seigneur messire Aymeri d'Amboise, grant maistre dudict Rhodes, car ledict Souldan s'estoit complainct au Roy, disant sadicte armée avoir esté prinse et deffaicte soubz umbre de paix et saufconduict (qui n'estoit pas vray.) Et le prioit comme prince treschrestien pourveoir à ce que ... ses dommaiges et interestez il fut satisfaict. Et, en ce faisant, luy faisoit offre du Sainct Sepul-chre.* (4–5)[31]
>
> ... carrying letters to the Sultan of Egypt and Babylon who was detain-ing the guardian and the clerics of Jerusalem, after removing them from the Holy Sepulchre and closing it to the Latins; who similarly was detaining the consul of the French and Catalans, Philippe de Peretz, and with him several merchants and merchandise that happen to be in his land, country, and ter-ritories, after the noble Knights of Rhodes (unwavering columns of the faith) had defeated his fleet, burnt boats, killed Mamlūks and captains, at the gulf of Ayas, by order of the most venerable lord Aymeri d'Amboise, grand master of Rhodes. For the Sultan had complained to the King saying that his army had been captured and defeated in times of peace and truce (which was not true). And he was asking the most Christian prince ... to compensate him satisfactorily while offering him the Saint Sepulchre.

According to Thenaud and unlike Lemaire, who is silent about this aspect of the embassy, the negotiations were extremely difficult and put the French delegation under stress.[32] Nevertheless, the Mamlūk ruler offered France unprecedented and advantageous travel and economic agreements that can be viewed as antecedents to the Capitulations that were devised between the French kingdom and the Otto-man Empire some 20 years later.[33]

In addition to Cairo, a second political destination appears in the *Voyage*: Per-sia. While Louise de Savoie requested Thenaud to fullfill a religious mission, her son and future king of France, Francis, Count of Angoulême, asked the pilgrim to establish preliminary contacts with Shah Isma'il. Thenaud states that the king "vouloit que fisse mon effort pour aller en Perse veoir Sophy et sçavoir quelle estoit sa court" (3) (wanted me to go to Persia to see Sophy and to know more about his court). In power since 1494, Shah Isma'il occupied the Ottomans on the southeastern front of their empire and was seen as a potential ally for the French—against the Ottomans, the pope, or both, as Lemaire's *Traicté* shows.

Although for some unspecified reasons, Thenaud will never meet Shah Isma'il,[34] he claims to have, by chance, encountered a Persian princess fleeing persecution. Seeking protection from Qānsūh al-Ghawrī, she joins Thenaud's caravan momentarily. With the notable exception of female mystics like Hildegard of Bingen, Margery Kempe, or Marguerite Porete, travel and pilgrimage narratives of the medieval and early modern periods rarely include women as narrator or character. Thenaud's "dame de Perse" is thus a rare and notable female manifestation in the *Voyage*. Mysterious and invisible like the territory she incarnates, Thenaud's princess remains inaccessible to both traveler and reader, but her company tells of her grandeur. Fifty camels carry her bags; she is protected by 20 bodyguards and accompanied by the women of her court; a blind man sings the story of her ancestors and prays to God continuously. Her litter is "moult belle et riche" (118–19) (extremely beautiful and rich), her food delicate and refined, and her caravan continuously lit at night. The Muslim women—be they Egyptian or Ottoman— described decades later by Pierre Belon and Nicolas de Nicolay are very tangible, observed (admittedly) directly by the French travelers. Literally engraved in their accounts, they are portrayed twice, in words and in woodcuts. Thenaud's text, on the contrary, proposes the hazy portrayal of a Persian lady with an ethereal manifestation. The dreamlike vision constitutes a welcomed pause in the narrative, a literary respite that speaks and perhaps responds to a future monarch's wishes and political needs—for if Shah Isma'il resembles this noble, wealthy, and devout Persian princess, Thenaud suggests, then France should feel welcome to pursue contacts with the Safavid dynasty and eventually associate with Persia. For the time being, such a political collaboration would remain in the realm of the imaginary. Thenaud's description of his encounter with the ephemeral princess represents an unrealized and unofficially formulated wish on behalf of French royals to engage with Shah Isma'il.

After Cairo and Persia, Thenaud takes his readers to the Arabic peninsula. This time, the reader is invited to walk, mentally, to Mecca and Medina. A caravan of Muslim pilgrims met in Cairo brings the two most important places of pilgrimage for Sunni Muslims to the *cordelier*'s mind. Heavily borrowed from Ludovico de Varthema,[35] this episode allows Thenaud to map the wide surroundings of the road to Jerusalem. After a political Cairo and an imaginary Persia surface the literary and religious sister cities of Mecca and Medina. Six pages suffice to take the reader to uncharted territories for Christians and to round up this brief but extraordinary interlude on Islam, which is supported by short remarks throughout the narrative— a preacher heard in Foue, a mosque sighted in Damascus, veiled women, and dietary rules. During this digression, Thenaud juxtaposes Islam with Christianity. Around the Ka'bah, pilgrims turn to "gaigner les pardons" (39) (earn forgiveness) and when they splash themselves with Zamzam water, it is as if they are purifying themselves with holy water, or being baptized. The Islamic rituals are thus decoded using a grid familiar to Christian readers.[36] By including a second pilgrimage— to Mecca and Medina—within the pilgrimage to Jerusalem, Thenaud multiplies sacred places, thereby de-emphasizing the centrality of the Holy Land and opening the narrative to new horizons, at once religious, political, and economic.

Rather than following closely a well-traveled path, rather than establishing a frontier or a border between Christian and Muslim territories and religious practices, Thenaud seeks to multiply geographic destinations. He assimilates Islamic and Christian rituals of pilgrimage and expands French horizons—both spatial and religious—by stretching the genre of pilgrimage narrative. The steps he takes are certainly small and hesitant. The narrative's digressions implying 'third spaces'[37] are always brief, safely kept at a distance by way of politics, imagination, or religion, and sometimes borrowed from previous authors. Nevertheless, in the *Voyage*, Thenaud confirms that it is possible to envision a larger and less constricted world, one which, without focusing directly on the Ottomans, invites them in.

"Des Senteurs, des Pierreries, des Soyes, des Toilles, des Drogues, des Tappiz": From Religion to Commerce

What connects the web of *loci* identified and described by Thenaud—Egypt, Persia, Arabia, and less explicitly but as surely Ottoman lands—is commerce. In the *Voyage*, the Muslim pilgrims' caravan heads toward Mecca for business as much as religious devotion: "[la] compaignie qui estoit allée à la Mecque tant pour le faict de marchandise que pour voyager" (33) ([the] group that had gone to Mecca as much for commerce as for travel). It carries "grande quantité d'espiceries, drogues, pierres precieuses et odeurs" (37) (a great quantity of spices, drugs, precious stones, and perfumes) to be sold *en route* or in Mecca itself, since around the Ka'bah "se vendent les senteurs comme castor, ambre, musc, lignum aloes et aultres maintes choses dont l'air est tout odorant" (38) (are sold perfumes like castor, amber, musk, lignum aloes, and many other things whose smells fill the air). Pilgrimage turns to trade. Despite dangerous routes,[38] merchants trade widely in Arabia including in Djedda, the Red Sea port through which merchandise passes between India, Ethiopia, Persia, Arabia, and Europe. Similarly, on the Red Sea, boats abound carrying "drogues et espiceries qui de là se transportent au Cayre, puis en Alexandrie" (80) (drugs and spices that are, from there, transported to Cairo, then to Alexandria).

During the medieval period, European merchants were active participants in the spice trade, many having settled in Alexandria or Cairo. Thenaud's narrative corroborates the continued presence of French merchants in Egypt in the early sixteenth century. During his 1511 mission, Le Roy hopes to free "plusieurs marchans et marchandises" (4) (several merchants and merchandises) and Thenaud mentions two Frenchmen by name: Richard Marie, a merchant from Lyon, and Francis de Lalle, from Montpellier, now a resident of Damietta where

> *le pays . . . est moult bon et fertile en bledz, sucres, pastures, chairs et poissons. Aussi de Grece, chascun jour sont amenées grandes marchandises de vin, huylle, . . . fromaiges, boys, miel, cyre et drapz. A ceste cause sont là plusieurs Grecz demourans . . . sur lesquelz est ung consul Venicien et sur aultres marchans. Lequel ne me voulut loger, prester vestemens pour dire messe, ne faire aulcune charité pour le temps que estoye là. Parquoy me retiray ches*

ung More où estoit logé messire Francisque de Lalle, marchand de Montpel-
lier, qui chargeoit casse, fistulle et aultres marchandises. (122)

the country . . . is very good and fertile in wheat, sugar, pastures, meat, and
fish. And so from Greece, every day, are brought great quantities of wine,
oil, . . . cheese, wood, honey, wax, and cloth. Several Greeks stay busy with
this trade . . .; a Venetian consul oversees them and the other merchants. He
did not accept to host me, nor did he lend me clothes to perform a religious
service, neither was he charitable while I was there. For this reason, I went to
a Moor's house where Sir Francisque de Lalle, a merchant from Montpellier
trading cassia fistula and other merchandise was staying.

Competing openly with Venetians, French merchants were neither the oldest nor
the newest comers in Egypt and the Levant. Whereas the French and the Greeks
seemed to trade exclusively on and around the Mediterranean, the Portuguese had
begun to bypass other Europeans as well as merchants from the Islamic world
in the spice trade thanks to their recent circumnavigation of Africa. Thenaud
acknowledges what he and Muslim traders of the period consider the disruptive
role the Portuguese played in the Levant trade when he mentions that Egyptian
galleys attempted to stop Portugal "de plus aller ès Indies, car il degastoit son
trafic de marchandise et celuy de la Mecque. Aussi avoit jà conquis plusieurs
choses en Arabie la Fertille, Ethiope et Indie" (64) (from going further to India,
for it ruined its [Egypt's] trade and that of Mecca while it had already conquered
several things in Arabia Felix, Ethiopia, and India). By bringing the reader's attention to old and new trade routes as well as economic competition among French,
Portuguese, Mamlūks, Venetians, and Greeks, the *cordelier* stretches geographical space and draws a map of connected cities and ports expanding beyond the
Mediterranean and well into the Indian Ocean.

Furthermore, adds Thenaud, in the peripheral regions mapped in his *Voyage* as
well as in Alexandria, Christians are not always well tolerated but "le prouffict
à celuy qui scet le traffic de marchandise est si grant que les marchans ont, tout
temps, vouloir de retourner, car ilz gaignent cent pour cent et plus, en marchandises que icy sont desperées et de peu de valeur" (27) (the profit, for whoever
knows how to trade, is so significant that merchants have always wanted to go
back, for they earn one hundred percent more from goods that are not wanted
and of small value here). The result of this extensive commerce is wealth for the
merchants as well as for the economically thriving ports and cities. Cairo, for
example, is

plus riche que aultre pour la fertilité du pays et habondance de marchans qui
y viennent chascun jour. Car y font baasas et halles appropriées à chascune
marchandise en particulier, comme la halle d'or et d'argent, la halle des
senteurs, des pierreries, des soyes, des toilles, des drogues, des tappiz et ainsi
de toutes choses. (48)

richer than any other because of the country's fertility and the abundance
of merchants who come there every day. For there open and covered markets

adapted to each merchandise are set up, like the market for gold and silver, the market for perfumes, stones, silks, cloth, drugs, carpets, and so on and so forth.

It was not unusual for Europeans to comment on spices and goods available in faraway lands, and this is certainly not the first time that a European traveler raves about Egypt's riches, real or imagined.[39] The insistence with which Thenaud maps trade routes, however, shows the *cordelier*'s awareness in the geopolitical changes and the economic exchanges that brought Christians and Muslims into contact in and around the Mediterranean. It also indicates the interconnectedness of trade, politics, and religion in the early sixteenth century. European travelers did not wait until the seventeenth century to focus on trade, as Wolfzettel's analysis tends to suggest. Useful as it may be, his classification creates artificial distinctions between medieval pilgrimage, sixteenth-century humanist travel, and seventeenth-century commercial voyage. Indeed, traveling in the late medieval and early modern period was rarely limited to pilgrimage, diplomacy, or trade, and travelers who went on a pilgrimage to the Holy Land were also involved in political missions and interested in the spice trade. Thenaud is a perfect example of the multifaceted dimensions of travels in the early modern period when religion, politics, and commerce overlapped. Hence in the *Voyage*, Cairo (36), Damascus (113–14), and Bethlehem (93) rival each other in natural beauty and resources that are, on the one hand, the unstated conditions of economic wealth and opportunity, and, on the other, the sign of God's preference. Further south, "la sterilité de la terre assez monstre l'yre et indignation de Dieu sur icelle, parcequelle est salée et rien n'y peult fructifier" (38) (the soil's sterility, because it is salty and barren, demonstrates God's anger and indignation with the land). Thus the only frontier that Thenaud establishes in his narrative is the one separating fertile and sterile lands, the chosen lands and those that have been ignored by God. Following the divisions established by the Ancients, he restricts the territory of Islam to the Arabia Desert and claims that, past Egypt, Syria, the Holy Land, Arabia Petraea, and Arabia Felix, the Arabian Peninsula is a harsher place. By pushing Islam back into distant geographical areas untouched by trade routes, Thenaud brings the 'Souldan' and Egypt closer to his European audience. So much so, in fact, that a Frenchman would feel quite at home on the Egyptian coast.

As soon as Thenaud and his retinue reach Alexandria, they are told to rest "asseurez comme si nous estions en France" (22) (assured as if we were in France). At their first meeting with the Sultan, the latter urges the visitors not to worry about their safety. Consequently, Thenaud feels safe—"nous estions aussi seurement en ses terres comme en France en noz propres manoirs" (46) (we were as safe in these lands as we are in our own manors in France)—and quite at home in Cairo:

> *après ce que eusmes oultrepassé une grande rue aussi longue comme celle de Paris qui est de Sainct Jacques à Sainct Denis, tant continuellement plaine de monde que est la salle de Palais de Paris ès jours que arrestz sont pronuncez,*

vinsmes au palais du Souldan qui n'est gueres moins spacieulx que la ville d'Orleans. (44)

after crossing a large street as long as the one that goes from Saint Jacques to Saint Denis in Paris, as continuously full of people as the Palais de Paris in the days when sentences are pronounced, we went to the palace of the Sultan which is slightly less spacious than the city of Orleans.

Later in the text, a similar comparison appears: "Ceste cité [Le Caire] unie et assemblée est trois foys aussy grande que Paris et peuplée cinq fois plus; et croy que en ycelle se brusle autant d'huylle qu'il se boyt de vin à Orleans" (46) (this city [of Cairo] as a whole is three times bigger than Paris and its inhabitants five times as many; and I think that in it as much oil is burnt as wine is drunk in Orleans). Even the Egyptian monuments, so distinct from European architecture, recall France. The pyramids "y sont tant de pierres si grosses, pollies et bien assises que je croy que en deux citez comme Paris n'en auroit tant" (53) (consist of so many stones that are so large, polished, and well placed that I think that in two cities like Paris there would not be as many) and Isis's statue "se monstroit plus haulte que les tours Nostre Dame de Paris" (54) (showed itself to be higher than the towers of Notre-Dame in Paris). According to Thenaud, Cairo is a microcosm of the world; bigger and more cosmopolitan than Paris, the Egyptian city invites merchants, diplomats, and pilgrims alike, both Muslim and Christian.

Focusing on the First-Person Narrative:
The Parenthetical "I"

As he decenters geography and religion, Thenaud zooms in on himself as narrator. The pilgrimage's collective experience related in the *Voyage* is punctuated by personal anecdotes[40] and colored by interferences from Thenaud as a first-person narrator. With the exception of the narrative's beginning, where the *cordelier* identifies himself and the various reasons for his travels to the Levant, Thenaud is rarely visible in his text. His textual apparitions as narrator are all the more telling. The first one is literally parenthetical. When he explains André Le Roy's mission, Thenaud refers to the Knights of St. John as "inconcussibles coulompnes de la foy" (4) (unwavering columns of the faith), a side comment offered to the reader in parenthesis. Additionally, Thenaud portrays himself as judge to Qānsūh al-Ghawrī's version of the incident for which Le Roy was sent as a negotiator: "ledict Souldan s'estoit complainct au Roy, disant sadicte armée avoir esté prinse et deffaicte soubz umbre de paix et saufconduict (qui n'estoit pas vray)" (5) (the said Sultan had complained to the King, saying that his said army had been captured and defeated in times of peace and truce [which was not true]). These two short parenthetical observations give the *cordelier* a voice that delivers a personal commentary on events that are otherwise related quite neutrally.

Furthermore, a series of encounters narrated in the *Voyage* uncover Thenaud as an individual expressing himself in the collective mode of the pilgrimage narrative. Both happen on the way to Jerusalem, in the peripheral zone described earlier, and depict unexpected and tense situations. The first involves a *truchement*, a guide and interpreter, who accompanies Thenaud on his trip. In Suez, Thenaud meets Adela, "ung mammelu qui avoit longuement demouré en Languedoc, lequel avoit esté prins par les Mores à Tripolis de Barbarie, puis circuncis et donné à l'admiral d'Alexandrie" (63–4) (a Mamlūk who had long lived in Languedoc and been captured by the Moors in Tripoli on the Barbary Coast, then circumcised and given to the admiral in Alexandria). Adela's secret wish, Thenaud tells us, is to return to his native Christian lands. Delighted by the opportunity, the *cordelier* works towards freeing his new friend. As Bartolomé Bennassar and Lucile Bennassar have demonstrated, captivity was a real danger for Christians living in coastal areas and for those traveling into Muslim territories in the early modern period[41]—as it was for Muslims stumbling upon Christian pirates or the Knights of St. John. At one point in the narrative, Thenaud mentions avoiding a wreck. He heaves a sigh of relief: "si naufrage se fust faicte, nous estions tous esclaves" (116) (if we had capsized, all of us would have been taken captives). At another time, he notes that "plusieurs chrestiens estoient enchesnez, reservez pour en icelles [les galères du sultan] ramer et naviguer" (64) (several Christians were in chains, meant as oarsmen and sailors for these [the sultan's galleys]). In Christian lands also, Muslim captives were used as slaves. In Rhodes, Thenaud claims, there were "pour lors environ cent Mores et Turcs esclaves qui faisoyent les fossés, murailles et aultres forteresses de la ville" (134) (at the time about one hundred Moors and Turks used as slaves to maintain the walls, the ditches, and other strongholds of the city). According to Thenaud, helping a Christian slave return to his original land and to his faith was even more perilous than being captured in a *razzia* (maritime raid) for "Si nostre entreprise eus testé sceue, luy et moy eussions esté ars et brulez vifz" (64) (if our plan had been discovered, he and I would have been burned at the stake). Nevertheless, the brave *cordelier* details his success in taking Adela to Rhodes where he "fut reconcilié à l'eglise" (64) (was reconciled with the church).

The fortuitous encounter is as beneficial to Adela as it is for Thenaud who, thanks to the reluctant renegade, can show his wits. In what amounts to his confession, Thenaud admits: "et croy que Dieu, Nostre Dame et saincte Katherine lors me l'avoient envoié pour me secourir ès inevitables dangiers èsquels j'estoie, lequel faignoit (par mon conseil), estre plus devot en la loy Mahommetiste que nul autre" (64) (and I believe that God, Our Lady, and Saint Catherine had sent him to me to rescue me from the unavoidable dangers in which I found myself. [On my advice] he pretended to be more devout than anybody else in the Muhammadan law). Once again the parenthetical note is crucial to the unveiling of Thenaud as individual: to avoid the dangers associated with traveling, the *cordelier* suggests to Adela that he disguise himself, not with clothes, but culturally and religiously. He pushes the guide, who had converted to Islam outwardly, to show that he is a true Muslim. On the one hand, the trick allows Thenaud to prevent worries associated with Muslim thieves during the journey, and on the other, it lets Adela return to Christianity. The plan's success proves that this follower of God and royal envoy is a trickster quite capable of directing his voyage, destiny, and narrative in a truly unique way.[42]

Thenaud highlights his shrewdness a second time during an encounter with Arab thieves. After making their demands known to Adela, the Arabs choose to ignore the interpreter and to turn instead to the *cordelier* who becomes their primary interlocutor—and hence the main character of the encounter. Adela disappears from the location and the narration entirely and Thenaud acts as a go-between. It is thus the *cordelier*, and not Adela, who recounts the verbal exchange using some of the Arabic spoken during the encounter: "puis me demanderent laet, bait, c'est à dire chair ou oeufs. Esquelz respondy: 'memphis,' c'est à dire je n'en ay point" (67) (then they asked me *laet, bait*, that is to say meat or eggs. To which I responded: 'memphis,' that is to say I do not have any). Having replaced Adela, his *truchement*, Thenaud has become his own interpreter and negotiator. After the thieves have long disappeared, convinced by the *cordelier* that there was nothing to steal from the caravans, Adela reappears and delivers a confident monologue that must be read ironically as a failed act of bravery. In turn, the pilgrim's humility is a thinly disguised affirmation of his linguistic skills as a cultural broker.

A last peculiar anecdote is incorporated in the *Voyage*, showing once again Thenaud as a strong individual who operates within a generic tradition while being very much in charge of his trip and his narrative. During his travels, an Arab prince invites the *cordelier* for a meal. The reader is led to believe that, for a short while, the traveler will be observed by the curious Arab. In other words, whereas it was Thenaud who, until now, has reported on local customs,[43] the *cordelier* is about to be seen and studied by another. The prince appears anxious to learn about living and dietary customs in Christian lands. Thenaud, the reader thinks, will let the prince question him and will answer obligingly. However, from object of the gaze, the traveler surreptitiously becomes the agent of the narration and a judge of the Arab culture. Thenaud therefore uses this episode to solidify his position as first-person narrator. In his narration, he ignores the prince's question entirely and chooses to comment instead on his host's less than appetizing meal and his rustic environment:

> *Sondict logis estoit tel que il luy falloit entrer à quatre piedz, et en icelluy logis se tenir à genoulx, car ce n'estoit fors une belle regnardiere. Touttefois, c'estoit le mieulx logé qui fust au pays. Puis, sur deux ou troys pierres plates qui estoient au soleil et presque ardentes de la grande chaleur du soleil, mit du beurre et de la paste et nous fit cinq ou six crespes cuyttes au soleil, en nous donnant des pommes qui n'estoient demy meures ; lequel nous demandoit si estions en chrestienté aussi aysés et si nous avions telles viandes; puis me convint payer pour icelluy dix medins qui vallent douze sols six deniers. Car il luy estoit advis que nous ne vivions que de racines et fruictz saulvaiges comme sangliers. Puis, me collaudoit celluy pays. Ledict banquet parachevé, fuz remonte avecques mon truchement au monastere.* (77–78)

His house was such that he had to enter on all fours and be on his knees inside for it was nothing but a fox's lovely den. However, his was the best house in the country. Then, on two or three flat stones that were in the sun and almost burning because of the sun's heat, he put butter and some dough and made us five or six crepes that cooked in the sun, while giving us apples that were not half ripe; and he asked us if we, in Christendom, were as wealthy as he and if we had such food; next, I had to give him ten *medins* for this which is the equivalent of twelve *sols* and six *deniers*. For he thought that we only lived off roots and wild fruits like boars. All the while he was talking about this land. Once the banquet was over, I went back up to the monastery with my interpreter.

In this episode of failed encounter, the prince's curiosity, even if present at first, ends up being lost behind Thenaud's sly commentary on the lack of sophistication of his host. Like a fox, the Arab prince lives in a nice but narrow den and feeds on unripe fruit. Whereas he thinks that Christians live off roots and wild berries like boars, he is less a man and more an animal himself, insinuates Thenaud. The term "banquet" at the end of the passage is ironic, undoubtedly, and reinforces the Christian visitor's cultural superiority. In this passage, Thenaud could have let the prince direct the conversation in his own voice and provide the reader with his perspective. Instead, Thenaud turns the situation around and offers his own description of and commentary about Arabs who are, here, unflatteringly compared with foxes and, in a later passage, with Jews.[44] The praise concerning the living quarters of the prince is, in fact, another ironic comment on Thenaud's part, leaving the reader to imagine what the living conditions of the average Arab must be like.[45]

Of Changing Times: The *Voyage*'s Present

Much more than a collective and atemporal religious pilgrimage, the *Voyage* relates trade conditions throughout the Levant and beyond while singling out a first-person narrator telling a number of singular adventures. Thenaud's account also includes several political missions that correspond to particular needs and opportunities for early sixteenth-century France. Clearly marked by André Le Roy's 1511 embassy in Egypt, Thenaud's report contains personal anecdotes in the Levant that, ultimately, do not propose significant, new, or even valuable information about either the Arabs, the Mamlūks or the Safavid shah—as opposed to Lemaire's *Traicté*. The *Voyage*, however, reinforces the idea of an alliance, particularly economic, with a Muslim power. By focusing on the commercial exchanges he witnessed and by mapping the periphery of the traditional pilgrimage route, Thenaud invites the French into narratives of the future as well as into diplomatic circles far away from France.

Thenaud's *Voyage* is neither anti-papal nor as deeply entrenched in prophecies, millenarism, universal religion, and crusade as Lemaire's *Traicté*. Nevertheless, it remains solidly anchored in its own time, the 1510s of course but also the 1520s. Printed more than 10 years after Thenaud's travel but during his lifetime,[46] the narrative includes several elements that insist on the historical timeframe of its composition. First dedicated to Louis XII, the account is then addressed to Francis I who becomes the real *destinataire* of the work since Louise de Savoie's son is actually the first royal figure mentioned in the text: "mon treshault, trespuissant et tresillustre seigneur à present treschrestien et tresserenissime roy et empereur de la sacrée monarchie Gallicane" (2) (my almighty, powerful, and illustrious lord, presently Christian and august king and emperor of the sacred Gallican monarchy). Although the narrative is set in the past of a fulfilled pilgrimage and the political negotiations of 1511, the 1520s and the immediacy of that decade are very much stressed. With the inclusion of 'à present' in the dedicatory address, the *Voyage* shows concerns about the present's presence. Accordingly, Louis XII, who died in 1515, four years after Thenaud's travel, is only mentioned by name after Francis I, Louise de Savoie, Marguerite de Navarre, and even her *secrétaire*, Françoys de Bonjan. Having written extensively for the king and his family,[47] Thenaud now expressed his allegiance to the youngest of the Valois.

Between the early 1510s and the time of the *Voyage*'s publication some ten years later, the Franco-papal relations did not improve and the spice trade remained contested among Portuguese and Muslim powers. A new French king had acceded to power, however, and he had to be rightfully celebrated as such. Just as important, on the Islamic front Qānsūh al-Ghawrī was defeated by Sultan Selim in 1517, bringing Cairo, but also Mecca and Medina, into the Ottoman fold. Moreover, in 1524 Shah Isma'il of Persia died, and with him the temporary respite offered to Christian Europe. With two Muslim opposition rulers subdued, the Ottomans could resume their attacks on the Christian West and imagination where they would soon become "incontournables columnes" (unavoidable pillars) themselves, particularly for the Knights of St. John of Jerusalem. Whether the Ottomans would emerge as crows or doves is what the next chapter tells.

Notes

1 Ayas is near Alexandretta, known today as Iskenderun, in Turkey. On the Mediterranean, see recent works by: David Abulafia, *The Great Sea: A Human History of the Mediterranean* (Oxford: Oxford University Press, 2011); Peregrine Horden and Nicholas Purcell, *The Corrupting Sea: A Study of Mediterranean History* (Oxford: Blackwell, 2000); and Eric Dursteler, "On Bazaars and Battlefields: Recent Scholarship on Mediterranean Cultural Contacts" in *Journal of Early Modern History* 15, no. 5 (2011): 413–34, which gives an overview of recent scholarship on contacts in the Mediterranean.

2 On Shah Isma'il's momentary destabilization of the Ottomans see Mantran, *Histoire de l'empire ottoman*, 39.

3 The first and most complete edition comes from Etienne Baland in Lyon in May 1511. Jennifer Britnell used this edition as the basis for her critical edition of Jean Lemaire de Belges, *Traicté de la différence des schismes et des conciles de l'Église* (Geneva: Droz, 1997).

4 In his history of the color black, Michel Pastoureau notes that "the sixteenth and seventeenth centuries gradually witnessed the establishment of a kind of black-and-white world." See Michel Pastoureau, *Black: The History of a Color* (Princeton, Princeton University Press, 2009), 115.

5 Britnell uses this expression; see Lemaire, *Traicté*, 44.

6 Lemaire, *Traicté*, 57. On the various editions of the work and their slow degradation, see 47–76.

7 Obviously, Lemaire considered popes useful sometimes.

8 The *Traicté* would be recuperated by Protestants, not only because of its sharp criticism of the papacy, but also because it advocates the marriage of priests.

9 Jennifer Britnell, "The antipapalism of Jean Lemaire de Belges' *Traité de la Différence des Schismes et des Conciles*" in *Sixteenth Century Journal* 24, no. 4 (1993): 783–800 and "Jean Lemaire de Belges and Prophecy" in *Journal of the Warburg and Courtauld Institutes* 42 (1979): 144–66.

10 The French, though, might have been more interested in an invasion of Italy than in a crusade. See Introduction.

11 The Bible stresses the presence of pure and impure animals aboard Noah's ark in Genesis 7:1–10. The crow is mentioned as being impure in Leviticus 11:15. Raven and dove are discussed in Genesis 8:6–12.

12 The visual representation of the Biblical passage is entitled "Comment Noe laissa aller le corbin et la columbe." François Garnier, ed., *Thesaurus iconographique* (Paris: Le léopard d'or, 1984) image 64, p. 58; bibliographic information, p. 218.

13 Pierre Jodogne, *Jean Lemaire de Belges, écrivain franco-bourguignon* (Bruxelles: Palais des Académies, 1972), 344–57. Rota was a Venetian doctor who spent several years in Aleppo; the Doge asked him to report on his experiences in the East.

14 Peter Burke, "The Renaissance Translator as Go-Between" in *Renaissance Go-Betweens: Cultural Exchange in Early Modern Europe*, ed. Andreas Höfele et al. (Berlin: Walter de Gruyter, 2005), 1–14. Burke talks about the freedom and liberty of the Renaissance translator on page 26.

15 "*Et de là vient que l'armée de Syach Ysmail est toute sans ses despens ou gaiges, ainsi comme se fait la croisée entre nous pour aler contre les infideles, et à ceste cause de tous les quartiers d'Asie les hommes de sa secte courent à lui avec tous leurs biens et toute leur famille*" (248–9) (And from this comes the fact the Shah Isma'il's army is easily raised, as is for us the crusade against the infidels, and the reason why men from his sect come from all over Asia rushing to him with all their goods and family).

16 "Le baptesme de Sophie roy de Perse" cited by Jean-Pierre Seguin in *L'information en France avant le périodique, 517 canards imprimés entre 1529 et 1631* (Paris: Maisonneuve et Larose, 1964), 64. In another piece, Shah Isma'il's perceived love of Christianity has him attend mass in 1516; see the *canard* "Nouvelles bonnes lesquelles sont produictes et venues dorient. . . ." in Seguin, *L'information en France*, 79.

17 In his *Ressource de la chrestienté* (1494), La Vigne pushes a similar program; see Chapter 1. Cynthia Brown has analyzed "La complainte de Grèce" and *Ressource de la chrestienté* along with Lemaire's *Concorde du genre humain* in "The rise of Literary Consciousness in Late Medieval France: Jean Lemaire de Belges and the *Rhétoriqueur* Tradition," *Journal of Medieval and Renaissance Studies* 13, no.1 (1983): 51–74.

18 Quoted by Jacques Abélard in "Les *Illustrations de Gaule* de Jean Lemaire de Belges—Quelle Gaule? Quelle France? Quelle nation?" *Nouvelle Revue du Seizième Siècle* 13, no. 1 (1995): 7–27. In the 1520s, another historiographer, Jacques de Bourbon, will lament Christianity's inner troubles and wish for Christian unity. See next chapter.

19 Vihlo Harle, "On the concept of the 'Other' and the 'Enemy'," *History of European Ideas* 19 (1994): 27–44.

20 Charrière, *Négociations*, 1: 45–46.

21 Margaret Meserve, *Empires of Islam in Renaissance Historical Thought* (Cambridge, MA: Harvard University Press, 2008).

22 Jean Thenaud, *Le voyage d'outre mer*, ed. Charles Schefer (Geneva: Slatkine Reprints, 1971).

23 Ibid. 74–75.

24 Wes Williams, *Pilgrimage and Narrative in the French Renaissance* (Oxford: Clarendon, 1998).

25 Friedrich Wolfzettel, *Le discours du voyageur: Pour une histoire littéraire du récit de voyage en France, du Moyen-Âge au XVIIᵉ siècle* (Paris: Presses universitaires de France, 1995). Chapter 1 gives an analysis of medieval pilgrimage narratives.

26 Schefer points to such early travelers and literary predecessors in the introduction to his edition of Thenaud's *Voyage*.

27 "[so that they] *y aillent par esprit, en la meilleure forme qu'il leur sera possible*" (94) (go there in spirit, in the best shape possible) Thenaud, *Voyage*, 94.

28 See Frédéric Tinguely on the rise of curiosity in pilgrimage accounts and on Thenaud in Chapters 1 and 2 respectively of his *Le voyageur aux mille tours: Les ruses de l'écriture du monde à la Renaissance* (Paris: Champion, 2014). These chapters were previously published as "Janus en Terre Sainte: La figure du pèlerin curieux à la Renaissance" in *Revue des Sciences Humaines* 245 (1997): 51–65 and "Une tradition réorientée: Pèlerinage et gallicanisme chez Jean Thenaud" in *Versants* 38 (2000): 91–102.

29 Amy Turner Bushnell and Jack P. Greene give an overview of the center-periphery approach in "Peripheries, Centers, and the Construction of Early American Empires" in *Negotiated Empires: Centers and Peripheries in the Americas, 1500–1820*, ed. Christine Daniels and Michael Kennedy (New York: Routledge, 2002), 1–14.

30 On the importance of Egypt, particularly Alexandria and Cairo, as economic and political centers, see Domenico Trevisan's own *Voyage* in Schefer's edition of Thenaud, *Voyage*, 147–226, specifically 170–81 for Alexandria and 181–214 for Cairo. See also Stéphane Yérasimos, "Les voyageurs du XVIᵉ siècle en Égypte ottomane (1517–1600): Essai de typologie," in *D'un Orient l'autre*, ed. Irène Fenoglio-Abd El Aal and Marie-Claude Burgat, 301–15.

31 Lemaire de Belges gives additional details peppered by rather subjective comments about Le Roy's mission and the reasons for the falling-out between Rhodians and Egyptians in his *Traicté*. For instance, he accuses the Ottomans and the Mamlūks of plotting to destroy Rhodes: they "*s'estoient aussi raliiez et contrebendez entr'eulx, et avoient conspiré de destruire premierement Rhodes, comme celle qui trop les grieve et assubgetist*" (264) (had gathered and allied together and plotted to destroy Rhodes that aggravates and subdues them first). After finding excuses for the Knights' attack on Egyptian vessels, Lemaire interprets the Mamlūk sultan's overture toward the king of France as the result of Louis XII's reputation, the French delegate's diligence, and God's will.

32 Thenaud, *Voyage*, 43–44, 57–59, 86, 96, 119–20. Lemaire, *Traicté*, emphasizes the advantage that the agreement affords the French over the Venetians. Giving them the keys to the holy places means:

> *ouvrir dutout le passaige d'oultremer pour les pelerins et marchantz, lesquels y pourront doresenavant frequenter seurement, au tresgrant honneur, prouffit et consolation du roy et de toute la nation françoise et gallicane, voire de toute Chrestienté, et n'y a nul qui ne s'en doibve resjouyr, synon les Veni
tiens, lesquels souloient avoir ceste prerogative, et maintenant ilz en sont forcluz et alienez par leurs demerites* (268).
>
> opening wide the passage in the Levant for pilgrims and merchants who from now on will be able to circulate safely with great honor, benefit and joy for the king and the entire French gallican nation as well as the entire Christendom, and everyone will rejoice except for the Venetians who wanted to have to have this right but now are excluded and alienated because of their misconduct.

33 See Introduction.

34 "*Maintes choses me empeschoyent le susdict voyage*" (many things prevented the journey described earlier), says Thenaud enigmatically in *Voyage*, 3.

35 See Schefer's introduction to Thenaud's *Voyage*. La Broquère also reports an encounter with Muslim pilgrims that leads to the sighting of a Turkish lady and to the meeting with a renegade slave named Abdullah. See La Broquère, *Le Voyage d'Orient*, 72. Thenaud may have been aware of La Broquère's account.

36 And particularly Italian ones, as the mosque in Mecca is compared to the Colloseum in Rome. This analogy, of course, comes from Varthema.

37 This term is borrowed from Homi Bhabha, *The Location of Culture* (London: Routledge, 1994).

38 Wind, lack of water, quicksand, and looters abound in the *Voyage* as in other pilgrimage and travel narratives of the period.

39 One thinks of Marco Polo of course. Since the thirteenth century, Egypt is acknowledged as being affluent. See Jacques Paviot's "D'un ennemi l'autre: Des Mamelouks aux Ottomans. Voyages de renseignement au Levant, XIIIe–XVIIe siècles" in *D'un Orient l'autre*, eds. Irène Fenoglio-Abd-El Aal and Marie-Claude Burgat (Paris: Centre National de la recherche scientifique, 1991): 317–28.

40 Thenaud, *Voyage*, for example, relates his encounter with Nâsir al-Din, an interpreter from Jerusalem (48–9), and Antoine Passerot, a crypto-Christian (114–16). He also describes a street quarrel started by a hat (58) and recalls a theft (122–24).

41 Bartolomé Bennassar et Lucile Bennassar, *Les chrétiens d'Allah: L'histoire extraordinaire des renégats, XVIe et XVIIe siècles* (Paris: Perrin, 1989).

42 Al-Hasan al-Waazan, known in the West as Leo Africanus, offers a reverse example of cultural negotiation. See Natalie Zemon Davis, *Trickster Travels: A Sixteenth-Century Muslim between Worlds* (New York: Hill and Wang, 2006).

43 In Alexandria, for example, he comments on the transportation of luggage: "les coffres et bagaiges furent conduictz dès le port audict logis par deux cameaulx pour lesquelz furent payez cinquante seraphs d'or, car telle est la coustume" (22) (from the port, trunks and luggage were transported on the back of two camels to the said house; for this, we paid fifty gold seraphs, as is customary).

44 Thenaud, *Voyage*, claims that the Jews *"font assavoir ès ennemys et adversaires tous les secretz de la Chrestienté et du royaulme auquel sont aussi utiles que regnardz en poullailliers"* (7) (make known all the secrets of Christendom and the kingdom to our enemies and adversaries, in which way they are useful as a fox in a chicken coop). In his judgement, he echoes Lemaire and most Europeans commentators of the time.

45 The *cordelier* has little esteem for those he calls Arabs: as guides, they regularly seek to harm him and other travelers including Muslim pilgrims. Thenaud's Arabs are nomads, Bedouins; his Moors, on the contrary, are sedentary dwellers. At times though, Thenaud uses the terms 'Arabs' and 'Moors' interchangeably.

46 Titia Schuurs-Jansenn gives 1523–1530 as the time frame for the *Voyage*'s publication date in her edition of Thenaud's *Triumphe des vertuz* (Geneva: Droz, 1997), xlii.

47 Thenaud's first works, *Margarite de France* and *La Lignée de Saturne*, date from 1508 to 1509 and were meant for the royal family. *Le triumphe des vertuz* is dedicated and presented to Louise de Savoie in 1517 and 1518. *La saincte et treschrestienne Cabale metrifiee* was published in 1519 but did not satisfy its *commanditaire*, Francis I, who requested another attempt. The *Traité de la Cabale en prose* appeared in 1520–1521. See Schuurs-Jansenn's introduction.

3   A Sultan for a Master

Jacques de Bourbon Counters Lame Ducks

On December 25, 1522, the Ottomans were celebrating. For Christians in Europe, however, Christmas 1522 would not be remembered as a time of joy. In one sentence, the grand master of the Order of St. John encapsulates the mood: "Ce jour de Nohel ledit grand Turq entra dedans la ville, et le premier jour de l'an avons faict voyle noz navires désarmez, et aprez avoir passé en mer plusieurs fortunes, sommes arrivez tous espars en ceste isle de Candie"[1] (On this Christmas day, the Great Turk entered the city, and on the first of the year our disarmed ships set sail. After having countered several misfortunes at sea, we arrived, disheveled, on the island of Candia). What Philippe de Villiers l'Isle-Adam summarizes in just a few words is the loss of Rhodes to the Ottomans. After months of fierce battle, the city and the island had given up arms to Sultan Süleyman and his troops, causing a long-standing and powerful Christian organization whose members were suddenly forced into exile to reexamine its *raison d'être* and its image. For two centuries, the island of Rhodes in the Aegean Sea had been the Order's base against those whom the Knights liked to call infidels; as such it represented Christendom's oriental frontier to many in Christian Europe. In late 1522, while Christmas celebrations were about to start, a young king from the East was conquering the most invincible fortress in the Christian world, giving some reason to rejoice and others reason to despair.

In 1480 Rhodes had already withstood a first siege, from which Pierre d'Aubusson, grand master from 1476 to 1503, had emerged as the perfect defender of Christianity, reinforcing the mystique of Rhodes, of the Order, and of himself.[2] The siege of 1522 lasted five long months. Unlike that of 1480, it was a resounding success for the Ottomans and in particular for Süleyman, who had come to power two years earlier in his mid-20s. Preceded by the capture of Belgrade, the fall of Rhodes indicated to Christian Europe that the new, young Ottoman leader had quickly and beautifully stepped into the shoes of his father and predecessor, Sultan Selim. Thanks to two consecutive military successes, Süleyman turned the Ottomans into a most serious concern for Christian Europe, which feared that the 'Turks' might indeed arrive "iusques aux portes de Romme." Using these unambiguous terms was Jacques de Bourbon, a Knight of St. John and the author of the chronicle detailing the fall of Rhodes that is the subject of this chapter. Bourbon writes with a distinctly apocalyptic tone about the menace he perceives.

For the chronicler, the Ottomans' progress in the eastern Mediterranean signaled Christianity's loss of territorial and spiritual influence and pointed to its possible demise. Hence Bourbon witnessed "les ennemys de iour en iour prosperer & gaigner sur les chestiens"[3] (the enemies prosper daily and overtake Christians). In his journal written from Marseille, Honorat de Valbelle shares similar worries: "si la France et l'Espagne ne s'accordent point, ce Turc va se rendre maître de toute la chrétienté, et il en a déjà pris le chemin. Dieu, dans sa miséricorde, veuille nous venir en aide, car nous en avons bien besoin !" (If France and Spain do not unite, this Turk will become master of the entire Christendom. He is well on his way to doing just that. May our Merciful God come to our aid, for we truly need help).[4] The Ottomans' victory in Rhodes coincided with the weak papacy of Adrian VI, a non-Italian pope who succeeded Leo X on January 9, 1522 and died just a few months later on September 14, 1523. Writing the day after the pope's death, grand master Villiers l'Isle-Adam hoped for a new pontiff who would work toward "la union et augmentation de la chrestiente"[5] (the union and the rise of Christendom). His wish was granted in November when Giulio de Medici, Leo X's cousin, became Pope Clement VII, remaining in this position for over a decade. More importantly for Villiers perhaps, Clement VII was himself a member of the Order. Bourbon was confident in Clement's ability: "par sa prudence & vertu & bonne voulunte mettra transquilite paix et amour entre les princes chrestiens et generallement a toute la chrestiente: dequoy avons bien besoing" (50r-v) (with his prudence, virtue, and good will, he will bring love, peace and quiet among Christian princes and throughout Christendom, which we very much need).

The news of the fall of Rhodes quickly spread throughout Europe, particularly in French-speaking territories. The 'Belgians' Pasquier de la Barre and Antoine de Lusy mention it briefly in their respective diaries, but *Le journal d'un bourgeois de Paris* and *Le journal d'un bourgeois de Marseille* describe it in detail.[6] Besides stimulating the production of pamphlets warning the public about the irresistible advance of the Ottoman army in the Eastern Mediterranean,[7] the fall of Rhodes also prompted three narratives, two of them published in France. These important testimonies stem from Christian eyewitnesses and are counterbalanced by an Ottoman military journal and several contemporaneous narratives written by Ottoman chroniclers.[8]

The only narrative composed in French is signed by Jacques de Bourbon and entitled *La grande et merueilleuse et trescruelle oppugnation de la noble cite de Rhodes, prinse naguieres par Sultan Seliman a present grand Turcq, ennemy de la tres saincte foy Catholicque*. First published in Paris in 1525, the chronicle generated such interest that it was re-edited a year later and a third time in 1527. These successive editions are all Parisian and do not change much in content.[9] In the eighteenth century, the abbé de Vertot incorporated the 1527 edition into his voluminous history of the Knights.[10] The work has not been published since then and, despite being a crucial testimony on early Franco-Ottoman relations, it has received only scant scholarly attention. The Bibliothèque Nationale de France holds a 1525 volume of the *Oppugnation*. This chapter studies an edition that dates from 1525 held in the University of Virginia's Gordon Collection. The work is signed by "treshumble et tresobeissant relligieux et seruiteur frere, Jacques bastard de Bourbon, commandeur de sainct Mauluis doysemont, et fonteynes au prieur de France" (humble and obedient knight and servant Jacques, bastard of Bourbon, commander of Saint-Maulvis of Oisemont and of Fonteynes for the prior of France). About the author of the *Oppugnation*, we know little.[11] Born in 1466, he is the illegitimate son of Louis de Bourbon, Prince-Bishop of Liège, appearing in the Catalogue des imprimés de la Bibliothèque Nationale as "Jacques de Bourbon bâtard de Liège." Bourbon is thus a relative of Francis I, whom he meets for the first time in 1527, five years after the fall of Rhodes, for a mission on behalf of the Order. Few details are available to us about the time between his birth and his self-described appearance at Rhodes during the Ottoman assault, but we know that beginning in 1482, he lived with the Bourbon-Beaujeu, in Amboise notably, and in the shadow of the French court. Around 1503, he was inducted into the Order of St. John. After the capture of Rhodes, Bourbon moved among Viterbo, various commanderies of the Order in France, and later Malta and Paris, where he died in 1537, after having occupied increasingly important positions within the Order.

The *Oppugnation* is his only published work. It begins with a dedicatory piece to "tresreuerend et tresillustre seigneur monseigneur le grãd maistre de Rhodes Frere Philippe de Villiers lisleadam" (respected and illustrious lord, Sir grand master of Rhodes, Brother Philippe Villiers L'Isle-Adam). In the *Oppugnation*, Bourbon and Villiers L'Isle-Adam appear as religious and military brothers, the former offering his "petite oeuure" (small work) to his "superieur et redoubte seigneur" (superior and feared lord). An important political figure, Villiers Lisle-Adam is also a patron to whom the courtier-chronicler, inscribing himself in the lineage of historiographers like Guillaume Caoursin, presents his work.

The introductory *dédicace* of the *Oppugnation* is followed by a detailed table of contents of the narrative, which is divided into a hundred and eight short sections. In the margins, brief summaries of the main events punctuate the text. With an important exception to which I will return, the narrative follows the assault chronologically: first, it depicts the events that led to the siege; then, it describes the preparation for battle, the various assaults, the negotiations and the capitulation, and finally the departure of the Knights for an unknown destination. The narrative ends on January 25, 1524, as the Order leaves Rome to settle momentarily in Viterbo.

Marie-Paule Loicq-Berger thinks that Bourbon focused his narrative around the siege and that the analytically oriented preamble and the final segment of the work are secondary.[12] As this chapter shows, however, the dedicatory introduction is of utmost importance, not only because of its initial position,[13] but precisely because of its critical nature. The prologue introduces the main participants in the 1522 battle of Rhodes and sets the tone for the entire narrative by elucidating one of the principal reasons behind the composition of the *Oppugnation*—the need for a new base. In his introduction, Bourbon talks about "le grand désir que iay de faire chose qui soit agréable à ta seigneurie renommee" (the desire I have to please you,

esteemed lord), suggesting that his work answers a patron's request. It is not difficult to see how pressed the grand master must have felt after the Order's crushing
defeat. In need of a physical location from which to continue launching attacks
against Islam, the grand master also had to maintain and assert his authority as
head of an international Christian organization. Expressly dedicated to Villiers
Lisle-Adam, the chronicle is also meant for a larger audience, "princes chrestiens & aultres seigneurs" (Christian princes and other lords): the pope, of course,
who has supported the Order since its inception; Charles V of Spain; Henry VIII;
and above all the young Francis I of France, all of whom are mentioned by name.
Answering a command from Villiers Lisle-Adam, the Bourbon's chronicle calls
on Christian leaders of Europe, particularly the French king, to help the Order
regain a base and maintain its reputation.

Writing within the long tradition of crusade narratives, Bourbon divides the
various persons he introduces in his dedicatory preface into two distinct groups:
Christians—including himself as narrator, the grand master, all other knights, as
well as the public to which the *Oppugnation* is directed—and their military opponents and nemeses, the Muslims whom Bourbon calls "infidelles" and who are
symbolized by Süleyman, "le grand Turcq." The introduction, therefore, establishes a stark difference between Christianity and Islam, the latter being schematically constructed as the religion of the infidels. Just as the 'Turks' never appear
as Muslims in Bourbon's text, Islam is not named as such; instead it is presented
through descriptive and subjective notions such as sect, superstition, or "loy du
faux Mahommet" (law of the false Muhammad). In short, Islam is not the religion of Muslims; it is the religion of Christianity's most virulent opponents, the
non-Christians. As a Knight of St. John, Bourbon takes on the expected military
and religious role of the crusader. His text, thus, is a mix of detailed military
considerations and constant calls for help to God. Yet, the chronicler makes the
peculiar and chaotic situation of Europe's Christianity at the very beginning of
the sixteenth century omnipresent in the *Oppugnation*. He shows that European
Christendom is faced not only with a difficult transition in papacy and an external
menace—the Ottomans—but also, and perhaps more forcefully, with an internal one—disagreements and disputes among Christians themselves. Indeed the
conflict between Francis I and Charles V, elected Holy Roman Emperor in 1519,
exacerbated tensions that were already present and palpable within Christendom.
Bourbon laments that while the Ottomans are attacking Rhodes, Christian Europe
is fighting inner wars. Very much aware of not only past but present events, the
chronicler is a typical early modern Christian historiographer, an individual concerned with the future of his own religious community, implicated in the affairs of
his "nation," and far from neutral in his narration.[14]

It appears that for Bourbon, dissension in Europe is the main reason for Rhodes's fall in 1522. While he represents the Ottomans as a group by depicting Sultan Süleyman's traits, he shows the Christian camp as divided into competing
factions, on the one hand Philippe de Villiers l'Isle-Adam and his faithful friends,
on the other gossipers and traitors. Seeking to please the grand master, the knight
informs Christian Europe's highest officials about the unfolding of the siege, the

power of the "infidelles," and the need for assistance. But Bourbon, who seeks to honor the memory of those who died in the battle, also aims at "obuier aux calumniations et mauluaises parolles des mesdisans" (responding to the calumnies and the negativity of the gossipers), referring to European accusations against the Order following the loss of Rhodes. To accomplish this, he had to simplify and to carefully craft a master report that would counter such allegations by depicting the acts of treason some Christians committed. According to Bourbon, these traitors are the guilty ones. On the island, indeed, there were, Bourbon claims,

> *des grandes & abhominables trahysons que plusieurs faulx chrestiens qui estoient dedans ta ville ont faict et machine contre toy et ta saincte relligion. Entre les aultres celle dung de tes propres disciples et religieux: lequel ensuyuant le vray train de Judas ta vẽdu aux infidelles.* (*dédicace*)
>
> significant and abominable treasons committed by several false Christians who were within your city and who worked and schemed against you and your sacred religion. Among others, the treason of one of your own members who, following Judas' path, turned you in to the infidels.

According to the chronicler, slanderers—"peruerses et serpentines langues" (perverse, slithering tongues)—and traitors come from and belong to Christianity's side; they reside within Rhodes and belong to Christendom. These are the Order's biggest adversaries.

In this chapter, thus, I examine the representations of the Ottomans by an eyewitness of the 1522 assault. I ask if and how Christians—both the grand master of the Order and traitors—are equated with the Ottomans. I show that while a text like the *Oppugnation* contributed to the ambient fear surrounding the Ottomans in the early sixteenth century, at the same time it opened the door for an alliance between the kingdom of France and Süleyman's empire. More than the fall of Rhodes itself, it is Bourbon's rhetoric that might have had an impact on its French-speaking audience, and an unexpected one at that. The island, after all, was located far away in the eastern Mediterranean.

The Order of St. John and Rhodes

Before delving further into the *Oppugnation*, a few words on the Knights of St. John and Rhodes are in order. If the adjective "global" might be applied to the medieval and early modern periods, it could be in the context of the Christian enterprise that the Order of St. John had formed in and around the Mediterranean since the eleventh century.[15] Founded by one Gérard or Géraud from Martigues, the Order established itself first as a monastery and hospice in Jerusalem. Regularly expelled from their Levantine bases by Muslim armies, the Hospitallers settled in various locations in the Levant and the Mediterranean. After Jerusalem, Acra became the center of their religious activities, which had long before acquired a strong military tone; the Knights next established themselves in Cyprus before electing Rhodes as their base in the 1320s. They remained there until the Ottomans expelled them from the island in 1522. During their long presence in the

Levant and the Mediterranean, the Knights formed and consolidated ties with the Republics of Genoa and Venice, but also with the Mamlūks in Syria and Egypt, as well as with local Turkish rulers and the ruling Ottomans themselves with whom the *course* was regulated.[16] The Order also kept close contacts with Rome, which had sanctioned the organization early on—in 1113—and with the European powers upon whom it depended financially. In addition to numerous French *commanderies*, many of which are still standing today, a large number of its leaders, the grand masters, originated in France. D'Aubusson, previously mentioned, was one of its most emblematic leaders. Another Frenchman, Philippe de Villiers l'Isle-Adam—grand master from 1521 to 1534—is arguably the main figure of the *Oppugnation*. Villiers l'Isle-Adam had served as ambassador to Francis I under his predecessor, the Italian Fabrizio del Carretto.[17] During his tenure, he carried on a regular, if sparse, correspondence with the French monarch,[18] playing an essential role in negotiating the release of King Francis after his capture in Pavia in 1525. A well-known and unavoidable power in the Levant, the Mediterranean, and Europe, the Order is a perfect example of the intricacies and the interconnectedness of the late medieval and early modern world.

The Order's mission to sustain Christianity motivated the Knights to secure the safe passage of merchants and pilgrims to and from holy sites in the Levant. The reasoning went as follows: if Christian travelers could avoid capture by Muslim pirates or armies, it would no longer be necessary to pay ransom for them. In addition, potential conversions to Islam would be prevented, and Christian princes would then be able to invest in projects that would further strengthen Christendom. The reality on the ground was more complicated, given that the Hospitallers themselves did not hesitate to engage in piracy with Rhodes as their base.[19] Furthermore, from 1481 to 1495, they played the role of political broker with Cem, Sultan Bayezid's brother and contender to the Empire.[20]

In addition to being a safe harbor for pilgrims and pirates alike, Rhodes was a fortress, a port, and a vibrant city where commerce (of goods and men) thrived under the Hospitallers. We recall that Adela, in Thenaud's narrative, was reunited with his original faith in Rhodes, after having been bought back into Christendom.[21] The Order, then, under the guidance and influence of its military and spiritual leader, the grand master, radiated from one small geographic epicenter into the Muslim and Christian worlds at large. Much more than a peripheral element, the Order at Rhodes found itself at the intersection of several political and religious circles reaching far across the Mediterranean and beyond.

In the *Oppugnation*, though, Bourbon gives a much simpler image of Rhodes. Located at the crossroads of East and West, Islam and Christianity, Rhodes is a most favorable place mainly because of the Knights' presence. Its special status comes from the fact that the island prospered and triumphed gloriously over the "infidelles" for over two centuries. Rhodes is "la iadys honoree Et qui a prospere deux cens & quatorze ans en triumphe et gloire a loccasion des belles et honnorables victoires quelle a eu sur les infidelles" (once honored, having prospered for two hundred and fourteen years of triumph and glory thanks to the beautiful and honorable victories it claimed over the infidels). According to Bourbon, "en toute la crestiente ne a lieu ne place de quelque qualite ou force que lon la sceult

nommer" (1 r-v) (there is no place of such quality and strength in all Christendom). Rhodes is a stronghold and the ideal place from which to launch attacks
against Islam. It is also the

> *clef es parties doriẽt de la republicque crestiẽne esperance des fidelz tumbez*
> *es mains des turcqs . . . soullagemẽt & repos sur des pelerins de la terre*
> *saincte a leur aller, & tourner, recueil & adresse de tous chrestiẽs: marchãs*
> *trafigans en leuant propugnacle, & boullouuard de larchepellago & mer*
> *mediterrane.* (1r)
>
> the Christian republic's key in the Orient, the hope for Christians who have
> been captured by Turks . . . the solace and resting place for pilgrims going to
> and returning from the Holy Land, the meeting point for all Christian mer-
> chants trading in the Levant, a fortress and stronghold of the archipelago and
> of the Mediterranean.

Under the Hospitallers then, Rhodes is a safe harbor for pilgrims on their way to
and back from the Holy Land and for merchants buying and selling goods in and
around the Mediterranean. The island's reputation is undeniable; its people are of
high rank, and everyone including the sultan knows it.

In the late fifteenth century and early sixteenth century, however, Rhodes was
characterized by a significant religious and ethnic diversity. A culturally var-
iegated island in the middle of an Islamic sea, its population comprised Jews,
Latins, Greeks, and Muslims who mixed with Knights born in Western lands.[22]
Rhodes was synonymous with fluidity. In the *Oppugnation*, the constant movement of interpreters, envoys, and spies from one camp to the other during the
siege is testimony to the multitude and the intricacy of exchanges happening in
the Rhodian zone. During the assault, emissaries, observers, and men of all standing go back and forth between the fortress and the Ottoman camp, between what
Bourbon perceived as the territory of Christianity and that of the 'infidelles.' Rhodes was a busy place, an anthill from which certain men circulated easily and
where ethno-religious lines blurred. Depending on the circumstances, the Rhodians could belong to one camp or another. The author of the *Oppugnation* is uneasy
about such a possibility and such a lack of clarity. For him, the island belongs
entirely to Christendom. While giving access to a territory that is not Christian,
Rhodes is situated inside Christendom and within Christianity. For Bourbon, Rhodes is a door, a gate, a bridge allowing and at the same time preventing access to
the Islamic world, always preserving Christianity pure and untouched.[23] In Bourbon's chronicle, there is first and foremost a *here*—"deça"—largely made up of
Christian nobles. The *there*—"delà"—and the diversity of the Rhodian population itself are hinted at, but the reader is never transported into an Islamic land
and remains firmly anchored in a familiar Christian environment, even though
Rhodes, like many locations in the Levant and the Mediterranean, was religiously
and culturally varied. Although followers of Islam and Judaism do occasionally
appear in Bourbon's text, he does not discuss religion in its complexity. Was the
richness and multiplicity of the island so customary for Bourbon that he did not

care to describe it? Did he take it for granted and ignore it, he who belonged to the privileged? Or did he want to stress other issues in his text? All three of these possibilities are at play in his *Oppugnation*. The latter, however, prevails.

The Grand Master

For Bourbon, then, Rhodes's geographic and geopolitical situation remains exceptional, but not because of its religious and cultural diversity. The standing of the island is matched by Philippe de Villiers l'Isle-Adam, grand master, whose reputation in the late 1500s is intact, judging by André Thevet's comments in his *Pourtraits*.[24] According to Bourbon, Villiers l'Isle-Adam is prudent, devoted, and courageous. Dismissing the skeptics who advise him to not worry about a possible attack, the grand master anticipates the Ottomans' assault "non voulant estre surpris" (4r) (not wanting to be caught off guard). He fortifies the city and collects food and weapons long before the start of the siege. Goodhearted, diligent, dexterous, he asks that his men parade in combat uniform, preparing them psychologically and physically for the siege. He delegates and puts men in charge, but never ignores his responsibilities. In addition to mobilizing the entire island, Villiers l'Isle-Adam sends delegates to alert the pope and Christian princes about the imminent attack. According to Bourbon, a certain Frère Claude is sent to Francis I, "le prince en qui elle [la religion] auoit toute sa principalle esperance" (12r-v) (the one prince in whom it [the Order] had hope). Although the king responded positively by requisitioning his fleet in the Provence area, bad weather prevented any French ship from ever reaching Rhodes.[25] The Knights would not receive more help from the pope, the Emperor, or the English king.

Once the Ottomans begin their attack, the grand master visits the fortress regularly and courage emanates from him:

> *Sil nestoit il point oysif de sa personne, car luymesmes alloit en personne visiter les guetz des murailles auant la mynuyt, & apres & a lheure que deuoit reposer il estoit debout: & estoit la vigilance dudit seigneur si grãde que les ieunes gẽs estoiẽt biẽ empeschez de le suyure: & pour parler a la realle verite de la paine dudit seigneur: ie ne sache ieune hõme de xxv ans qui ait plus endure de travail iour & nuyt en ce siege depuys le cõmẽcemẽt iusques a la fin sans se trouuer mal, qua fait ledit seigneur, graces a nostre seigneur qui luy a dõne ceste bõne dispositiõ quãt il a este de besoing & necessite de la familiarite quil auoit auec trestous, et de bonnes parolles que dõnoit pour mettre le cueur aux gẽ iamais seigneur ne feist mieux sõ deuoir.* (7v)

He was not idle: he would visit the walls' watches in person before and after midnight and, when he could have been resting, he was up. The lord's vigilance was so great that young men had a hard time keeping up with him; and to further speak about the trouble that he was taking, I would add that I did not know of any young man of twenty-five years or so who, during the siege, worked as hard day and night from the beginning to the end, without fail, as the lord did thanks to our Lord who gave him this disposition, when it is needed, to speak and act with affection to all, thereby warming people's hearts. Never did a lord accomplish his duty better.

Villiers l'Isle-Adam is portrayed as a perfect knight. Wise, tireless in spite of his 58 years of age, the grand master gives courage to his troops by being present and active among them. He is a natural leader whose qualities seem to emanate from God, with whom Villiers l'Isle-Adam shares the same title, that of lord—"seigneur."

While Bourbon mentions by name and praises other specific knights who behaved most courageously during the siege, he focuses on Villiers l'Isle-Adam, who is among the first to fight:

> *a tous assaultz il estoit tousiours le premier ou des premiers tãt quil fust en disposition & sante: avec ce quil est homme fort vigillant et de grand travail. Et de la sorte quil cest porte en ce siege soyt il de sa personne ou des charges quil auoit: nully ne sen peult que bien lauer & contenter.* (16r-v)
>
> He was always the first, or among the first, to respond to each and every attack, as long as his health and well-being allowed him; and he was very vigilant and hardworking. So much so that during this siege he behaved according to his position and his duties and one can only praise and be content with him.

In early August when the *porte d'Angleterre* is under assault, he leaves a more comfortable location to participate in its defense (18r). Later, carrying the cross, he rescues a place after two hours of combat, the Ottomans returning to their trenches "auec perte, honte, et dommaige" (21v) (with loss, shame, and destruction). Again, moving from the *porte d'Angleterre* to the wall of Spain, Villiers l'Isle-Adam saves the day, his sheer presence galvanizing his troops and bringing victory to the Christians: "aussi la venue & presence dudit tresillustre seigneur nous dõnerent la battaille gaignee" (24v) (also the arrival and the presence of the illustrious lord gave us victory in battle). In the fall, a wall is breached; Villiers l'Isle-Adam stays more than a month at that vulnerable place fighting against the Ottomans and risking his life each day: "bien souuent le bõ seigneur se mettoit plus auant que besoing nestoit pour limportance de sa personne. Mays il le faisoit pour donner cueur & bon vouloir a tous les gens de se deffendre" (31v) (very often the good lord was on the forefront, more than was necessary for someone of his importance. But he was doing it so as to give all the people the heart and the will to defend themselves).

Leading by example, Villiers l'Isle-Adam gives courage to his knights while scaring his enemies. The grand master postpones the ineluctable defeat on several occasions. When he is unable to reverse a difficult situation, a heavenly-sent downpour saves the Christians. God, it is inferred, is on the Knights' side:

> *Laquelle iournee se peult dire tresheureuse, & tresfortunee pour nous graces a dieu. Car nully ne pensoit ce iour la eschapper: mais tous mourir et perdre*

*la vie. Touteffois le voulloir diuin par sa grace & misericorde: le voullut aul-
trement: & furent les ennemys dechassez et vaincus.* (35r)

One can call it a happy and lucky day for us, thanks to God. For no one
thought we would escape that day, but rather that we would all die and lose
our lives. However, God's will, his grace, and mercy wanted a different outcome and the enemies were pushed back and vanquished.

In spite of the overwhelming number of Ottomans,[26] the Christians resist thanks
to the grand master and God. Villiers l'Isle-Adam's perfection is depicted as
divinely ordained.

Furthermore, in Bourbon's portrait of the grand master, Villiers l'Isle-Adam
appears sensible and respectful of the Order's rules and regulations (39r). Following the principles of chivalry, he gathers his council before making important decisions, notably when civilians come and ask him to stop the fight (36v).[27]
He tries everything before negotiating with the assailant for, according to him,
"ville qui parlemête est a demy perdue" (36r) (a city that negotiates is half lost).
Once convinced that there is no way out, however, he behaves as a perfect Christian who obeys God's will: "il se mist au voulloir diuin . . . et presse de tous
costez de faire appoinctement a grand regret & a douleur inestimable de son noble
cueur donna sa parolle de rendre la ville auec les pactz a luy presentez que fut le
xx de decembre" (43v) (he surrendered to God's will . . . and, pressed from all
sides to reach a truce, with great regret and pain, he gave his word to turn in the
city according to the conditions that were presented to him, which was done on
December 20). Bourbon extrapolates on his grand master's reaction: "tout con-
sidere: ta seigneurie renommee se doibt soubzmettre au vouloir diuin: lequel don-
nera remede a tout sil luy plaist auec le temps" (*dédicace*) (all things considered,
your renowned lordship must surrender to God's will for God can find a cure to
everything if He so pleases). If God's will is to have the Ottomans take Rhodes,
so be it since the Christian must resign himself to His power. Turning his back on
the crusade, Bourbon accepts the Ottomans as being part of God's plan. In this
respect, he singularly echoes contemporary leading Protestants such as Luther and
Erasmus who, when debating the necessity of fighting the Ottomans, tended to
view the latter as God's punishment against a quickly dechristianizing Europe.[28]

Far from accusing Villiers l'Isle-Adam of negligence during the siege of Rhodes in 1522, Bourbon avoids pointing fingers and chooses instead to highlight his
superior's numerous qualities, while somewhat surprisingly accepting the Ottomans into the Order's fold as it were. The only slight criticism, or rather regret,
expressed by Bourbon in his chronicle is a technical one, the fact that Rhodes did
not have covered trenches, but only open ones (20v).

When, despite Rhodes's exceptional location and the grand master's talents as
a leader, the Ottomans capture the island and impose a setback on the Order, the
legend around the Knights is upset. Bourbon, by depicting a perfect grand master, obviously attempts to keep that legend alive. The *Oppugnation*, however, is
a particularly complicated communications campaign since the ever-so-fervent
Knights lost the battle, and also since ill-intentioned reports flourished rapidly

after the military loss. Not only must the Order find itself another center, it must also maintain its aura and the grand master's reputation while countering rumors.[29] For Bourbon, it was necessary that "les princes chrestiens & aultres seigneurs soient mieulx informez de la verite des choses passees au siege" (Christian princes and other lords be better informed about what truly happened during the siege). As far as the chronicler is concerned, his presence at Rhodes during the siege legitimizes his version and perfectly positions him to tell the details of the battle. He asserts: "Voulant fidelement, et a la verite rediger par escript, le grand & merueilleux siege . . . Je declareray ce a quoy personnellemẽt me suis trouue" (1r) (wanting faithfully and truthfully to report in writing about the great and marvelous siege . . . I will state what I personally found myself confronted with). In addition, the Knight was able to speak directly to other reliable informants who were, like him, familiar with the island and the assault:

> *Et quãt au demeurãt pource quil est impossible que ieusse este present a tout ce quil est fait pendant le siege (durant lequel nay point este absent dudit Rhodes) nescripray chose que nay sceu & entendu par gens de bien et si vertueulx que ie nadiouste pas moindre foy a leur relatiõ que a ce que ay veu de mes yeulx.* (1r)

> And while it is impossible for me to have been present during each and every action of the siege (during which I was never absent from Rhodes) I will not write anything that I did not know or hear said by virtuous and noble people whom I trust as much as I trust my own eyes.

For Bourbon, truth derives from knowledge, which can only come from autopsy. Seeing and hearing allow discernment. The chronicler thus claims to transmit what he has been told including what the "turcqs qui estoient en ce siege mont racompte" (1v) (the Turks who were present during the siege told me). Emphasizing his unique position as eyewitness, Bourbon suggests a desire to write the most complete, if not objective, account, one that incorporates the Ottomans' description of the siege. Moreover, his status within the Order provides him with the credibility and the standing necessary for his testimony to carry weight.[30]

Evidently, Bourbon's 'true' account is neither absolute nor more objective than any other report of the siege, for the historian's discourse which seeks to describe the *Other* is first and foremost his own discourse.[31] Nevertheless, Bourbon builds his account on a variety of Western and Ottoman testimonies from eyewitnesses who were present in Rhodes during the siege and who hence, according to the knight, produced reliable commentaries. Bourbon's own account is to be viewed as the most complete and far superior to the ones written and circulating in Europe. He saw and heard, therefore he knows; therefore he is better qualified to testify. Those who were not in Rhodes during the siege can only be "ignorans de laffaire" (uninformed about the situation) and "mesdisans" (slanderers). By composing the *Oppugnation*, Bourbon goes against all those lame ducks who wish to "parler contre les nobles et vertueulx faictz" (speak against the noble and virtuous facts).

Bourbon is not the only one to worry about the transmission of facts. In a letter addressed to Montmorency and dated July 8, 1523, Villiers l'Isle-Adam, too, mentions critics who discredit the Order: "J'ay entendu que aucunes gens qui n'ont pas grandement affaire, poursuyvent envers le roy avoir nos commander-ies et prétendent de deffaire la religion"[32] (I heard that some people who don't have much to do are pressing the king in order to have our *commanderies* and to dismantle the Order). The Knights of St. John could not have forgotten that an organization similar to theirs, the Order of the Templars, had been dissolved and seen their assets confiscated two centuries earlier. The Hospitallers were undoubt-edly under pressure in 1523 after the loss of their island. In a concerted effort to keep (or regain) the prestige of the Order, Villiers quiets his adversaries by asking Montmorency to ensure that such men don't have further access to the king while Bourbon propagates the 'true' account of the assault.

Telling the story of the defeat of Rhodes was a perilous enterprise. While accus-ing Christian Europe of disunity, Bourbon could not put the blame too heavily on princes since they were the only ones who could remediate the forced exile that in early 1523 was plaguing the Order. Soon after the loss of Rhodes in Decem-ber 1522, the Order was looking at the kingdom of France as a potential financial and political supporter even though Francis had not helped the Knights when they were besieged. A new base, a place "convenable pour exercer les armes contre les ennemys de la foy chrestienne" (51r) (suitable to fight the enemies of the Chris-tian faith) had to be found to resume the crusading activities of the Knights; yet, some of them were ready to accept the Ottomans' victory as a sign of God's will. In the *Oppugnation*, Bourbon manages to focus the attention of Europe on its own disarray and on the Order while criticizing the indifference of Christian princes. Furthermore, he suggests that the Ottomans might be the solution to Christen-dom's problems.

Le Grand Turcq

Facing Villiers l'Isle-Adam on the battlefield, Sultan Süleyman first appears as his nemesis. Symbol of his army and of his faith, he is the infidel *par excellence*. Bour-bon introduces him in the dedication in the most striking manner. He speaks of

> *la grande et increable puissance et fureur en laquelle le peruers et san-guinaire ennemy de la foy chrestienne, le grand Turcq est venu assieger ta ville de Rhodes, lequel (tanquam leo rugiens circuit querens quem deuoret) ne demande sinon croistre et augmēter la faulce et mauldicte secte et super-stition. (dédicace)*
>
> The great and incredible power and anger with which the perverse and bloodthirsty enemy of the Christian faith, the Great Turk, has come to assail the city of Rhodes and (like a roaring lion hoping for a meal), wanting to see the false, evil sect and superstition grow and augment.

Using a metaphor taken from Peter's first epistle—"Votre adversaire, le diable, rôde comme un lion rugissant, cherchant qui il dévorera" (5:8) (your enemy, the devil, prowls like a roaring lion looking for what it will devour)—Bourbon depicts Süleyman as a lion ready to devour his prey. Vivid adjectives complement nouns that underline the power and cruelty of the sultan, as well as his religious misgivings. Undoubtedly, Bourbon's initial description of Süleyman impresses upon the reader that the sultan represents the heretical non-Christian world. And yet as the narrative unfolds, the malevolent Süleyman becomes a Christ-like figure who mirrors no other than Villiers l'Isle-Adam. From menacingly roaring lion, the sultan becomes majestically leonine, hence embodying the dual symbolism of the lion characteristic of the medieval period.

According to Norman Daniel, cruelty is one of the main characteristics of Muslims in medieval times.[33] In an initial reading of Bourbon's text, Süleyman's savagery is undeniable. If Christians refuse to surrender, the punishments awaiting them would be extremely severe, the narrator explains. In a letter addressed to the grand master before the attack, Süleyman makes it clear that resisting his army would lead to the destruction of the castle, enslavement, and death for the Knights and the Rhodian population at large: "ferons renuerser les fondemens de vostre chasteau sans dessus dessoubz: & vous ferons esclaux & mourir de male mort" (10v) (we will destroy the foundations of your castle and will enslave and kill you). As victory nears, menaces are reiterated. If Rhodes refuses to capitulate, no one, including cats, will escape unscathed.[34] But what exactly happened after five months of intense battle and the sultan's victory? Bourbon claims that the Ottomans did indeed plunder the city, specifically targeting its churches, the "hospital," as well as the tombs of the grand masters (45v–46r). Some ships were also destroyed (47r). Ottoman accounts agree with Bourbon's assessment of the situation and do talk about a certain degree of uncontrollability on the part of the janissaries. Both Ottoman and European texts, however, nuance the responsibility of Süleyman in the looting that immediately followed the victory: "si ce fust par sõ cõmãdemẽt [celui de Süleyman] ou des baschaz ie nen scay riẽ" (45v) (if it was by his [Süleyman's] order or by that of the pashas I do not know), Bourbon affirms. The Knight even adds that Ahmet Pasha, obeying the sultan's orders, put an end to the pillage of the Order's ships and refurnished them (47r).

Examples of the sultan's supposed cruelty abound in the *Oppugnation*, but they all are systematically repackaged. Süleyman is said to have executed a Christian prisoner; Bourbon, though, indicates that this was in response to the capture of an Ottoman soldier and the decapitation of another (18v). The chronicler, who claims that Ottoman soldiers cut the noses, fingers, and ears of Christian envoys, emphasizes that they are obeying orders from, not the sultan, but the second in command, Ahmet Pasha (43v). With regard to his own troops, Süleyman is certainly demanding, but no more than Villiers l'Isle-Adam, whose tireless involvement in the battle is matched by the Ottoman soldiers' relentless work on trenches. When Sultan Süleyman sees that he is unable to obtain the quick and tangible results promised by Mustapha, he gets irritated and threatens to kill his pasha, whom he now sees as incapable and responsible for his going to war. Bourbon, however, notes that Süleyman eventually regained his calm after the other pashas pointed out that the death of such an important figure could only hearten their opponents. Bourbon suggests a second explanation, that Mustapha's wife, Süleyman's sister, would have intervened personally to save her husband. According to this explanation, the sultan would have listened to his sister and henceforth moderated his first reaction. In either case, claims Bourbon, the sultan is a sensible man who, instead of killing his pasha, simply exiled him to Cairo.

Violence was unquestionably an integral part of medieval and early modern life and the Rhodian clash did not occur without heavy loss of life. Expected as it was, violence happened in predictable forms and with clear societal purposes.[35] Süleyman's cruelty was not purely imaginary, but it has sometimes been overemphasized and dehistoricized by modern scholars. For Bourbon, Süleyman was just, sensible, accepting of weakness, and able to control his troops' outbursts of violence. His cruelty might appear excessive to a modern reader, but it was not out of order. Besides, it was matched by that of Villiers l'Isle-Adam, who does not hesitate to hang a deserter, hoping to foster unconditional obedience and support from knights and civilians at a time when the fate of the island was looking grim (41v).

Violence notwithstanding, the sultan's admirable qualities allow him to be at the helm of an army that is entirely devoted to him. The unconditional obedience of the Ottoman army is a trope in European commentaries. La Broquère mentions it twice in his *Voyage*.[36] Over 100 years later, Montaigne invites the French youth of his time to recognize and ponder "la discipline des armées Turkesques, car elle a beaucoup de differences et d'advantages sur la nostre"[37] (the discipline of the Turkish army, for it has many differences with and advantages over ours). For Bourbon, impressed by the number of Ottoman soldiers who can relay one another on the battlefield, "la verite est telle quen nulle seigneurie du monde: il ny a telle obeisance: ne sy bien gardee que celle des turcqs enuers leur seigneur: la rayson y est pource quil est seul seigneur en tous ces pays" (11v-12r) (the truth is that the Turks' observed obedience toward their sultan is found nowhere else in the world and the reason for it is that he is the only lord in all these territories). The chronicler suspects that the obedience and the discipline of the Ottoman army derive from the authority of the sultan, which is seen as desirable, especially for a Christian Europe plagued with internecine wars. There is no Ottoman tyrant in Bourbon's *Oppugnation*, simply an exemplary military leader.

The Ottoman soldiers' serene attitude is matched by their endurance, which the quantity and variety of their ammunition allows.

> *Les ennemys auant les susditz assaultz, et depuys iusques a la fin ont fait chose increable . . . cest que des le premier iour et heure qui commencerent a tirer artillerie contre la ville, depuys nont cesse de tirer, ou bombardes grosses, ou pieces moyennes, ou mortiers . . . ou de saper la terre, de faire mynes, tranchees . . . sans laisser iamais heure ny demye ny quart, ny interualle matin ou soir, ou a heure de menger.* (25v)

> Before the assault and up until the end, the enemies did something incredible . . . from the time they started to attack the city with their artillery, they did not stop firing their big and medium-size bombards or mortars . . . or digging the ground, working on mines or trenches . . . without ever allowing for an hour, or even half an hour, or a quarter of an hour, or a minute, morning and night, to eat.

A powerful army and an unlimited reserve of men characterize the Ottomans' "merueilleuse puissance & non acoustumee armee maritime & terrestre" (1r) (marvelous power and unusual maritime and land army). Their artillery is impressive and the casualty caused by the Ottomans "une chose fort inhumayne & espouuantable" (15r) (a very inhuman and frightening thing). The sultan's army is almighty according to Bourbon, who is visibly impressed by these determined, obedient, and well-equipped soldiers who built marvelously high walls to attack the city (16v). In these pages, the conqueror is neither the Ottoman nor the infidel, but a stronger opponent capable of taking advantage of a delicate situation in Rhodes aggravated by Christianity's internal disputes. Confronted with such an opponent, Bourbon asks, what could the Knights have done? For the Rhodians who are under constant pressure, it looks as if the assailants never take a moment to rest or sleep (28v). Furthermore, the loss of their own galvanizes the Ottomans who do not fear death: "et quăt nostre artillerie leur faisoit plusgrăd meurtre de gens: a ceste heure la ilz gettoient grans crys de ioye" (26r) (and when our artillery caused them much death, at that time they shouted with joy). In opposition, on the Christian side, only the grand master seems ready to die for the faith (31v).

The Ottomans are organized soldiers who take the time to strategize. When a wall has fallen, enabling them to enter the city without any difficulty, they pause to better organize themselves "cŏme gens de guerre faisoiĕt leurs choses auec le poys de la raison" (34r) (as military people do their things, with reason) and set up several camps on the opponent's ground. The Knights, sensing their impending defeat, send an envoy to Ahmet Pasha to see if the sultan would accept money in compensation for war expenses. The pasha responds that "semblables parolles & offres dargĕt nestoient poĩt pour estre dictes ny presentees au grăd seigneur sur peine de la vie: car il regardoit plus a lhonneur que a tous les biens du monde" (43v) (such words and financial propositions were not to be said or presented to the sultan for fear of death, for he [the sultan] looked after his honor more than the world's riches). Süleyman is disinterested in material matters, a trait he shares with Villiers l'Isle-Adam, who "nestimoit ne or ne argĕt: nŏ plus que pierres ou feues comme chose decente a ung prince, principallement estant aux affaires et tribulation de la guerre" (7v–8r) (did not care about gold and silver any more than he cared about precious stones, which were not decent things for a prince involved mainly in matters of war).

In addition, the sultan generously proposes his own ships to help people leave the island if they so wish. He swears that he will not take the artillery from Christian ships and that he will keep anyone who wants to stay on the island safe and exempt from any imposition, including child levy, or *devshirme*. The janissaries' pillaging was thus counterbalanced by acts of civility. Süleyman may boast of "vayne gloire & . . . superbe" (2r) (vain glory and . . . pride), but he is a great military leader who practices charity just like a Hospitaller. Of course, for practical as well as ideological reasons, it was more advantageous to preserve as much of the Rhodian infrastructure as possible and to treat islanders decently if they were to become a part of the Ottoman administration.[38] Nevertheless, what is important here is that Bourbon emphasizes the sultan's qualities over the shortcomings of his troops.

To summarize, the sultan is cruel, but the grand master can be too. If the latter is ready to die for his cause, the same is true for the former; neither Villiers l'Isle-Adam nor Süleyman cares about material wealth. Although the sultan is first introduced as the antichrist in Bourbon's text, he emerges as just, tolerant, generous, and charitable. Furthermore, he is obeyed by a formidable and united army. Both competent, the grand master and the 'great Turk' are two remarkable leaders, two exceptional figures separated only by religion which, ultimately, does not matter much in Bourbon's narrative.[39] Villiers l'Isle-Adam and Süleyman are powerful lions fighting for their respective causes. Although one might have expected otherwise, Süleyman's portrait and Villiers l'Isle-Adam's in the *Oppugnation* are not based on radical differences. Bourbon attempts a rapprochement between the two men who share major characteristics and represent rather distinct worlds, societies that, for the chronicler at least, have nevertheless a knightly and military ethos in common. Instead of developing his initial portrait of the sultan as antithetical to the grand master, Bourbon ultimately likens the sultan to the leader of the Hospitallers and erases what might have distinguished the two men, religion.

This literary rapprochement might be an attempt to translate the foreign in what François Hartog calls an "opération de traduction"[40], whereby the Sultan acquires the characteristics of a Christian Knight so that he can be understood by a western audience. Rather, I propose that we view Bourbon's strategy as a sign of possibility, more specifically the possibility of common ground between Ottoman and French military (and potentially political) societies.

Deciphering the reasons Bourbon gives for the siege in the *Oppugnation* helps to pinpoint that both Ottomans and Hospitallers shared an understanding of the fall of Rhodes; it also reveals one major divergence in their interpretations of the event. In the chronicle, the motives for Sultan Süleyman to take Rhodes are manifold. In a letter he addressed to Rhodes prior to the assault, the Ottoman sultan tells of the damages the Knights had done to his empire: "[nous] voulons auoir ceste isle, pour les grands dommaiges, et oeuures mauluaises quen auons tous les iours" (10r) ([we] want to possess this island because of the great harm and troubles it [the Order] inflicts on us every day). Bourbon himself develops Süleyman's argument, acknowledging its validity:

> *Et oyant iornellement plainctes, lamentations, & crys de ses subgectz, tãt de turquie que Syrie des prinses que faisoyent iornellement ceulx de ladicte religion par mer & par terre de leurs personnes & biens: au moyen de quoy estoyent tellement contrainctz, quil ne pouuoyent plus guyeres nauiguer. Et que plus est en sõ particulier se trouuoit ledict turcq tresfort empesche & trouble entant que touchoit le gouuernement de la Syrie, par ce que par mer qui est le chemyn plus expedient & bref (obstãt ce que dessus est dit) ne pouuoit bonnemẽt dresser ses affaires sans despenses excessiues. Ains estoit contrainct continuellement entretenir grosse armee de mer pour le traffic de la turquie en Syrie. Ce cõsidere est resolu assaillir ceste religion & cite de*

Rhodes, iugeant & ayant ferme opiniõ que icelle subiuguee & mise en son obeyssance pacifieroit & mectroit en seurete perpetuelle, tous ces pays & estat quil a en ce leuant. (1v)

Hearing complaints, grievances, and grumbles daily from his subjects in Turkey as well as in Syria about captures of men and goods by the Order both on land and at sea, so much so that the Turks could no longer sail. Furthermore, the said great Turk was much bothered and troubled by the fact that he could not take care of the administrative affairs in Syria effectively by sea which is the shortest and most expedient route (as was stated above). He simply could not conduct business without heavy expenses. And so he was obliged to keep a large fleet to protect the Turkey-Syria route. All this considered, he was resolved to attack the Order and the city of Rhodes judging and believing firmly that once it was captured and subdued he would pacify and bring perpetual security to all the countries and states he has in the Levant.

According to Bourbon then, Süleyman wanted to put an end to the Knights' piratical activities in the Mediterranean, particularly the Euboea,[41] for piracy prevented the transportation of goods and people between different Ottoman territories, causing insecurity among the sultan's subjects as well as expenses for the empire. Nicolas Vatin agrees with Bourbon's interpretation and adds that the public opinion in Ottoman lands was more in favor of attacking Christian Knights than Safavids who were Muslim.[42]

Bourbon suggests a second reason for the assault of Rhodes. The Ottomans, claims the chronicler, are conquerors by nature and Süleyman comes from a long lineage of military holy warriors, or *ghazi*.[43] Detailing the genealogy of the sultan, Bourbon legitimizes, accentuates, and actualizes Süleyman's presence in his text. The origins of the sultan establish his pedigree and *label de qualité*. The sultan becomes more authentic, more powerful as his lineage, his ancestors and their military accomplishments are careful recorded. Recalling the Ottomans' recent victories, Bourbon starts with the oldest and most symbolic, that of Constantinople in 1453: "Sultan mahõmet le tresfellõ & belliqueux: lequel print constantinoble & lisle de negrepont & depuys passa en Europe" (1v) (Sultan Mehmed, the infidel and warmonger, who captured Constantinople and the island of Negrepont, and since then moved toward Europe). He continues with Mehmed's successors "sultan bayazet qui print . . . Le pantho & modon" (Sultan Bayezid who took Lepanto and Modon), and "magnanime & victorieux seigneur Sultã Sellin son pere" (the magnanimous and victorious lord, Sultan Selim, his father) who defeated the Safavid Shah and conquered Tabriz and Egypt.[44] Given this illustrious ancestry, Süleyman could easily call himself "Sultan Soliman par la grace de dieu tresgrand empereur de Cõstãtinoble de lune & lautre Perse, Arabye, Syrie, Lameeque, Jhierusalẽ, Dasie, Europe et de toute legypte: et de la mer seigneur et possesseur" (10r) (Sultan Süleyman, by the grace of God emperor of Constantinople, Persia, Syria, Mecca, Jerusalem, Asia and Europe and all of Egypt, and ruler and lord of the sea).

Following his ancestors' *ghazi* mentality, Süleyman wants to "ensuyure les vestiges & faictz de ses antecesseurs" (1v) (follow the steps and deeds of his ancestors), particularly those of his father, Selim, who was about to attack Rhodes in 1520 when he suddenly died. Before his death, Selim would have composed a will specifying his desire for his son to "faire apres sa mort deux entreprises premieres & principalles. Lune contre belgrado. Lautre contre Rhodes" (1v–2r) (embark on major enterprises after his death, one against Belgrade and the other against Rhodes). Bourbon mentions the success regarding the first one and insists that the "persuasion paternelle facillement entra & fust imprimee au cueur & iuue-nille volante dudit Selimã son filz" (2r) (the paternal words easily convinced his young son, Süleyman, and entered his heart and will, where they were imprinted). Süleyman is not only the shadow of his father as André Clot claims,[45] he is his faithful inheritor and executor, the next in a line of fine military rulers.

Süleyman's presence in Bourbon's text is accentuated by the inclusion of his ultimatum, one in which the sultan tells the grand master, his knights, and the civilians in Rhodes to surrender (10v). Süleyman is literally inscribed in Bourbon's narration. His letter, which is provided verbatim, functions as tangible proof of his existence and makes his presence ever more real for readers of the *Oppugnation*. The letter is given in French, suggesting an erased act of translation. Commentators have reproduced the sultan's message partially or in its totality.[46] When comparing it to other pieces of correspondence said to have come from Süleyman, Charrière judges that only the one included in Bourbon is authentic because of the terms used. The original is not known to us, but it is entirely likely that the sultan wrote such a message. Who translated it into French? Could Bourbon have memorized it when, as he says, it was read publicly (10r) or did he have access to a copy? We do not have answers to these questions. Regardless, the inclusion of the letter makes the sultan appear as if he is speaking directly to the reader. Letters from high-ranking officials can manifest the power of the despot who rules thanks to his writing.[47] For Bourbon, however, the letter functions differently: instead of pointing to the tyrant, it gives an aspect of familiarity to the Ottoman sultan. Of course, Süleyman is obeyed unconditionally by his troops and he imposes his rule by communicating his orders in writing. But these are qualities that a prince, Christian or Muslim, was expected to have and, as Bourbon suggests, early sixteenth-century European rulers could and should have taken notice and followed Süleyman's model.

The French, Francis I in particular, must have understood what was at stake: a young sultan coming from a formidable lineage wants to fulfill his father's wishes; he can count on his powerful and orderly army and he is helped by the fact that disunited Christians will not support the Order whose piracy troubles his economy in and around the Mediterranean. Disunity among Christians seems to have been a happy coincidence for Süleyman. Unlikely to count as a serious motivation for the Ottomans, it is a reason that Bourbon stresses by underscoring the presence of traitors in the text. For Rhodes is not only a bridge toward the Ottoman Empire; it is also a microcosm of Christendom. On the island as in Europe, dissension happens—Knights and civilians do not always agree and within the Order itself there is such tension that some Christians will be led to treason.

Turk to Traitor

Bourbon highlights two episodes of treason, the first one allegedly committed by a Jewish doctor and the second by a high-ranking knight. The narrator mentions these two cases right from the outset and describes them in detail in the initial chapters of the *Oppugnation*. The first of the traitors is never named, only identified by his profession and his religious affiliation. He would have been baptized in order to better hide his actions, claims Bourbon. He most likely came from Ottoman lands since the chronicler mentions that the doctor settled in Rhodes after been asked to do so by Sultan Selim. Once the spy was implanted, Süleyman would have reactivated him by sending some presents through a mysterious and unidentified man from Lyon who would have moved freely between Muslim and Christian worlds. Only through this case of treason does the reader get a furtive glimpse at Rhodes's ethnic and religious diversity and its constantly evolving configuration. The Jewish doctor is accused of spying on behalf of Süleyman, whom he would have kept informed about the casualties suffered on Rhodes (2r–v). As he is about to be executed though, "ledit iuifz se confessa & comme bon chrestien voulut finer ces iours" (23v) (the said Jew confessed and wished to end his life as would a good Christian). A liminal subject in Bourbon's text, the Jewish doctor converts *in extremis*.

The second traitor on which the *Oppugnation* insists is named André d'Amaral—de Mérail in the text. Unlike the Jewish doctor, d'Amaral is a Christian: "ung cheualier portugaloys chãcelier de nostre religiõ hõme dauctorite & scauoir & des principaulx seigneurs du conseil" (2v) (a Portuguese knight, chancellor of our Order, a man of authority and knowledge and one of the most important members of the council). A respected *seigneur de la grande croix* (7r), d'Amaral will be named during the siege as one of four *capitaines de secours*. According to Bourbon, it is precisely the influential position he occupies within the Order that allowed d'Amaral to spy and act against Christians with impunity. It was he, for example, who, before the assault even began, prevented brave and daring merchants from taking risks and fetching wine from Candia (4v–5r). Contrary to the doctor, whose identity, including his religious identity, remains unclear and questionable, d'Amaral is identified by name, religious affiliation, positions, and titles within the Order.

Bourbon considers d'Amaral as more dangerous than the Jewish doctor, more dangerous even than Süleyman, the apocalyptical infidel. In the *dédicade*, Bourbon states the presence of "faulx chrestiens" among whom one "de tes propres disciples et religieux: lequel ensuyuant le vray train de Judas: ta vĕdu aux infidelles" (*dédicace*) (of your own members who, following Judas' path, turned you in to the infidels). As Judas betrayed Jesus and gave him away to the Jews, the consequence of d'Amaral's treason is the surrendering of Villiers l'Isle-Adam to his enemies. Conveniently, this remark by Bourbon exonerates the grand master for, if Jesus did not prevent Judas's betrayal and allowed himself to be sacrified, how could Villiers l'Isle-Adam have opposed God's will?

On several occasions in the text, Bourbon reiterates the parallel between Judas and d'Amaral, until he surpasses it:

> *Et en ce mauldit & diabolique vouloir sans repẽtance fina ces iours le mal-*
> *heureux traistre, duquel la trahison ie croy auoir este plus grãde que celle de*
> *Judas pour les maulx qui en sont venus et viendront. Car la trahyson de Judas*
> *a la fin redonda a bien et a la saluation du gerre humain, mais ceste cy a este*
> *loccasion principalle de la perte de Rhodes. Et si dieu ny met remede, sera la*
> *perdition de toutes les isles de leuant pource que infinies ames de chrestiens*
> *seront prinses & mises hors de la foy chrestieñe & reduictes a la loy du faulx*
> *mahõmet.* (33r)

And with this damned and diabolical will, without repenting, this poor traitor ended his life, he whose betrayal I consider greater than that of Judas because of all the evils that have come from it and all those that will come. For Judas's treason turned out to have a positive outcome since it saved the human race; but this one was the main reason for the fall of Rhodes. And if God does not remedy the situation, it will be the end of all the islands of the Levant because an infinite number of Christian souls will be captured and taken away from the Christian faith and reduced to the law of the false Muhammad.

Here d'Amaral is associated with the end of times. He is described as false, damned, and diabolical, just as the sultan is in the *Oppugnation*'s first pages. However, unlike Judas' treason—which allowed Jesus to be sacrificed according to God's plan, thereby saving Christians—d'Amaral's might signify the end of Christianity. Bourbon suggests that a Christian, d'Amaral, is more responsible than a Muslim, Süleyman, for Christianity's demise.

The narrative structure of the *Oppugnation* stresses Bourbon's position with regard to d'Amaral. Distinguishing between *temps discursif* and *temps des choses*, Michel de Certeau has shown that discursive time is based upon, but not synonymous with, the time of events.[48] In other words, the narrative Bourbon wrote depends on and reflects the *temps des choses*, which is simultaneously being re-evaluated and modified by the chronicler. Linear for the most part, the narrative breaks away from the chronology when it deals with traitors, particularly d'Amaral. Bourbon takes pains to recount and rework the story of d'Amaral following a chronology that does not entirely correspond to the *temps des choses*. According to Bourbon himself, d'Amaral's culpability was established in October 1522. The chronicler, however, mentions the Knight's responsibility for the fall of Rhodes right from the *dédicace* and develops the idea prior to describing the preparations for the battle the previous spring. When it comes to traitors then, time is not only shortened or dilated as in any historiographical narrative, it is completely distorted by Bourbon in order to stress what he considers essential— the treason of a Knight.

Three temporal movements are visible in Bourbon's narration. The first is the one that follows the events chronologically. It can be schematically summarized by a succession of events—the preparation of the assault in the spring; the battle in summer; the discovery of d'Amaral's culpability in the fall and his execution; the surrender and the loss of Rhodes in winter. The second temporal movement is derived from the judicial trial that happens on the island following the suspicion surrounding d'Amaral. This movement follows a reverse chronological order. As Bourbon states, the trial starts in October and goes back in time to try to establish what happened, when, and where. Step by step, events are clarified until enough proof is collected to show the innocence, or in this case the culpability, of the suspect. The third movement is discursive time, in other words, the literary time that depends on Bourbon's subjectivity. This is where the narrator gathers the two preceding movements and creates a third new one, reconstituting and presenting the reader with a new timeline. Aware of the preceding movements, the narrator uses their respective chronologies as a base for his narration while including a number of details known to him only thanks to the judicial trial. Unlike a journal where the moment of the event coincides, more or less, with the moment of the writing of the event, the *Oppugnation* is a text in which facts are deliberately organized depending on the utility they have *a posteriori*. Bourbon respects the chronology of events overall; yet, in his narrative, he puts forward what he views as the essential reason for the loss of Rhodes, d'Amaral's culpability. Loicq-Berger seems to overlook Bourbon's authorial intervention when she claims that "le trait le plus frappant de cet ensemble, c'est la rigueur de sa composition, simplement fondée sur l'axe chronologique, exempte de tout pathos et conduit par un sévère souci d'objectivité" (the most striking element of the narrative is the rigor of its composition simply founded upon the chronological axis, exempt of pathos, and driven by a strict concern with objectivity).[49] The narrative is indeed mostly grounded in the chronological *temps des choses*, but not simply. Often unbiased and relatively objective, as when it details the Ottoman army's uninterrupted assault, the narrative also follows a chronology of morality, demanding that facts like d'Amaral's treason be given special consideration and thereby be asserted from the very beginning.

And indeed, the traitor's culpability is hammered right from the start of the narrative. Without mentioning that only in October will the witnesses to d'Amaral's treasonous act be interrogated, Bourbon gives numerous details at the very beginning of his *Oppugnation* about the affair and the personality of a man for whom he clearly has no sympathy. According to the chronicler, d'Amaral is a jealous man who could not accept Villiers l'Isle-Adam's election to the position he himself was eyeing. In spite of the honors he had already accumulated within the Order,

> *enflambe dambicion & conuoytise de paruenir a telle dignite . . . print si grãde enuye & par consequent inimicitie & mal veillance, non seullement contre ledit seigneur, mais contre toute sa religion parquoy mist son estude & fantasie de la trahir & vendre aux infidelles.* (2v-3r)

fired up with ambition and envy, wanting to achieve such status . . . he took so poorly to the news that he showed unfriendliness and evil thoughts towards not only the lord but the entire Order, against which he devised eerie plans of betrayal to the infidels.

Bourbon chooses to start his narration with this severe remark although, according to the time of events, the culpability of the Portuguese is still unproven. He does not spare any details either. He claims that d'Amaral, once deprived of the title and position of grand master, could not hide his evil intentions: "il dit a ung commandeur de la nation espaignolle homme de bien & amy sien, que ledit seigneur esleu grand maistre, seroit le dernier maistre de Rhodes" (3r) (he said to a commander of the Spanish nation, a man of good intentions and a friend of his, that the lord who had been elected grand master would be the last master of Rhodes). In a sense, he was right of course, since the Order, after losing Rhodes, had to leave the island and move through a series of temporary bases until settling finally in Malta in 1530. Affected by what he considered a setback, d'Amaral shows "dyable ingratitude & fureur" (diabolical ingratitude and furor) as the Ottomans approach and wishes for the Order and Rhodes to be lost. This sixteenth-century Ganelon went on to send letters to the Ottoman pashas encouraging them to lay siege to Rhodes and keeping them abreast of the state of the fortifications. In all fairness, Bourbon does confess that these facts will not be known for several months—even several years—after the attack, but he does so toward the end of his narrative, once his biased presentation is long finished. Accentuating the "mauldit vouloir" (evil intentions), "meschant couraige" (impetuous courage) and "deshŏnestes propos" (dishonest discourse) (3v) of d'Amaral, Bourbon condemns the Portuguese knight right from the start. Declared at the beginning of the *Oppugnation* and hammered in several subsequent passages, d'Amaral's culpability is not given to readers to contemplate but to accept and acknowledge. Miles away from Rhodes, in Marseille, Honorat de Valbelle was convinced.[50]

Later in the narrative, Bourbon gives additional details regarding d'Amaral's treason, in particular the content of the letters the knight had sent to the Ottomans. This time, he notes that in September there was no suspicion regarding the Portuguese; since then, however, "on trouua depuys le dessusdict frere Andre de merail escript une lettre aux baschas les ennortant de demourer & leur disant que au long aller la ville seroit a eux" (27r) (since then a letter written to the pashas was found on Brother d'Amaral informing them to stay put and telling them that in the long run the city will be theirs). Furthermore, Bourbon suggests that, among all the letters received by the pashas from various informers, d'Amaral's message carried the most weight. Because an influential knight informed them of the situation in the Christian camp, the Ottomans were convinced to continue the siege and to wait.

In spite of the certainty Bourbon felt regarding d'Amaral's culpability, his treason was established based only on the accounts of his servant, the Spanish commander, and the chaplain. The tribunal, composed of two lords of the *grande croix* and the judges of the *castelaine*, called for d'Amaral and his servant "dauoir les

testes tranchees comme traystres. Et puis apres estre mys en quatre quartiers"
(32v) (to have their heads cut off as traitors do and next to be quartered). Questioned and tortured like his servant, d'Amaral denied the accusation. His servant was executed on November 6. Two days later came d'Amaral's turn. Before
being executed, the Knight was stripped of his clothing as, the narrative suggests, d'Amaral did not deserve to wear the Order's cross on his chest any longer.
Unworthy of his uniform and title, he was symbolically banished from Christianity. Contrary to his servant, he neither confessed nor looked at an image of the
Virgin presented to him before his death. He died, therefore, as "faux chrestien,"
Bourbon concludes.

The question of d'Amaral's culpability has prompted many commentaries.
Eric Brockman and Claude Petiet have summarized the arguments of those who
believe in his innocence and of those who do not.[51] Whether guilty or not, for
Bourbon, d'Amaral represents the destructive "fausseté" that is in all of us. More
than religious alterity, the term refers to a lack of the loyalty expected from a
member of a community such as the Order of St. John. The chronicler thus demonstrates that there are many kinds and degrees of infidels. In this particular case,
the infidel is not the Ottoman sultan but rather d'Amaral, a more menacing and
most dangerous enemy for the Order and Christianity.

With d'Amaral then, the defeat and the danger are not only military and religious; they are also related to protonational identity politics. The Order is clearly
a pan-European organization; its members are united by one religion, Christianity—more specifically Catholicism—which is the *raison d'être* and the goal of
their actions. However, Bourbon mentions that d'Amaral is Portuguese whereas
Villiers l'Isle-Adam is French, therefore emphasizing that they belong to two different 'nations,' or *langues* to use the Order's vocabulary. The rivalry between the
two men was apparently long-standing since scholars report a first disagreement
in 1510 when they were under the orders of Emeri d'Amboise, another Frenchman who was grand master from 1503 to 1512.[52] This first divergence could be the
reason why d'Amaral ran for the position of grand master at d'Amboise's death,
certainly an unusual step that coincided with Charles V and Francis I's tussle over
Italy.[53] Bourbon does not mention this first disagreement. In fact, he denies rumors
of a rebellion among the Knights of the *langue d'Italie* (3r–v). According to him,
it is an invention by d'Amaral himself. We know, however, that 'nationalism'
weighed on the Order as soon as it settled in Rhodes.[54]

In his *Oppugnation*, Bourbon seeks to give a unified and idyllic image of the
Order faced with a Christian Europe in disarray. But is this perfect image of the
organization believable? Gathering eight *langues*—Provence, Auvergne, France,
Italy, Aragon, England, Germany, and Castille (in which Portugal was included)—
the Order represented the entire Christendom; it gave livelihood to many, prestige
to some, and often the opportunity of crossing the seas. And yet, influential as it
was in the wider Mediterranean, the Order depended upon Europe, which gave
it men and financial support. It was therefore at the mercy of European politics,
especially the politics of emerging nations. For Bourbon, Christian Europe's disunity was one of the main causes of the Order's defeat in Rhodes. Linking what

went on in Europe and in Rhodes, he acknowledged the possible consequences of Christianity's conflicts on the Order, but he was not able to fully comprehend the wide systemic changes that were taking place in the 1520s. The part treason plays in the *Oppugnation* is testimony to Bourbon's deep concern with the danger it posed. In 1525, who could understand that better than Francis I, who had lost his army chief to Charles V in 1523?

Conclusion

Bourbon's *Oppugnation* is apparently based on a fundamental and quite banal dichotomy with Christians on one side and infidels on the other. At first glance, barriers between these two camps seem immovable and one could think that the text makes yet another call for crusade. In his narrative, however, Bourbon quickly goes beyond his original frame. On the one hand, he brings the infidel, Süleyman, close to Villiers l'Isle-Adam and paints him as a remarkable chief whom Christian princes should value and emulate if Christendom does not want to succumb to Islam entirely. On the other, he insists on the treason of one of the Order's most respected members, hinting at the fact that alterity might be found in nationality more than religion. In the *Oppugnation*, the *Other* can be the non-Christian, whether Muslim or Jew, but it is also the non-French, particularly the Portuguese or the Spanish. In Europe as in Rhodes, this 'nation'-based *Other* fractures what Bourbon idealistically and simplistically conceives of as Christendom's unity.

Notes

1 Letter to the seigneur de la Rochepot dated February 7, 1523, in Charrière, *Négociations*, 1: 94–95. This chapter is a reworked and translated version of my article, "Du Turc au traître: Les chevaliers de Saint-Jean-de-Jérusalem, les Ottomans et la France de François Ier dans *L'oppugnation* de Jacques de Bourbon" in *French Historical Studies* 30, no. 3 (2007): 427–49.

2 The success of the Knights was immortalized by Guillaume Caoursin in a beautiful manuscript with striking illustrations now preserved in the Bibliothèque Nationale de France (Latin 6067). One of its illustrations shows Caoursin kneeling and presenting his work to d'Aubusson (3v). For further details on Caoursin's life and literary production, see Nicolas Vatin, *Sultan Djem* (Ankara: Türk Tarih Kurumu Basimevi, 1997), 89–102.

3 Jacques de Bourbon, *La grande et merueilleuse et trescruelle oppugnation de la noble cite de Rhodes prinse naguieres par Sultan Seliman a present grand Turcq ennemy de la tressaincte foy Catholicque* (Paris, 1525), 1r–v. All references are to the volume held in the Gordon Collection of the University of Virginia, GORDON1525.B68. When quoting the text, I have replaced slashes by commas and resolved abbreviations concerning relative pronouns.

4 Valbelle, *Histoire journalière*, 1: 108.

5 Letter written to Montmorency from Rome and dated September 15, 1523, in Charrière, *Négociations*, 1: 110.

6 Pasquier de Le Barre, *Le journal d'un bourgeois de Tournai: Le second livre des chroniques de Pasquier de Le Barre (1500–1565)*, ed. Gérard Moreau (Bruxelles: Palais des Académies, 1975), 237–38; Antoine de Lusy, *Le journal d'un bourgeois de Mons, 1505–1536*, ed. Armand Louant (Bruxelles: Palais des Académies, 1969), 213;

Le journal d'un bourgeois de Paris sous le règne de François Premier (1515–1536), ed. Ludovic Lalanne (New York: Johnson, 1965), 114–18; Honorat de Valbelle, *Histoire journalière*, 108–9.

7 Rouillard lists pamphlets written in French between 1525 and 1535 (*The Turk*, 64–65 and 647).

8 On Ottoman accounts of the fall of Rhodes, see Vatin, *Ordre*, 343–60 and "La conquête de Rhodes" in *Soliman le Magnifique et son temps*, ed. Gilles Veinstein (Paris: Documentation française, 1992), 435–54. The other Christian narratives of the fall of Rhodes are in Latin. The first is by Thomas Guichard and is entitled *Oratio . . . coram Clemente VII Pont. Max.*. It appeared simultaneously in Rome and Cologne in 1524, then in Paris in 1527. The second, *De bello rhodio libri tres*, is by Fontanus and was published in Rome in 1524.

9 Loicq-Berger, " 'L'Oppugnation de Rhodes' de Jacques de Bourbon: Un texte à découvrir," *Revue Belge de Philologie et d'Histoire* 69, no. 4 (1991): 905–24, here 905–6. Rouillard talks about two editions for 1525 (*The Turk*, 64, 647) and Loicq-Berger mentions one 1531 edition in Malta.

10 Abbé de Vertot, *Histoire des chevaliers hospitaliers de S. Jean de Jerusalem: Appelles depuis chevaliers de Rhodes, et aujourd'hui chevaliers de Malte* (Paris: Rollin, Quillau père et fils, Desaint, 1726). Bourbon's narrative is in volume 2, 622–88.

11 The following biographical elements are taken from Loicq-Berger, "Un 'Liégeois' au siège de Rhodes de 1522," *Revue de Philologie et d'Histoire* 67, no. 4 (1989): 714–47.

12 *"Entre le préambule, de caractère plutôt analytique que narratif, et la partie terminale, simple survol de la première année post-rhodienne, c'est manifestement au récit de* L'oppugnation *proprement dite que l'auteur entendait réserver le meilleur de ses soins."* Loicq-Berger, "*Oppugnation*," 908.

13 On the importance of introductory pieces, see Gérard Genette, *Seuils* (Paris: Seuil, 1987).

14 D.P. Chattopadhyaya, "Itihasa, History and Historiography of Civilization" in *Cultural Otherness and Beyond*, ed. Chhanda Gupta and D.P. Chattopadhyaya (Leiden: Brill, 1998), 43–74.

15 The Order exists today still, albeit with a lesser political significance. On the history of the Order, see: H.J.A. Sire, *The Knights of Malta* (New Haven: Yale University Press, 1994); Jonathan Riley-Smith, *The Knights of Saint John in Jerusalem and Cyprus* (London: Macmillan, 1967); Anthony Luttrell, *The Hospitallers in Cyprus, Rhodes, Greece, and the West, 1291–1440* (London: Variorum Reprints, 1978); and Luttrell's collection of essays entitled *The Hospitallers of Rhodes and their Mediterranean World* (Burlington, VT: Ashgate, 1992), particularly "The Rhodian Background of the Order of St John on Malta."

16 Vatin, "Conquête," 445. Vatin also reproduces several pieces of correspondence between Pierre d'Aubusson and Sultan Bayezid in *Ordre*, 400–403, 404–8, 419–20, 429–32.

17 Loicq-Berger, "Liégeois," 731.

18 Charrière reproduces two letters from Villiers l'Isle-Adam addressed to King Francis after his election, one written in Marseille right before his departure for Rhodes, one once he had arrived on the island (*Négociations*, 1: 87–89).

19 On Rhodian piracy, see Vatin, *Ordre*, 79–129.

20 Vatin, *Sultan Djem*.

21 See Chapter 2.

22 Vatin, *Ordre*, 26–37 and 377–83. On the roles that islands under Ottoman control played up until the nineteenth century, see the collection of essays entitled *Insularités ottomans*, ed. Nicolas Vatin and Gilles Veinstein (Paris: Maisonneuve et Larose, 2004).

23 On the paradox and the richness of the border, see Étienne Balibar's works, particularly *Droit de cité* (Paris: Presses universitaires de France, 2002).

24 Thevet, *Pourtraits*, talks about the "*vertueux & magnanime Philippes de Villiers*" (372) and the "*venerable vieillard*" (373). Judging by the details given by the cosmographer, he was perfectly aware of the 1522 events and could have had access to Bourbon's *Oppugnation*.

25 Bourbon, *Oppugnation*, 12r–v.

26 Bourbon states that they were "*mille contre ung*" (22v). This estimate must, of course, not be taken literally. Nevertheless, the numerical superiority of the Ottomans was certain. See Vatin, "Conquête."

27 The Ottoman sources claim that the Rhodians bypassed the Knights and negotiated the conditions of defeat directly with the Ottomans. See Vatin, "Conquête."

28 See C.A. Patrides, "'The Bloody and Cruell Turke': The Background of a Renaissance Commonplace," *Studies in the Renaissance* 10 (1963): 126–35 and Norman Housley, "A Necessary Evil? Erasmus, the Crusade, and War against the Turks" in *Crusading and Warfare in Medieval and Renaissance Europe* (Burlington, VT: Ashgate, 2001), 259–79. For a summary of Luther's change of heart—he first opposed a war against the Ottomans, then accepted it under specific conditions—and Erasmus's uncertainty with regard to the 'Turks,' see Timothy Hampton, *Literature and Nation in the Sixteenth Century* (Ithaca: Cornell University Press, 2001), 44–45.

29 On rumors and strategies of communication in the medieval period, see Jean Verdon, *Information et désinformation au Moyen–Âge* (Paris: Perrin, 2010).

30 On early modern eyewitnessing, see Andrea Frisch, *The Invention of the Eyewitness: Witnessing and Testimony in Early Modern France* (Chapel Hill: University of North Carolina Press, 2004).

31 Michel de Certeau says, "*le discours [de l'historien] destiné à dire l'autre reste son discours*" (the [historian's] discourse meant to speak of the *other* remains the historian's discourse), *L'écriture de l'histoire* (Paris: Gallimard, 1975), 48.

32 Charrière, *Négociations*, 1: 108.

33 Norman Daniel, *Islam and the West: The Making of an Image* (Oxford: Oneworld, 1997), 147–48.

34 "*Iusques aux chatz tout seroit mys en piece*" Bourbon, *Oppugnation*, 40v.

35 On the evolution of violence in French society, see Robert Muchembled, *Une histoire de la violence: De la fin du Moyen-Âge à nos jours* (Paris: Seuil, 2008). Muchembled posits that starting in the early sixteenth century with publications like Castiglione's *Courtier* and Erasmus's *La civilité puérile*, "la civilisation des mœurs" began to be imposed on young people, leading to state control and ultimately a state monopoly on violence (456).

36 La Broquère, *Voyage*, 164 and 192.

37 Montaigne, *Les essais*, "De la phisionomie" 3:1042.

38 Vatin, *Ordre*, 359–60.

39 At the end of the sixteenth century, André Thevet would erase the religious difference almost entirely in his *Pourtraits*, presenting Sultan Süleyman as a connoisseur of the Christian religion: "*De faict sçay-je bien que c'estoit le Prince, qui prenoit grand plaisir à entendre discourir des points de la religion Chrestienne, mesmes en parloit-il autant pertinnement, que pouuoit luy permettre sa lourdise Mahemetée* (436–7) (I know for a fact that he was a prince who enjoyed hearing about the articles of faith in the Christian religion; he even talked about them as pertinently as his coarse Muhammadanism allowed).

40 The scholar talks about "passer l'autre au même." See François Hartog, *Le miroir d'Hérodote: Essai sur la représentation de l'autre* (Paris: Gallimard, 1980), 249.

41 On the period leading up to war on Rhodes, see Vatin, *L'Ordre*, 329–42. On the Ottoman reasons, practical and ideological, see Vatin, "La conquête," particularly 446–47.

42 This was not always the case, of course, since the Ottomans had fought the Safavid Shias and defeated them at the battle of Chaldiran in 1514. Here again, though, the

Ottomans were less interested in religion and territorial acquisition than in psychological victory.

43 Paul Wittek applied the *ghazi* mentality to the Ottomans in 1938. It has been much debated by historians since then. The thesis is valid only to the extent that one focuses on a certain type of source, including certain passages from Bourbon's *Oppugnation*.

44 Bourbon, *Oppugnation*, 1v.

45 Clot, *Soliman le Magnifique* (Paris: Fayard, 1983).

46 Clot, *Soliman le Magnifique* gives an excerpt (64), Claude Petiet (350–51) the entirety. See Claude Petiet, *Des Chevaliers de Rhodes aux Chevaliers de Malte: Villiers de l'Isle-Adam* (Paris: France-Empire, 1994). Charrière gives it an undeniable "caractère d'authenticité," as he does with the other documents he includes in his *Négociations*, 91–92.

47 Grosrichard, *Structure du Sérail*, chapter on "Le regard et la lettre," 71–90.

48 Certeau, *L'écriture de l'histoire*, 104.

49 Loicq-Berger, "Oppugnation," 908.

50 Even though he tellingly misinterprets the name of the traitor: "*c'est ce traître d'amiral qui fut cause de tout*" (109) (it was this traitor, the admiral, who was responsible for everything) Valbelle, *Histoire journalière*, 109.

51 Eric Brockman, *The Two Sieges of Rhodes, 1480–1522* (London: Cox and Wyman, 1969),146–48 and Claude Petiet, *Des Chevaliers de Rhodes*, 238–39.

52 Petiet, *Des Chevaliers de Rhodes*, 161–62 and Brockman, *The Two Sieges of Rhodes*, 107–8.

53 On the Franco-Spanish war between 1519 and 1523, see Chapter 8 of R.J. Knecht's *Renaissance Warrior and Patron: The Reign of Francis I* (Cambridge: Cambridge University Press, 1994).

54 Petiet, *Des Chevaliers de Rhodes*, 323–25 and 339–41.

4   Of Pigeons

Rabelaisian Spaces

"- Mon amy dont vous viennent ces pigeons icy?
- Cyre (dist il) ilz viennent de l'aultre monde."

"My friend, where do these pigeons come to you from?"
"Sire," said he, "they come from another world."
—François Rabelais, *Pantagruel*[1]

Symbolizing passage from one geographical space to another, pigeons open new worlds—physical as in this quote from *Pantagruel*, as well as fictional and philosophical. In the medieval and early modern periods, pigeons were valued for both their wholesome and savory meat and their smelly yet precious droppings, which were widely used as natural fertilizer. Country nobles kept the birds in *colombiers*, pigeon houses often detached from other buildings; some of them are still visible in France, where they are commonly known as *pigeonniers*. If pigeons were prized for their nutritious and agricultural qualities in medieval and early modern Europe, Easterners used them mostly as a means of communication. Arabs and Persians were experts at raising and using homing pigeons, also called carrier pigeons, the former appellation indicating the fact that the birds would fly long distances to return home to their familiar *colombier*, the latter insisting on the communicative potential of what are now called in French *pigeons voyageurs*. Pliny mentioned homing pigeons, but they were rediscovered by Europeans in the sixteenth century. As Michael Screech suggests in his reading of the *Sciomachie*, François Rabelais might have been aware of what was, up to the sixteenth century, a strictly Oriental use of pigeons.[2] Following Screech's supposition, I posit that Rabelais knew of the many usages of pigeons in his own country, France, as well as in the East. This chapter therefore is about pigeons and passage, the passage of spaces, and also the passage of narrations and of meanings. As Rabelais inscribes the Ottomans in *Pantagruel*, he invites readers to reexamine their preconceptions and to ponder their ability to surpass personal and societal mental constructs.

The following pages unveil the limits and disintegration of identities and of spatial and cultural boundaries in Rabelais's narrative, a narrative that plays with linguistic and visual echoes and superimposes different geographical referents, thereby generating new horizons and possibilities. By repeating specific words and concepts and by recalling parallel images occurring in different sets of cultures, Rabelais calls to mind and conflates three physical spaces into a whimsical one. The Ottoman Empire, the New World, and France join in a literary creation that criticizes early sixteenth-century abuses of power and that, rather than being Orientalist in Said's understanding of the term, stresses relativism, communality, and humbleness. At once raucous and subtle, the representation of the 'Turks' in *Pantagruel* is constantly challenged and redefined. Fleeting, changing, it incessantly passes from one level to another, allowing in the process the creation of a third space that privileges ludic questioning (*serio ludere*).

References to the Ottomans are rare in Rabelais's works and personal contacts with them undocumented before the publication of his first book, *Pantagruel*, in 1532. However, judging from long paragraphs about world politics in his correspondence with Geoffroy d'Estissac, Rabelais was keenly aware of and interested in Ottoman politics in the 1530s. As he accompanied Jean Du Bellay in Italy,[3] Rabelais informed d'Estissac about the military defeat of the Ottomans in Persia and Barbarossa's subsequent retreat to Constantinople.[4] He even mentioned a portrait of the pirate that he would have sent his protector.[5] This artwork is unfortunately lost; yet it is safe to say that when Rabelais looked East, he did not limit himself to Italy and, like the pigeons he mentions in *Pantagruel*, the author freely explored other worlds, words, and significations.

Unsurprisingly, Rabelais's fictions contain discrete but sustained traces of the Orient and particularly of the Ottoman East that concerns us here.[6] In chapter 14 of his *Pantagruel* the author situates an entire episode of Panurge's life in Ottoman lands. "Comment Panurge racompte la maniere comment il eschappa de la main des Turcqs" (How Panurge relates the way in which he escaped from the hands of the Turks) begins with a reference to the failed attack on the city port of Mytilene in 1501 and tells the fabulous adventures of Panurge captured by the 'Turks.' Several pages later, in Chapter 32, Rabelais returns to the Ottoman Empire with his narrator, Alcofrybas Nasier, seeking refuge under the giant's tongue. In "Comment Pantagruel de sa langue couvrit toute une armée, et de ce que l'auteur veit dedans sa bouche" (How Pantagruel with his tongue covered a whole army, and what the author saw inside his mouth), Rabelais takes readers simultaneously to a new world evoking the recently discovered American continent and to Constantinople by comparing Pantagruel's mouth to Hagia Sophia.

Rabelais's Herrings: *Iocus* and Communal Space

In Chapter 14 of *Pantagruel*, Panurge tells of his astonishing encounter with the Ottomans and of his no less astounding escape from their *roustisserie* (roasting). The trickster explains that, while fighting as a crusader in Mytilene, he was captured by the "Turks."[7] Wrapped in bacon and put to the flame, he manages to reverse a critical situation by putting his captor on the skewer. Escaping first an entire city engulfed in flames, then a "villain petit Turq bossu" (266) ("one ugly little Turk, hunchbacked in front" [181]), a courtesan, and thousands of dogs,

Panurge eventually regains Christian lands. The grotesque situation, its startling reversal, and its extraordinary developments accentuate the first comical detail of Chapter 14, which is the thematic point of departure for the following reflection: Panurge's comparison with an elongated, dried, and pungent smoked herring— Panurge being "eximé comme un haran soret" (263) ("as dry and emaciated as a red herring" [178]).

Terence Cave, Timothy Hampton, Frédéric Tinguely, Scott Juall, and more recently Phillip Usher have examined Panurge's encounter with the Turks from the perspective of alterity.[8] In his analysis of Chapter 14, Hampton uses the prism of humanist thought to show that Panurge's story illustrates the limits of humanism when faced with a religious *Other* such as the Muslim 'Turk.' Hence, in Hampton's words, Chapter 14 gives us a "perspective on the uneasy alliance between prose fiction and humanism in the face of alterity."[9] For this critic, Panurge's inability to express gratitude toward the 'Turks' who save him from the flames is a central scene underlining the absence of Christian charity, a key tenet of humanism and the principal agent of community, community being understood in Hampton's analysis as fundamentally Christian.[10] In my analysis of Chapter 14, I would like to build on Hampton's considerations and to consider Rabelais's narrative as profanatory. By profanatory, I do not refer to some sort of *incroyance* on the part of Rabelais,[11] but rather to the creative force of the narrative that extirpates us out of the limiting space of the sacred and brings us into a new sphere unaffected by religious and political forces. In other words, I examine the liberating aspect of Rabelais's discourse rather than its limitations. For if *Pantagruel*'s author shows the limits of humanist thinking in Panurge's story, he also provides a solution to the vexed confrontation with the Islamic other. I focus therefore on Panurge's playful liberation and specifically on Rabelais's linguistic games, an essential element of the narrative.[12] More specifically, I am interested in Rabelais's herrings, the literal as well as metaphoric ones, including the red kind. I uncover the humorous and rich associations that the author establishes between man and fish and I explore the resonating force of the herring so as to demonstrate how Rabelais's *iocus*, or linguistic game, liberates from the sphere of oppressive power (including humanist thought) and opens up a (re)new(ed) communal space, one that is characterized by the lack of confessional boundaries. Following Giorgio Agamben's interpretation of the *jeu*, I show Rabelais's profanation through his linguistic game with herring.[13]

Herring, particularly salted or smoked herring, was consumed widely in Europe in the late medieval period and during Rabelais's time, especially for Lent and the numerous "jours maigres" (lean days) of the Christian calendar when meat was forbidden.[14] "Haran soret," in modern French "hareng saur," refers to herring that has been smoked with oak or beech, a technique that assures its long preservation, the possibility of transportation deep into continental Europe, and thereby its regular presence on early modern tables throughout the continent, including areas close to the Mediterranean Sea. Caught in the Atlantic Ocean, particularly in the Channel and the Northern Sea, herring made its way to continental Europe through ports like Boulogne-sur-Mer in northern France, today the country's biggest center for the fishing industry and already in the medieval period a thriving port that focused its activity on that small fish. Unlike most early Renaissance food, then, herring was rarely a local product for most consumers. Nevertheless, it was regularly and commonly appreciated throughout Europe not only for its nutritious value but also for its medicinal properties against leprosy and abscesses. Indeed, the ubiquitous fish held a special place in the medieval imagination.[15] Recognized as foreign in origin, it was nevertheless not considered exotic.[16]

Panurge, like the Renaissance herring, is an oddity. In Chapter 9, when he first appears in Rabelais's novel, his foreignness, exemplified by his unimpressive physical presence and reinforced by the multiple languages he speaks, is coupled by a familiarity that does not escape *Pantagruel*'s narrator: "Un jour Pantagruel . . . rencontra un homme beau de stature et elegant en tous lineamens du corps, mais pitoyablement navré en divers lieux" (246) ("One day Pantagruel . . . met a man of handsome stature and elegant in every bodily feature, but pitiably wounded in various parts" [163]). The giant himself immediately recognizes something familiar in the rugged man:

> *Voyez vous cest homme qui vient par le chemin du pont Charanton? Par ma foy il n'est pauvre que par fortune: car je vous asseure que à sa physionomie nature l'a produict de riche et noble lignée, mais les adventures des gens curieulx le ont reduict en telle penurie et indigence.* (246)
>
> Do you see that man coming along the Charanton Bridge road? 'Pon my word, he is poor only in fortune, for from his physiognomy I assure you that Nature brought him forth from some rich and noble line, but the accidents that happen to the adventurous have reduced him to such penurie and indigence. (163)

An unintelligible and unrecognizable traveler at first, Panurge finally reveals himself by declaring that he speaks French:

> *Si faictz tresbien, seigneur, respondit le compaignon, Dieu mercy: c'est ma langue naturelle, et maternelle, car je suis né et ay esté nourry jeune au jardin de France, c'est Touraine.* (249)
>
> "Indeed I do very well, My Lord," replied the fellow, "thank God. It's my native mother tongue, for as a youngster I was born and brought up in the garden of France, that is to say Touraine." (166)

The reverse image of the Renaissance herring, Panurge, under the guise of worldly polyglotism, is French. Raised in the garden of France, he traveled the world and added languages and adventures to his initial repertoire before returning to his place of origin. More importantly perhaps, this anecdotal episode with which *Pantagruel* opens suggests that Panurge, just like the Silène in *Gargantua*'s prologue, is a riddle that demands the reader's attention. His outward appearance, "eximé comme un haran soret," may hide a "sustanticfique mouelle" (7) ("substantific marrow" [4]). Like a shriveled smoked herring that provides sustenance, there is more to the tall, thin, and dried-up Panurge than meets the eye. Might his adventures with the Ottomans also contain a deeper meaning than what has been acknowledged thus far?

A set of dichotomies punctuates Chapter 14 of *Pantagruel*. Most are religiously motivated and support the opening allusion to the 1510 crusade-like assault on Mytilene. These oppositions set two characters apart: Panurge on the one hand, and his executioner turned victim, the pasha, on the other. Panurge, a Frenchman from Touraine, is Christian: "Mon vray et propre nom de baptesme est Panurge" (264) ("my real proper baptismal name is Panurge" [166]). Accordingly, Panurge calls on God and all His saints when in a dire situation:

> *Comme ilz [les 'Turcs'] me routissoyent, je me recommandoys à la grace divine, ayant en memoyre le bon sainct Laurent, et tousjours esperoys en Dieu, qu'il me delivreroit de ce torment.* (264)
>
> Even as they were roasting me, I was commending myself to the Divine Grace, keeping in mind good Saint Lawrence, and I kept hoping in God that He would deliver me from that torment. (179)

In constrast with Panurge, the pasha and his peers, "ces diables de Turcqs," call on devils when they need help:

> *Voyant mon Baschaz, que le cas estoit desesperé, et que sa maison estoit bruslée sans remission, et tout son bien perdu: se donna à tous les diables, appellant Grilgoth, Astarost, Rappullus et Gribouillis par neuf foys.* (265)
>
> Then my pasha, seeing that the situation was desperate and his house was burned beyond reprieve and all his property lost, gave himself up to all the devils, calling Grilgoth, Astaroth, Rappullus, and Gribouillis, each nine times. (180)

Neither the geographical location nor the national origins of Panurge's 'Turks' are mentioned, but their title—pasha—and the names of the gods they worship suffice to locate them in a non-French and non-Christian land and culture. Rabelais reinforces the opposition between the Christian Panurge and his non-Christian captors by having Panurge emphasize the fact that the latter prefer water over wine: "Ces diables de Turcqs sont bien malheureux de ne boire goutte de vin. Si aultre mal n'estoit en l'*Alchoran* de Mahumeth, encores ne me mettroys je mie de sa loy" (263) ("Those devils of Turks are not to drink a drop of wine. If there were no other harm in Mahomet's *Alcoran*, still I would hardly place myself under his law" [179]). Thus the very beginning of the story suggests that Panurge could have escaped being roasted had he agreed to convert, which he is unable to do because of his unconditional love of wine. Describing his subsequent plight, Panurge calls it a "torment, auquel ces traistres chiens me detiennent, pour la maintenance de ta loy" (264) ("torment in which these treacherous dogs are holding me for maintaining Thy law!" [179]). Therefore, after his capture in Mytilene, Panurge finds himself facing a forced conversion or death, a common plight for victims of Ottoman military raids in the early modern period.[17] For him, religious differences are irreconcilable; a French Christian is not a Muslim pasha from Mytilene or Constantinople.

Conversion is what is at stake in Chapter 14 of *Pantagruel* and Panurge does not consider it an option. What happens in the course of the narration, however, is as close to conversion as can be. As characters trade places over the coals—literally and figuratively—the reader is left to wonder who is Christian and who is not. This slippage, aptly described by Tinguely as "altérités croisées," or crossed alterities,[18] occurs not only at the physical level, but more importantly at the linguistic level, allowing a passage from the religious and the sacred to the profane and the (re)opening of a space that religion had appropriated for itself. As Hampton has shown, by the end of Chapter 14, the metaphors have come alive: the *paillards* have materialized into the *paillasse*; the devils have taken the form of the pasha and his companion, and Turkish dogs are chasing Panurge out of the city. More importantly, Panurge has also effectively turned into the pasha. He has become as *paillard* as the 'Turk.' Commenting on Panurge's half-roasted skin, Rabelais uses the same adjective he had chosen earlier to describe the "paillards Turcqs" (263) ("blasted Turks" [179]): Panurge is now characterized by a "paillarde chair demy rostie" (267) ("wretched half-roasted flesh" [182]).[19] Not only are metaphors taking flesh as Hampton says they do, but Panurge's identity and the pasha's collide.

The blurring culminates over the roast pit. In a striking visual role reversal, it is Panurge who now cooks the pasha. In Chapter 14, the *roustisserie* is the boundary that separates but also potentially connects life and death, Christianity and Islam. It is also the place and the moment when words coalesce and the red herring is exposed. The scene deserves a close look. Panurge provides the following details about his adventures:

> *Les paillards Turcqs m'avoient mys en broche tout lardé, comme un connil, car j'estois tant eximé que aultrement de ma chair eust esté fort maulvaise viande, et en ce poinct me faisoyent roustir tout vif.* (263–64)
>   The blasted Turks had put me on a spit, all larded like a rabbit, for I was so emaciated that otherwise my flesh would have made very bad meat; and in that state they were having me roasted alive. (179)

Panurge compares himself to a rabbit, *un connil*, whose naturally dry and bland meat needs to be flavored and made juicier by adding pieces of bacon to it. Why does Panurge resemble a rabbit? Because he is *eximé*, skin and bone. The initial encounter between Pantagruel and Panurge, in Chapter 9, makes no mystery about the reason for Panurge's skinniness—he is undernourished: "j'ay necessité bien urgente de repaistre, dentz agues, ventre vuyde, gorge seiche, appetit strident" (250) ("I have a very urgent need to feed: sharpened teeth, empty stomach, dry throat, clamorous appetite" [166]). Panurge's defining characteristic, his thinness, explains why he is carefully prepared by the 'Turks.' The pasha, once on the pit, is being roasted by Panurge "comme on faict les harans soretz à la cheminée" (266) ("as you do red herrings in the fireplace" [181]). Panurge's identity and the pasha's blur as they share the same physical position on the fire. This is the moment when they begin to share similar physical characteristics. Both are described as herrings.

Interestingly, the image of the roasted herring also appears in Chapter 5 of Rabelais's work as Pantagruel is touring French universities, long before his encounter with Panurge. The giant travels to La Rochelle and Bordeaux before stopping in Toulouse, where he learns how to dance and fence with both hands like students customarily do in that city. Despite the obvious entertainment value of Toulouse, Pantagruel does not stay long in the southern city for "il vit qu'ils faisoyent brusler leurs regens tout vifz comme harans soretz" (231) ("he saw that they had their teachers burned alive like red herrings" [148]). *Écoliers toulousains* were known for demonstrating, often violently, against their pro-Catholic *parlement* and were accused of heresy as early as the 1530s,[20] but Pantagruel's remark could be a reference to Jean de Cahors's execution.[21] Accused of having presided over a Lutheran banquet, the law professor had been condemned and burned at the stake in June 1532, some six months before the publication of *Pantagruel*.[22] Three years earlier, in 1529, Louis de Berquin had also been burned, in Paris this time, for having being a sympathizer of Erasmus. Etienne Dolet would follow in 1546. In his *Pantagruel* then, Rabelais points out that both in Ottoman lands and in the French kingdom men are put to death by fire for not wanting to conform to religious beliefs.[23] France and the Ottoman Empire coalesce because of a common practice, death by fire on the *bûcher*. Purportedly focusing on and denouncing the Ottomans' cruelty, Rabelais alludes to the religious persecutions that occurred in France in the late 1520s and the 1530s, a period when the *Parlement* did not refrain from openly criticizing a rather tolerant royal policy toward Reformers. Whereas Panurge attempts to keep the 'Turks' at a distance by insisting on cultural and religious differences, Rabelais associates the giant with his Ottoman pasha: both share *paillardise*, devilishness, scrawny animality, and above all fire. The *bûcher* is the common place *par excellence* in the early sixteenth century, and Rabelais says so unequivocally. Rabelais's herring, then, are not solely entertaining and comical; the *iocus* is also a very serious game, one that denounces religious intolerance and abusive political power, which are found in both Ottoman and French cultures. But Rabelais does not stop at a bleak accusation. His linguistic game offers his readers the opening of a new space, one of contestation, opposition to orthodoxy, and reflection through laughter.

It is at this point in the narrative that pork takes on a whole new dimension. Like wine, pork is strictly prohibited in Islamic law and informed early modern Europeans knew as much. Rabelais, however, neglects[24] this commonly held precept and understanding, and has Panurge roasted unscrupulously like a dry-fleshed rabbit seasoned with slices of bacon for "ces diables icy sont frians de lardons" (265) ("these devils have a taste for lard strips" [180]). After stressing the water/wine dichotomy, Rabelais tackles an irreconcilable religious opposition by totally disregarding an equally well-known fact. Rabelais separates water-drinking 'Turks' and wine-thirsty Christians to better emphasize their commonalities when it comes to meat. Rabelais's 'Turks' enjoy their game juicy and tasty and therefore flavor it with bacon, like the French. The Ottoman in Rabelais's *Pantagruel* is thus a composite being, a Muslim who abstains from wine, but also practices French, and therefore Christian, culinary arts.[25]

Panurge's episode with the 'Turks' takes readers away from the sacred, not only by referring to the materiality of the herring and to the commonality of the fire and the forced conversion in both Ottoman and French worlds, but also by playing with words that punctuate several passages of *Pantagruel*. Rabelais, thereby, neutralizes principles of domination and restitutes (and creates new) spaces for the common good.[26] His profanatory herrings indict a stifling political and religious order while pointing to what Michael Randall calls a Gargantuan polity, a place where the abusive powers of the sacred and the political are deactivated because of individuals who work within and in favor of a communal space.[27]

In a last semantic play, Rabelais seemingly takes his readers back into Panurge's binary world of Christians and Muslims. Pantagruel's companion explains that he saved himself from his 'Turkish dogs' by throwing pieces of bacon to them, thereby satisfying their cravings for pork while distracting them from himself, a poor skinny rabbit. Once saved by bacon, Panurge confesses that he now keeps on him at all times a "flacon soubz la robbe, et quelque morceau de jambon: car sans cela jamais ne alloit il, disant que c'estoit son garde-corps, aultre espée ne portait il" (267) ("a flagon and an odd piece of ham; for without that he never went out, saying it was his bodyguard. No other sword did he wear" [182]). Bacon being Panurge's talisman against the 'Turks,' it can become a protection for all other Christians against the Muslim Ottomans who, it is implied, remember Panurge's trickery and escape, but above all against the fate the pasha suffers. The trickery of a Christian Panurge who defeated a Muslim pasha is a sure sign that Christianity may envision a possible halt, if not a conquest, of Islam, which had been knocking at Europe's door since 1453. As on many other occasions in his narrative, Rabelais reinvents beginnings by giving fantastic meaning to this passage. Under his playful pen, rules of 'halalness' do not stem from a religious restriction but rather from the fear Panurge instilled in the Ottomans. It is because of and after Panurge that Muslims do not eat pork, Rabelais fancifully and fantastically posits in this chapter. Bacon can, therefore, be used to keep Muslims at bay.[28] One could read this final commentary as expressing the limits of Rabelais's narrative, the author showing himself as ultimately Christian and superior, if only by his tricks, to the Muslim Ottomans. Christians, incarnated by Panurge, will ultimately prevail as Ottomans are subdued and annihilated. A foreign cultural element—the interdiction against consuming pork—is disregarded as religiously motivated and explained by a clearly fantastical and fictional episode that shows the intellectual power of the Christian world over a less sophisticated and more animalistic Ottoman society. However, the conclusion of this episode might be read as more ambiguous and open. Less a moral and a prediction, the last detail given by Panurge about the protective qualities of bacon appears to complicate things further for Rabelais's recipe, for countering the pressing Ottomans by way of a talismanic piece of bacon is clearly absurd and fatally futile.

Canis, **Cannibals**

If the roasting pit is the hinge that connects and divides worlds, religious conversion is its mechanism. Cannibalism is a second device Rabelais uses to question identity and socio-political power in *Pantagruel*. As we have already seen, Panurge's Ottomans figure as cannibals for whom the Frenchman's bland rabbit-like flesh would not have tasted good save for the bacon that accompanied it. Panurge's condition, then, may be reminiscent of St. Lawrence; it also recasts the recurrent questioning on food that punctuates Rabelais's works. Many other religious groups have been accused of cannibalism throughout history: Jews in the medieval period, Catholics during the wars of religion.[29] In Matthew Paris's thirteenth-century *Chronica Majora*, Tartars are depicted as cannibals (Figure 4.1). While the man on the left is busy cutting body parts with an axe, another next to him devours a leg; a third one to the right, seated on two human heads, is turning a spit on which a man has been tied and skewered. At the beginning of the sixteenth century, however, cannibalism is no longer considered an Eastern practice but one of the New World, as Frank Lestringant has shown.[30] In both Amerigo Vespucci's and Christopher Columbus's travel accounts, cannibalism takes center stage.[31] In an anonymous map dating from the early 1500s, a man is being roasted by a Native American (Figure 4.2). One of the earliest depictions of the New World, this map locates cannibalism on the American continent and uses human flesh consumption as America's main narrative.[32] The similarities between the two illustrations are striking. The mechanism of cannibalism in the early sixteenth-century map is identical to the one depicted by Matthew Paris. The human body, being roasted on an open fire suggested by flames, has been pierced through with a skewer while its limbs are bound with ropes. The anthropophagic cook is located on the right-hand side, toward the victim's feet. He is holding and turning the skewer. In the case of the Tartars, however, the cook is sitting, whereas on the early modern map he is kneeling. Also noticeable in Matthew Paris's illustration are the hands of the Tartars' victim. Roped, they join together in a gesture evoking prayer. This slight hint of the victim's Christianity is absent from the New World illustration, suggesting perhaps that religious clashes have subsided or taken a new turn on the American continent. The most interesting difference between the two illustrations is the verticalization of the roasting pit in the depiction of the American cannibalism. This reorientation of cannibalism on the map expresses its passage and therefore its transformation from East to West, which is nothing but the East to a western West. Rabelais would have been aware of the passing of cannibalism from East to West and his *Pantagruel* reflects the movement of cannibals visible in maps of the medieval and the early modern periods. By way of a flawed etymology—*canis*, cannibals—Rabelais turns dogs into man-eating beings and applies an American *topos* to the Oriental setting it once occupied.

Except that cannibalism never fully exited the Oriental scene. The cruelty associated with anthropophagy stayed well anchored in the East, even arguably contaminating Europe. In other words, cannibalism never simply jumped over

Figure 4.1 Cannibals. Thirteenth-century *Chronica Majora* by Matthew Paris. Courtesy of the Master and Fellows of Corpus Christi College, Cambridge.

Figure 4.2 Early sixteenth-century map showing cannibals on the American continent. Courtesy of the Bayerische Staatsbibliothek.

Europe to find its new niche in the Americas. Rather, it contaminated the whole world. Cannibalism did not merely get displaced, it spread. In a different medium, in a different context, and with a new meaning, numerous sixteenth-century woodcuts portray images reminiscent of earlier illustrations used to portray cannibalism. One that is contemporary with *Pantagruel* is particularly telling. It shows the killing and rape of women by Ottoman armies alongside the slicing and impaling of European (Christian) children (Figure 4.3). Although there is

Figure 4.3 Atrocities committed by Ottoman armies. Woodcut by Erhard Schön. Courtesy of the Zentralbibliothek Zürich, Department of Prints and Drawings/Photo Archive.

no explicit cannibalism expressed in this 1530 woodcut by Erhard Schön, the suggested slicing of arms and legs is reminiscent of Matthew Paris's illustration of Tartars. Also significant is the shared verticality of the American and Ottoman scenes and the resemblance between the positions of the victims in both illustrations—each shows the point of the spit coming out between the victim's vertebrae and his left shoulder-blade. In Rabelais's words, in order to impale his incompetent "roustisseur," the pasha

> *passa la broche peu au dessus du nombril vers le flan droict, et luy percea la tierce lobe du foye, et le coup haussant luy penetra le diaphragme, et à travers la capsule du cueur luy sortit la broche par le hault des espaules entre les spondyles et l'omoplate senestre.* (264–5)
>
> ran the spit a little above the navel toward the right flank and pierced the third lobe of his liver, and the blow moving upward penetrated his diaphragm; and, running through his pericardium, the spit came out through the top of his shoulders between the spondyls [vertebrae] and the left shoulder-blade. (180)

Panurge completes the picture by skewering the pasha:

> *Je . . . vous le lye rustrement piedz et mains de mes cordes, si bien qu'il n'eust sceu regimber, puis luy passay ma broche à travers la gargamelle, et le pendys acrochant la broche à deux gros crampons, qui soustenoient des alebardes.* (266)
>
> I . . . tie him up saucily, hand and foot, with my cords, so thoroughly that he could not have resisted; then I thrust my spit through his throat and hanged him, attaching the spit to two big hooks that used to hold halberds. (181)

Rabelais's fiction combines horizontality and verticality, ancient and American worlds, cannibalism and Ottoman cruelty.

Pigeons in a Mouth

Rabelais conflates worlds again in Chapter 32 of *Pantagruel* when he reaffirms the back-and-forth movement between worlds and words. In "Comment Pantagruel de sa langue couvrit toute une armée, et de ce que l'auteur veit dedans sa bouche" (How Pantagruel with his tongue covered a whole army, and what the author saw inside his mouth), Alcofrybas Nasier reappears. Presented as *Pantagruel*'s narrator, Rabelais's anagrammatic alter ego resurfaces to tell the amazing story of his adventures in the giant's mouth. Alcofrybas explains that, as Pantagruel's army gets ready to fight the Almyrodes, a violent shower catches the soldiers by surprise. In order to protect them from the rain, the giant sticks his tongue out. All but one seek cover, Alcofrybas Nasier arriving too late and finding no more space left for him. This lack of physical space is what obliges the narrator to explore other places and to embark on a voyage of his own, the places he encounters being enigmatic and not easily accessible. The spatial restriction in fiction allows for the narrative to open into uncharted geographical and philosophical terrains. As Alcofrybas enters the giant's mouth where he hopes to find a refuge from the torrential rain, he discovers a world both strange and familiar,[33] a world unknown of which no one has ever written. The discovery of this brave new world gives Alcofrybas the occasion to write a book about it:

> *Veu que nul avoit encores escrit de ce pais là, auquel sont plus de. xxv. royaulmes habitez, sans les desers, et un gros bras de mer: mais j'en ay composé un grand livre intitulé l'Histoire des Gorgias: car ainsi les ay je nommez parce qu'ilz demourent en la gorge de mon maistre Pantagruel. (332–33.)*
>
> seeing that no one had yet written about that country, in which there are over twenty-five inhabited kingdoms, not counting the deserts and one great arm of the sea; but I have composed a book about it entitled *History of the Gorgias*, for thus I have named them because they live in the throat [la gorge] of my master Pantagruel. (240–41)

Playing on words with the name of the new people discovered, Alcofrybas names and appropriates for himself the inhabitants of Pantagruel's mouth and the space that they inhabit. The discovery lasts several months, during which the traveler walks through valleys and mountains and encounters a cabbage farmer, thieves, doormen, and a pigeon catcher. As Lestringant points out, this travel is more of an *itinéraire* or an *itinérance* than a pilgrimage or an odyssey like the one described in chapter 38.[34] Here, no one is accidentally eaten in a salad, although surprising encounters do happen.

This chapter recalls the recent discovery of a new continent. "Jesus (dis je) il y a icy un nouveau monde" Alcofrybas exlaims (331) ("'Jesus,' said I, 'then there's a new world here?'" [239]), the expression "nouveau monde" echoing the title of the letter sent by Amerigo Vespucci—*Mundus novus*—to Lorenzo de Pier Francesco in 1503. Later in the chapter, we learn of a "terre neufve" and of a "aultre monde" (331). The New World is not, however, the only place to which Chapter 32 refers. Other older, and resolutely Eastern, geographical areas are mentioned by the narrator. In addition to Poitiers and Lyon, Alcofrybas Nasier connects the world he is exploring in Pantagruel's mouth to Ottoman territory: "Mais o dieux et deesses, que veiz je là? Juppiter me confonde de sa fouldre trisulque si j'en mens. Je y cheminoys comme l'on faict en Sophie à Constantinoble" (331) (But, O ye gods and goddesses, what did I see there? Jupiter confound me with his three-forked thunder if I lie. I was walking along there as you do in Saint-Sophia in Constantinople [239]). Rabelais's reader is thus directed not only to the New World but also to France and to Hagia Sophia, the fourth-century Byzantine church adorning the capital of the Ottoman Empire. Pantagruel's mouth is where old and new, Orient and Occident intermingle.

The gigantism of Pantagruel's mouth described by Alcofrybas Nasier is a commonplace in both literary and visual representations of Hagia Sophia. On the literary side, many European travelers—pilgrims for the most part—left descriptions of Hagia Sophia that stress the church's size. In his 1336 *De itinere Terrae Sanctae liber*, for example, Ludolf von Sudheim mentions the possibility that a boat could fit into the church.[35] In 1403, Ruy Gonzales de Clavijo mentions the smallness of a man once inside the basilica,[36] reminding us that all throughout the western medieval world Hagia Sophia was known as the "Grande Eglise." As for artistic depictions of Hagia Sophia, they too insist on the size of the building. Cristoforo Buondelmonti and Giuliano da Sagallo depict a church that is easily recognizable because of its size and its imposing dome.[37] Mosaics and paintings were still visible inside Hagia Sophia until the sixteenth century, its central dome being adorned by an enormous Christ Pantokrator who would have dwarfed any person looking at it from the ground.[38] When, three centuries later, the Fossati brothers restored the church, they originated lithographs that illustrate the impression of *petitesse* one feels when inside the church. In their rendering of the building, minuscule men appear swallowed by the convex space of the domes above them. Additionally, the main porch gives the impression of an enormous open mouth above which one can see two small black eyes.[39]

Alcofrybas's initial comparison between Pantagruel's mouth and Hagia Sophia expresses the *elsewhere*, the *unknown* to readers who might have never gone beyond either the Pyrenees or the Alps and yet who would be familiar with literary and visual traditions pertaining to Hagia Sophia. Through authors and artists like the ones mentioned above or Robert de Clari who, in the thirteenth century, stressed the basilica's richness and its miraculousness,[40] Hagia Sophia exposes the East in its recognizable classical form. Comparing Pantagruel's mouth to Hagia Sophia is not an innocent choice. It brings 'Turquie,' France, and the New World closer from the start of the chapter, the Byzantine church being the focal point of the reader's gaze. This initial comparison allows a series of parallels and mingling between spaces, and also between Frenchmen and *Others*, testing the readers on their possible assumptions towards the Ottomans and the inhabitants of the New World.

When Alcofrybas expresses his surprise at encountering a "nouveau monde," he is told: "il n'est mie nouveau: mais l'on dist bien que hors d'icy y a une terre neufve où ilz ont et Soleil et Lune: et tout plein de belles besoignes; mais cestuy cy est plus ancient" (331) ("it's hardly new; but they do indeed say that outside of here there's a new earth where they have both sun and moon, and all sorts of fine carryings-on; but this one is older" [239]). Everything is relative and depends on one's perspective, it can be concluded. For Alcofrybas, the new world is Pantagruel's mouth but, for his interlocutor, the novelty lies in the world familiar to Alcofrybas—the one that resembles ours. The pigeon catcher encountered next by Alcofrybas claims that the birds he catches "viennent de l'aultre monde" (331) ("come from another world" [239]).

Alcofrybas's narration ends on another comparison, that of the giant's teeth and mountains: "À quoy je congneu que ainsi comme nous avons les contrées de deçà et de delà les montz, aussi ont ilz deçà et delà les dentz" (332) ("from which I learned that just as we have the countries on this side and on the far side of the mountains [the Alps], so have they on this side and on the far side of the teeth" [240]). After Rabelais's blurring of physical spaces and the opening of a third geographical and literary space, the "deçà" can no longer be understood as Pantagruel's world as opposed to the pigeon hunter's, or Christian Europe as opposed to the Islam-dominated Ottoman Empire or to an allegedly areligious New World. It could also refer to the French kingdom as opposed to Italy, as Frame's translation suggests, or to Spain, both located right past mountains, the Alps and the Pyrenees respectively. Rabelais simultaneously enlarges and reduces the field of the *elsewhere*. In his narrative, difference is not simply a matter of geographical distance, it is a matter of political divergence and that difference can be felt among peoples who are physically very close to one another. The *bergers* (shepherds) and the *fouaciers* who originate the Picrocholine war in Chapter 25 of *Gargantua* are such an example. Similarly, the French and the Spaniards too, although geographically very close, can be so dissimilar politically that they can be enemies and wage war, as was the case during the 1520s and the 1530s when Francis I came to power.

After his final relativist comparison, Alcofrybas innocently adds: "Mais il fait beaucoup meilleur deçà et y a meilleur air" (332) ("but it's much nicer on this side and the air is better" [240]). For the first time in his narration, Alcofrybas clearly positions himself in favor of the "deçà." This judgment, however, arrives after a methodical questioning and reworking of the "deçà," the "delà," and their limits. Acting as Montaigne will several decades later in his essay on cannibals, Rabelais ends his demonstration with a pirouette and a final check requiring his readers to test for themselves whether or not they have integrated his demonstration. For "Vérité en deçà des Pyrénées, erreur au-delà" (There are truths on this side of the Pyrenees that are falsehoods on the other) is precisely what Rabelais warns his readers about.[41] Testing and shaking his reader, Rabelais concludes with a preconception that he has painstakingly attempted to undermine throughout the episode of the world found by Alcofrybas in the giant's mouth. Rabelais makes his readers jump, disorients them one last time, and asks their involvement in defining the "deçà" and the "delà."

This checking necessarily affects the narrator's legitimacy. Eclipsed for many chapters after the prologue, the narrator resurfaces in Chapter 32, where the first-person pronoun "je" seems to impose itself. On several instances, Alcofrybas explains what he is being told by using interior monologue: "lors je pensay que, quand Pantagruel baisloit, les pigeons à pleines volées entroyent dedans sa gorge, pensans que feust un colombier" (331) ("Then it occurred to me that when Pantagurel yawned, pigeons in whole flocks flew into his throat, thinking it was a dovecote" [239]).[42] Alcofrybas's loss of power as the narration unfolds is noticeable: from narrator, he becomes simple character. More importantly perhaps, Alcofrybas turns into a reader, for, as he travels Pantagruel's mouth, he begins to read the world. Similarly, Alcofrybas takes the time to translate the scenery he encounters: the "grands rochiers" for example are the giant's teeth. These marks of authority could have made Alcofrybas a respected narrator. After all, he is the first and only one to have visited a new world—Pantagruel's mouth—at length and to have composed *l'Histoire des Gorgias* about it. His remarks, however, discredit him entirely. Still, he is depicted thinking about, analyzing, and drawing important conclusions about the world he encounters. "Là commençay penser qu'il est bien vray ce que l'on dit, que la moytié du monde ne sçait comment l'aultre vit" (332) ("At that point I began to think that it is very true what they say, that half the world doesn't know how the other half lives" [240]). Alcofrybas models readings for past, present, and future readers.[43]

As with Panurge in Chapter 14, Alcofrybas as narrator is ridiculed and his authority questioned by a second narrative voice that emerges from behind. At the same time, through Alcofrybas, Rabelais provides us with an example of a good reader. Rabelais's mastery emerges from his designated narrator—Alcofrybas in Chapter 32, Panurge in Chapter 14. Intervening in the narration, Rabelais manipulates readers and questions the presuppositions they may share with the respective narrators, with whom readers collide and identify in turn. Hence two different visions are superimposed in the Rabelaisian text: the simplistic and predictable vision of a self-identified and official narrator, and that of the author, a more complex and ambiguous vision. The reconcilability of these two visions is not proposed or even suggested, but simply left for readers to fathom, just as they are invited to create a hybrid space composed of Ottoman and American elements, with a European tinge.

Conversion is ever-present in Rabelais's text. Religious conversion, at first unimaginable, is ultimately evoked as a possibility as Panurge becomes as diabolical as the pasha who had condemned him and as the Catholics in Toulouse who burn perceived heretics of Protestantism. 'Turquie' and America also mutate into a new space that recalls sixteenth-century France. A narrative conversion takes place as Panurge and Alcofrybas give away their voices to another narrator, the author. The reader's conversion, of course, is implicit yet understood: at the end of the demonstration, the reader is no longer to believe that the Ottomans are the only barbaric people on earth.

But Rabelais is more than simply about conversion and opposing halves. If the Rabelaisian text is utopian, it is because it incarnates the border, a place of passage, of superimposition of spaces, of here and there, of "deçà" and "delà," a place where multiple voices are heard. Ambiguous and complex, the Rabelaisian text is, like a border, in the process of being defined and of happening for, by definition, it belongs to neither here nor there. Its pigeons symbolize the crossing of spatial as well as ideological borders, the overcoming of geographical and mental spaces.

Notes

1 All references to François Rabelais's works are from Rabelais, *Œuvres complètes*, ed. Mireille Huchon (Paris: Gallimard, 1994). I use Donald Frame's translation, *The Complete Works of François Rabelais* (Berkeley: University of California Press, 1991), here 239.
2 Michael Screech, *Rabelais* (Ithaca: Cornell University Press, 1979), 318–20.
3 On Rabelais's four voyages to Italy, see Richard Cooper, *Rabelais et l'Italie* (Geneva: Droz, 1991). The first of the voyages took place in 1534 and the last between 1547 and

1549. Thanks to connections and travels, Rabelais was aware of the interconnectedness between peoples.

4 Huchon, includes three letters Rabelais wrote to d'Estissac (*Œuvres*, 1000–1017), including Rabelais' discussion of the Ottomans' defeat (1002–1003). Cooper also reproduces these three d'Estissac letters (*Rabelais et l'Italie*, 107–59).

5 Huchon, *Œuvres*, 1009.

6 Of course, Rabelais's interest in the East was not limited to the Ottomans. In a recent paper presented at the annual meeting of the Modern Language Association in Seattle, Dorothea Heitsch highlighted the many Arabic influences on Rabelais, from his training at the Arabizing medical school of Montpellier to his possible knowledge of the Arabic language and his dispute with Symphorien Champier regarding medicinal simples and the role of Arabic medicine.

7 In a pseudo-crusade on the island of Lesbos, French and Venetians assailed the Ottomans, only to be severely countered. On the Mytilene attack, see René Favret, "Il y a cinq cents ans, la dernière croisade ou Panurge à Metelin," *Bulletin des Amis de Rabelais et de la Devinière* 5, no. 10 (2001): 663–79.

8 Terence Cave, "Travelers and Others: Cultural Connections in the Works of Rabelais," in Jean-Claude Carron ed., *François Rabelais: Critical Assessments*, ed. Jean-Claude Carron (Baltimore: Johns Hopkins University Press, 1995), 39–56. Timothy Hampton, "'Turkish Dogs': Rabelais, Erasmus, and the Rhetoric of Alterity," *Representations* 41 (1993): 58–82. Hampton reworked his article as Chapter 2 in his *Literature and Nation*. My analysis of Rabelais's fictional encounter with the Ottomans owes much to: Frédéric Tinguely, "L'*alter sensus* des turqueries de Panurge," *Études Rabelaisiennes* 42: 57–73; Scott Juall, "Early Modern Franco-Ottoman Relations: Utopian Mapping of Imperialist Encounters in François Rabelais's *Pantagruel*," *Études Rabelaisiennes* 44: 79–110; and Phillip Usher, "Walking East in the Renaissance," in *French Global: A New Approach to Literary History*, ed. Christy McDonald and Susan Rubin Suleiman (Columbia University Press, 2010), 193–206.

9 Hampton, "'Turkish Dogs'," 59.

10 Hampton says, "Panurge's blindness to generosity, then, can be linked to a failure to tread within the allegorical spirit of New Testament charity, the signs produced by the other" in "'Turkish Dogs'," 69.

11 On *incroyance*, see Lucien Febvre's *Le problème de l'incroyance au XVIᵉ siècle: La religion de Rabelais* (Paris: Albin Michel, 1968).

12 This approach is not new. Hope Glidden has discussed slippages in Rabelais's texts and the attentive "souplesse" required of the reader. "Digression, diversion, et allusion dans l'œuvre de Rabelais," *Revue des Amis de Ronsard* 12 (1999): 83–96.

13 Giorgio Agamben, *Profanations*, trans. Jeff Fort (New York: Zone Books, 2007). Giorgio Agamben, *Profanations*, trans. Martin Rueff (Paris: Payot et Rivages, 2005).

14 In Touraine, Rabelais's natal region, herring was a common staple until the nineteenth century. See Arlette Schweitz, *La maison tourangelle au quotidien: Façons de bâtir, manières de vivre (1850–1930)* (Paris: Publications de la Sorbonne, 1997), 197.

15 Herring was thought to feed exclusively on sea water. On herring's magical and medicinal properties, see Cécile Le Cornec, "Les vertus diététiques attribuées aux poissons de mer," in *Mondes marins du Moyen-Âge: Actes du 30e colloque du CUER MA, 3, 4 et 5 mars 2005* (Aix-en-Provence: Université de Provence, 2006), 273–83, here 280–81.

16 Salt was the other widely used commodity that traveled far and wide and was most likely not a local production. On the contrary, spices were rare and viewed as foreign and exotic.

17 A plight also shared by Muslims captured by Christian corsairs. Bartolomé Bennassar and Lucile Bennassar have shown the issue of conversion to Islam, forced or desired, to be central to the early modern period in *Les chrétiens d'Allah*.

18 Tinguely, "L'*Alter Sensus*," 63.

19 Panurge's rash behavior does not come as a surprise for the careful reader who has already witnessed an inebriated Panurge exclaim: *"je me donne au diesble"* (288). This exclamation comes before Panurge tells his story with the Ottomans, therefore reinforcing the fact that after this episode, Panurge has become like them.

20 Kevin Gould, *Catholic Activism in South-West France, 1540–1570* (Aldershot, UK: Ashgate, 2006), 112.

21 Rabelais, *Œuvres*, 1256–57. On Jean de Cahors's execution, see also William Monter, *Judging the French Reformation: Heresy Trials by Sixteenth-Century Parlements* (Cambridge, MA: Harvard University Press, 1999), 64–66.

22 Jean de Boyssoné, born in Castres and a fellow lawyer in Toulouse, was harassed all his adult life for his ideas, but he escaped a similar fate.

23 Tinguely emphasizes Rabelais's condemnation of Catholic intolerance in "L'Alter Sensus."

24 Agamben insists on negligence: "To profane means to open the possibility of a special form of negligence, which ignores separation or, rather, puts it to a particular use" (Agamben, *Profanations*, [trans. Fort], 75).

25 In traditional recipes—for example, "Lapin à la liégeoise"—rabbit is often, but not always, cooked with bacon. In this respect, my interpretation of food, more specifically of herring and pork, follows closely Timothy Tomasik's approach to Rabelais's work which posits that "food . . . is a discourse that . . . filters humanistic debates" (158) and provides "fodder for satire, parody, carnival, and Renaissance humanism" (164). "[Rabelais] invests himself in culinary discourse as a privileged space from which to draw both linguistic and literary inspiration" (164). See Timothy Tomasik, "The World in Pantagruel's Mouth: Alimentary Aesthetics and Culinary Consciousness" in *Approaches to Teaching the Works of François Rabelais*, ed. Todd. W. Reeser and Floyd Gray (New York: The Modern Language Association of America, 2011), 159–64.

26 *"[La profanation] désactive les dispositifs du pouvoir et restitue à l'usage commun les espaces qu'il avait confisqués"* (Agamben, *Profanations* [trans. Rueff], 97). "[Profanation] deactivates the apparatuses of power and returns to common use the spaces that power had seized" (Agamben, *Profanations* [trans. Fort], 77).

27 Randall, *The Gargantuan Polity.*

28 This proposition has been recently adopted, albeit in a far less humorous manner, by some in France who have organized 'wine and sausage' events that have been widely interpreted and denounced as stigmatizing the growing Muslim community.

29 Maggie Kilgour, *From Communion to Cannibalism: An Anatomy of Metaphors of Incorporation* (Princeton, NJ: Princeton University Press, 1990), 5.

30 Frank Lestringant, *Cannibals: The Discovery and Representation of the Cannibal from Columbus to Jules Verne*, trans. Rosemary Morris (Berkeley: University of California Press, 1997).

31 Tzvetan Todorov, *Les morales de l'histoire* (Paris: Grasset, 1991), 148.

32 Todorov reproduces this detail of the map in *Morales*, 152.

33 Erich Auerbach, *Mimesis: The Representation of Reality in Western Literature*. Trans. Willard R. Trask. (Princeton: Princeton University Press, 1953).

34 Frank Lestringant, *Écrire le monde à la Renaissance* (Caen: Paradigme, 1993). See "Dans la bouche des géants," 129–38.

35 J. P. A. van der Vin, *Travellers to Greece and Constantinople: Ancient Monuments and Old Traditions in Medieval Travellers' Tales*, 2 vols. (Leiden: Nederlands Historisch-Archaelogisch Instituut te Istanbul, 1980), 1: 580.

36 Ibid. 1: 631–32.

37 Patricia Fortini Brown, *Venice and Antiquity: The Venetian Sense of the Past* (New Haven, CT: Yale University Press, 1996), illustrations p.16 and p.91 respectively.

38 On the history of Hagia Sophia, see Gülru Necipoğlu, "The Life of an Imperial Monument: Hagia Sophia after Byzantium," in *Hagia Sophia from the Age of Justinian to the*

Present, ed. Robert Mark and A. S. Cakmak (Cambridge: Cambridge University Press, 1992), 195–225.

39 As visible on the front cover of Ilhan Akşit's *Treasures of Istanbul* (Istanbul: Haset Kitabevi Tünel, 1982) for example.

40 Robert de Clari, *La conquête de Constantinople*, ed. Jean Dufournet (Paris: Champion, 2004). See laisses 84–85.

41 This saying is from Pascal, see Blaise Pascal, *Pensées*, ed. Michel Autrand (Paris-Bordas, 1965), 108. However, before the seventeenth century, Rabelais and Montaigne had expressed the same idea. Montaigne wrote "Quelle vérité que ces montagnes bornent, qui est mensonge au monde qui se tient au-delà" in *Les essais*, 'Apologie de Raymond Sebond,' 2:579.

42 In a similar vein: "lors je pense et calcule, et trouve que c'estoit une puante halaine qui estoit venue de l'estomach de Pantagruel alors qu'il mangea tant d'aillade" (332) (Then I thought and calculated, and decided it was a stinking breath that had come from Pantagruel's stomach when he ate all that garlic sauce [240]).

43 As in many other passages from Rabelais's works, particularly the prologues of both *Gargantua* and *Pantagruel*.

5 The Hawk above Constantinople

Bertrand de La Borderie's Imperial Envy

. . . tout ainsi comme le jeune Autour
Volant de branche en branche tout autour
Des boys loingtains, qui esloigne son aire,
Se void laissé, & de pere, & de mere,
Et luy convient seul apprendre à voler,
A seul se paistre, à seul se consoler :
Ainsi à moy jeune de sens, & d'eage
Convient errer loingtain pelerinage,
Et loing d'amys, de voysins, & parens
Suyvre païs estranges apparens,
Mettre en oubly le naturel ramage,
Changer de mœurs, d'habitz, & de langage.
(vv. 21–32)

. . . just as the young Hawk,
Flying from branch to branch around
Faraway forests, leaving his territory,
Sees himself without father and mother,
And has to learn how to fly by himself,
Eat by himself, and find comfort by himself:
I, young in age and knowledge,
Am expected to travel blind on a faraway pilgrimage,
And far from friends, neighbors, and family,
Am expected to reach renowned foreign countries,
Forget natural feathers,
Change customs, dress, and language.
—Bertrand de La Borderie, *Le discours
du voyage de constantinoble*

Comparing himself to a chick that has flown out of his nest, the narrator of La Borderie's *Le discours du voyage de constantinoble*[1] summarily describes the difficult transformation that awaits him: helped by no one, the inexperienced young will be tested in foreign lands before becoming an adult. Only after a dramatic change will the chick be able to fly and turn into a powerful bird of prey. The metaphor, connecting bird and narrator, can also be applied to France in the late 1530s. Newly engaged in an uneasy and controversial alliance with the Ottomans, Francis I's kingdom was about to emerge as a great and independent nation—such were the hopes of Bertrand de La Borderie at least.

The 1530s witnessed dramatic changes in Franco-Ottoman relations. After 10 years of secret contacts, Jean de La Forest took up residence in Constantinople as French ambassador. In 1536, the French kingdom and the Ottoman Empire openly joined forces in trading, military, and religious agreements, the Capitulations.[2] A year later, La Forest accompanied the sultan on a first joint Franco-Ottoman offensive against Italy.[3] The French were to attack by land, while the Ottoman fleet was expected to strike from the sea. For the occasion, Francis I had sent a special envoy, Charles de Marillac, and possibly our poet, Bertrand de La Borderie, on a vessel captained by Baron Saint-Blancart, who was coordinating the French naval efforts on the Ottomans' side. The military offensive, the French king hoped, would destabilize Charles V and help him reconquer parts of Italy. The raid never took place however. Taking their French allies by surprise, the Ottomans decided to sack the small island of Corfu at the entrance of the Adriatic Sea instead of striking Italian interests and diminishing Habsburg dominance. In the *Discours*, La Borderie comments on this failed attack and the perceived treason of the Ottomans, the last act of betrayal in a long series that included high-profile traitors such as André d'Amaral,[4] the Connétable Charles de Bourbon who had defected to Charles V in 1523 before attacking Provence a year later, and Andrea Doria, who had abandoned the French fleet, thus causing the death of the Vicomte de Lautrec and his army in 1528. How to deal with France's newest allies, the Ottomans, and more specifically their unpredictability and inconstancy is thus the question raised in Bertrand de La Borderie's *Discours*. The poet provides an original answer to the dilemma caused by the French-Ottoman alliance by suggesting that the French ought to look beyond the 'Turks' toward their esteemed ancestors—the Greeks.

The journey of initiation described in the poem in general and in the verses beginning this chapter in particular is a ubiquitous one, a mixture of epic and romance *topoi* common in European literature of the Renaissance. The hero undergoes countless tests before reaching his goal and, more importantly, recognition by and undisputable standing in his society. First published in 1542 by Pierre de Tours,[5] La Borderie's poem narrates the departure of the young and inexperienced 'knight,' his painful separation from other human fellows, the solitary wandering in faraway lands, the numerous tests—". . . faim, soif, mer, feu, ventz, terre, ennemys" (v. 558) (. . . hunger, thirst, oceans, fire, winds, land, enemies)—and finally the sorrow and the fear of being forgotten. However, the narrative and the excerpt from the poem that begins this chapter both seem to be missing a crucial character: the beloved. As the full title of the poem indicates—*Le discours du voyage de constantinoble, Envoyé dudict lieu à une Damoyselle Francoyse*—the French lady comes second to both the "discours" and the "voyage," and the lover is eclipsed from both the passage cited above and the poem at large. The object of desire in the poem is not a woman; instead, it is Constantinople, the capital of the Ottoman Empire behind which emerges the Greek city of old. Like the lady of courtly love poetry, Constantinople is, then, to be conquered. A French hawk could accomplish this goal.

This chapter examines the poetics of conquest that underlies La Borderie's poem. It shows how the poet, under the guise of fiction as much as with its subversion and its help, speaks about early sixteenth-century Franco-Ottoman relations and finds a very practical response to a fiercely debated issue. Using the recognizable frame and *topoi* of courtly discourse, La Borderie (re)creates an earlier classical world as he invents the possibility of an empire for France. He erases the beloved to replace her with Constantinople, which he connects to France historically and linguistically. Focusing on the sixteenth-century Ottomans, the poet ultimately effaces them, allowing ancient places to emerge and classical heroes to populate the poetic voyage and the political discussion. Disappearances and emergences are, thus, the engine of a narrative orchestrated by the poet's careful use of words, their repetitions in various contexts, and the semantic changes that occur throughout the poem. Therefore, the "discours" of the title refers to both the narration of the travel and the journey itself. The *Discours* is a *carte postale*, a postcard informing the beloved of the narrator's progress in the eastern Mediterranean while surreptitiously reminding her of his presence, and a *carte routière*, a roadmap for future travelers. Similarly, in order to comment on the Franco-Ottoman alliance of the 1530s, the poet plays with the concept of the *infidèle* and the idea of servitude, skilfully merging ancient and modern genres, art forms, fiction and facts.

The Infidels and the Tyrant: Representing the Ottomans

Critics have been at a loss with regard to the *Discours*, a poem of some 1,768 decasyllables describing a trip to Constantinople. The lyric form is rather unusual for an early modern travel narrative[6] and it has troubled Victor-Louis Bourrilly, who speaks of its author as a verse maker obsessed with current love poetry and hampered by classical antiquity.[7] Yet Bourrilly recognizes the work's historical import, and several critics have gathered many biographical details concerning La Borderie from the *Discours*, suggesting that the poem is autobiographical and historically accurate. Danielle Trudeau, for example, claims that the poet participated in the expedition leading to the Ottomans in 1537 and that his acceptance of the mission obliged him to leave his wife-to-be in France.[8] Whereas La Borderie's presence alongside Marillac and Saint-Blancart seems quite certain,[9] a supposed connection between the narrator's love life and the author's seems farfetched. In all likelihood the beloved was but a pretext allowing the poet to bridge fiction and history.

Courtly poet that he was, La Borderie was well aware of the international context of the 1530s, in particular the Franco-Ottoman alliance and the controversy it was causing in the minds of some, like Valbelle. Indeed, details in the *Discours* suggest that the poet had excellent, if not first-hand, knowledge of the ensuing

1537 military mission. The poem includes the names of four men who participated in the venture: the "Duc de Somme" (v. 98), the Prince of Melphe (v. 97),
Baron Saint-Blancart (vv. 590 and 1114), Philippe de Villiers l'Isle-Adam, the
grand master of the Order of St. John of Jerusalem (vv. 758 and 1117), as well
as Barbarossa, the infamous North African pirate (v. 705).[10] In addition, the poet
alludes to the 1537 joint Franco-Ottoman mission twice, recognizing its novelty
and controversial aspect. Justifying the attack and thereby vindicating Francis I in
his rapprochement with the Ottomans, La Borderie states that Christianity as a
whole will benefit from a Franco-Ottoman strike against Italy. Therefore the alliance is well-founded. In the narrators's own words:

> . . . *nous estions (quelque chose qu'on tienne)*
> *La envoyez pour un effect semblable:*
> *A tous Chrestiens utile & proufitable* (vv. 184–86)
> . . . we had been (whatever people may think)
> Sent there for a similar purpose
> Useful and profitable for all Christians.

If France is dealing with the Ottomans, it is by necessity and for the public good,
the poet claims. If, for over a week in 1537, the French have sailed side by side
with the 'Turks,' it is only because they needed to work on "les affaires/Au bien
public de nous tous necessaires" (vv. 257–58) (the business/That is necessary to
our own public good). Openly accused by the Habsburgs of an unholly alliance,[11]
the French kingdom responds poetically via La Borderie who, while denying any
formal relationship with a people "contraire à moy de foy, & d'alliance" (v. 19)
(contrary to me in faith and alliance), confesses nevertheless "une amytié privée"
(v. 172) (a private friendship) with them.

The *Discours* contains an abundance of details that shows a growing familiarity with the Ottoman world. As such it anticipates more ethnographic accounts
such as Nicolas de Nicolay's. The striking ambiguity expressed in the poem with
regard to the new Franco-Ottoman alliance is not reflected in the treatment of
the 'Turks,' however. Their representation is negative overall and repeats the
diabolical association found in earlier works such as La Vigne's *La défense de
la Chrétienté*, Molinet's "Complainte de Grèce," and Bourbon's *Oppugnation*.[12]
Despite efforts at *mimesis*, La Borderie's depiction of the 'Turks' is neither historically accurate nor more tolerant than earlier or other contemporary accounts
such as Jean de Vega's.[13] In the poem, for example, the prospect of meeting with
the Ottomans is clearly not a cheering one for the narrator. Before the encounter,
he stresses the unknown[14] and its corollary: fear. Once sighted near Corfu, the
'Turks' are frightening:

> *Et la Turcquesque armée decouvrismes,*
> *Surgie en mer, en troupe espouventable,*
> *Dont le regard n'est pas moins veritable,*
> *Ne moins estrange à l'œil qui le contemple,*

Qu'est incroyable au monde le bruit ample
Des hommes, nefz, & galeres sans nombre,
Mettant le gouffre, & les poissons à l'ombre
Si qu'au travers, l'onde marine verte,
Ne pouvoit estre à mes yeulx descouverte.
Et me sembla des le premier arrest
Que je voyois une grande forest
Qui paroissoit couppée de nouveau,
Ou l'on avoit laissé maint baliveau.
. . . alentour de l'armée qui bruict
L'air est si plein, & de flamme & de bruict
Que l'on n'eust peu entendre Dieu tonner (vv. 218–43)
And we discovered the Turkish army
Coming out of the water, a frightening troop,
Whose look is neither less true
Nor less strange to the eye contemplating it
Than, to the world, the ample noise
Of men, boats, and countless galleys,
Shadowing gulf and fish,
So much that, through it, I could not
See the green sea.
And it seemed to me that since the first moment
I was seeing a huge forest
That appeared as if cut afresh,
Where many young trees were left.
. . . around the army that roars,
The air is so full of flames and noise
That one could not hear God's thunder.

The Ottoman fleet catches the narrator unaware: noisy, dark, massive and ghoul-ish, it resembles a freshly-cut forest. Subsequent contacts with the Ottomans accentuate this negative impression. As the narrator discovers the island of Chios, a Christian enclave among "nations barbares" (v. 1233), he cannot but wonder how its inhabitants manage to live peacefully among the 'Turks':

. . . nous nous esbahissons.
Non toutesfoys tant de leur nouveaulté,
Que de pencer celle communaulté
Povoir regner si longs temps belle, & riche
Parmy les Turcs, sans estre mise en friche,
Chose qui semble estre plus impossible,
Que la brebis povoir vivre paisible
Parmy les loups : car Turcs d'anciennet[é],
Sont pis que loups envers la Chrestienté. (vv. 1250–58)

> ... we are utterly surprised.
> About not so much their unexpectedness,
> But to think that this community
> Could reign for so long, rich and beautiful,
> Among the Turks, without being torn into pieces,
> A thing that seems even more unlikely
> Than a lamb living peacefully
> Among the wolves: for the Turks of old
> Are worse than wolves toward Christendom.

Everywhere in the Mediterranean, with the astounding exception of Chios, the 'Turks' are wild beasts who prey on innocent lambs, an obvious allusion to Christ and by extension to Christians. Mixed marriages offer another occasion of puzzlement for the narrator:

> ... *vous verrez en un mesme mesnage*
> *Souvent le Turc, & le Grec habiter:*
> *Chascun sa loy sans contraincte imiter.*
> *Si que j'ay veu maintes femmes Grecquesques*
> *Ayans maris subjectz aux lois Turcquesques.*
> *L'un Machomet par foy recongnoissant:*
> *L'autre adorant Jesuschrist tout puissant.*
> *Chose qui semble estre non moins estrange*
> *Que veoir ensemble un Dyable avec un Ange.* (vv. 1512–20)
> ... you will see in the same household
> Often a Turk and a Greek live,
> One imitating the other person's [religious] law freely.
> Indeed I have seen many Greek women
> With husbands who obey the Turkish laws.
> One believing in Muhammad,
> The other praying to Jesus Almighty.
> This does not seem less strange
> Than seeing together a Devil and an Angel.

Foreign and terrifying, the 'Turks' as a people are ferocious wolves or diabolical infidels. As for the sultan, he is a tyrant who enslaves everyone. French commentators of later centuries will largely dwell on this claim, but La Borderie is the first to point out Oriental despotism unambiguously. For example, after underlining what humanity owes Athens in terms of letters, philosophy, law, and science, the poet laments Athens' current situation:

> *Athenes serve, à present mise en friche,*
> *... est la plus immonde,*
> *La plus abjecte, asservie, & foulée*
> *Qui soit en terre, & la plus desolée.* (vv. 991–6)

Athens, enslaved, now torn into pieces
. . . is the filthiest,
The most abject, subservient, and repressed
On earth, the most desolate.

As for the Athenians, they are

>. . . *contrainctz à tous ars mechaniques*
>*Eulx asservir, selon les loix iniques*
>*Du grant tyrant, qui les detient petis*
>*Pour les renger plus serfz, & plus craintifz.* (vv. 1009–12)
>. . . forced to the mechanical arts,
>Serfs according to the iniquitous laws
>Of the great tyrant who keeps them small
>To make them even more subservient and more scared.

In short, the 'grand Turc' is a "grant tyrant," especially with regard to the peoples
of Greek heritage whose young he conscripts into his army:

>. . . *ces genissaires,*
>. . . *sont par la Grece levez*
>*Des leur enfance, & de la loy privez* (vv. 1722–4)
>. . . these janissaries
>. . . are from Greece leveed
>Since their childhood, and deprived from the [Greek] law

The sultan's family, too, is a victim of his despotism. La Borderie takes the occasion to comment on a second cultural detail unnoticed by earlier commentators
but stressed by many later ones, such as Gabriel Bounin.[15] Since Mehmed II, it
was customary for the new sultan to kill his brothers and half-brothers in order to
access and consolidate power. La Borderie's judgement of this fratricide is severe
and unequivocal:

>*[la coutume du fratricide] est un cas le plus abominable*
>*Qui soit au monde, & le moins raisonnable*
>*Car s'ilz estoient ou vingt ou trente freres*
>*Celuy qui peult gaigner les genisseres*
>*Et occuper le siege imperial*
>*De cueur felon, cruel, & desloyal*
>*Fera soubdain le reste mettre à mort:*
>*Sans de son sang avoir aucun remort.*
>*Ò loy perverse! ò tyrannie dure!*
>*Quand cruauté tant execrable dure!*
>*Que la grand fain de regner sur l'or cher*
>*N'a point d'horreur de devorer sa cher!* (vv. 1477–88)

[the fratricidal custom] is a most abominable case
And the least reasonable in the world,
For if there were twenty or thirty brothers,
The one who can win the janissaries
And occupy the imperial seat
With a treacherous, cruel, and disloyal heart
Will suddenly put everyone else to death
Without having any regret for his own blood.
Oh, perverse law! Oh, harsh tyranny!
How such heinous cruelty lasts!
How horrorless is the extreme hunger of him who, to rule over gold,
Devours its own flesh!

The narrator's indignation is obvious: this passage contains an accumulation of interjections; negative adjectives and nouns are reinforced by superlatives; finally, the fratricide is described as an act of cannibalism. Unsurprisingly then, it is the word 'tyranny' that closes a long enumeration that qualifies the sultan and functions as a first conclusion to the poem:

Consequemment de vous rendre raison
De tous estatz qui sont en la maison
De ce grand Turc, de son obeissance:
De ses tresors, de toute sa puissance:
De son recueil trop plus grave que humain
. . .
De ses deduitz, de ses garsons infames,
De ses jardins, de ses quatre cens femmes,
De ses statutz modernes, & anciens,
De quelles loix il gouverne les siens
De Machomet, de ses religions,
De ses confins, païs, & regions
De sa justice, & de sa tyrannie :
Il me fauldroit une Bible infinie. (vv. 1725–38)
Consequently, in order to let you know
About this great Turk, his obedience:
About his treasures, his great power:
About his demeanor too serious to be humane
. . .
About his entertainments, his shameful boys,
His gardens, his four hundred women,
His statutes, modern and ancient,
His law with which he governs his people
About Muhammad, and his religions,
About his borders, lands and regions,
About his justice and about his tyranny:
I would need an infinite Bible.

In addition to *devşirme* (the mandatory *levée* of Christian youth) and fratricide, the list of Ottoman evils includes sexual deviances and appetite ("garsons infames," "quatre cens femmes"), a heretical "Machomet," and despotism. In this long tirade, "tyrannie" is literally *le mot de la fin*. It closes the list and summarizes the most essential characteristic about the sultan according to La Borderie. Consequently, the reader is to conclude, if living conditions are indeed as hard in Ottoman lands as the narrator describes,[16] it is because of the sultan's tyranny. The only positive traits noted in the *Discours* are the strict obedience and the silence of both the janissaires and the common people whom the traveler observed at public audiences.

> *En celle court de peuple toute pleine,*
> *Les uns assis demeurent en silence:*
> *Autres debout sans aucune insolence.*
> *Coustume à eulx autant ou plus louable*
> *Que moins elle est à la nostre semblable.*
> *Car la verrez dix mille genissaires,*
> *Qui du seigneur sont gardes ordinaires,*
> *Assiz en terre croisant leurs genoulx,*
> *Ne faire tant de bruict que six de nous.* (vv. 1712–20)

> In this court very full of people,
> Some remain sitting in silence:
> Others are standing, never insolent.
> A custom of theirs all the more praiseworthy
> That is to us far from common.
> For there you will see ten thousand janissaries,
> The sultan's ordinary guards,
> Sitting on the ground, their knees bent,
> And not making more noise than six of us would.

Like Jacques de Bourbon, La Borderie comments enviously on the Ottomans' discipline and respect for the hierarchy. In the *Discours*, however, these qualities derive from what, in the European lore, would become the legendary Oriental despotism. Lucette Valensi noted that, among the Venetians, the Ottoman tyrant appears in the last third of the sixteenth century. Similarly, Alain Grosrichard has shown in *Structure du sérail* that the Oriental despot is present in French literature in the seventeenth and eighteenth centuries. As La Borderie's *Discours* clearly shows, the spectral prefiguration of the 'Turkish tyrant' is visible in France as early as 1542.

Looking Beyond the Ottomans: More Slaves, More Infidels

In the *Discours*, several kinds of servitude overlap. The sultan, as we have seen, is a tyrant who subjects his people to poverty, the levy of youth, fratricide, and sexual deviance. Two allegories reinforce the bleak atmosphere of the Ottoman world according to La Borderie. Death and her sister, Fortune, appear early in the poem and anticipate the narrator's encounter with the Ottomans. The personifications operate like the sultan, at the expense of both individuals and society. Stalking the narrator, Death and Fortune seek to harm him: "mes deux mortelles enemies,/À me guetter n'estoient point endormies" (vv. 371–72) (my two mortal enemies/Were not wasting time to locate me). More specifically, Fortune wants to enslave the narrator: "la fortune ennemie . . . souloit à me nuire pretendre . . . Et en ses fers esclave me tenir" (vv. 287–98) (Fortune, my enemy, . . . wanted to harm me . . . And to hold me captive in her prison). Like the elm overshadowing the vine, Fortune prowls. Her partner, Death, is not far behind and strikes the narrator's close relative, "un mien prochain parent/Qui de long temps par service apparent,/Avoit acquis honneur, bruit, & estime/Envers son Prince, & pays legitime" (vv. 345–48) (a close relative of mine/Who, for a long time, by his service/Had acquired honor, fame, and respect/From his Prince and true country). As Trudeau points out, this could be a reference to Ambassador La Forest, who died in 1537 in Albania. When transformed into a blood-thirsty sea monster, Death spots the narrator on Saint-Blancart's ship (vv. 589–94) and takes its next aim. The natural elements and the gods are raging: the tempest begins, and with it the travelers' prayers. The narrator himself offers two, a Christian prayer (vv. 501–6), and a second one addressed to Venus (vv. 640–50). The first supplication, a personalized 'Our Father,' expresses a servitude that, contrary to the one imposed by Death, Fortune, and the sultan, is welcome by the Christian narrator: "Seigneur, ton bon plaisir soit faict/Sur moy ton serf, de peché tresinfect" (vv. 501–2) (Lord, may your will be fulfilled/Upon me, your most sinful servant). Characterized by a wilful submission, this address comes from a Christian soul. The prayer addressed to Venus asks the goddess to send her child, Love, to save the narrator. In return, he promises to revere and pray to Venus, as he indeed does when sailing by Cythera (vv. 837–51). He also pledges allegiance to Love whom, among all the travelers, he is the only one to see (vv. 609–744): "tousjours son serf serois" (v. 737) (Always shall I be her servant). La Borderie conflates Christian beliefs with classical mythology in an almost syncretic gesture: in both cases, the servitude is voluntary and opposed to that imposed on him by Death, Fortune, or the sultan. The narrator surrenders to God and Venus, but rejects Death, Fortune, and the sultan as his masters.[17] France should follow suit.

Interestingly, when La Borderie mentions slavery in the *Discours*, he never depicts it as a consequence of Ottoman tyranny. The poet describes the enslavement of captives, practiced by both Europeans and Ottomans, without condoning the practice and stops short of condemning it. It is the occasion for the poet to elevate himself by differentiating between a Christian captive and a servant of (divine) Love. The living conditions of slaves are horrendous, claims La Borderie, but Love's bind is much worse, because it is agreed upon by the lover. The misfortune of the captives is evident when the wind stops blowing. This is when they must row day and night:

> *Ò sort inique ! ò gens infortunez,*
> *A tel labeur estans predestinez !*
> *Or pense (amye) icy la grand misere*
> *De ces forsatz condemnez en galere.*

Mais quant & quant veuilles penser aussi,
Que plus grand est mon mal que leur soulci :

. . .

Que plus dure est la mienne affliction,
Que n'est la leur serve condition.
Chascun d'eulx est nommé serf, & forsaire :
Serf non forsé je suis, mais voluntaire.

. . .

Les pauvres gens sont par serve rigueur
Liez au pied, & je le suys au cueur,
Qui est du corps trop plus noble partie.

. . .

Mais regardez lequel plus de mal sent,
Ou eulx pecheurs, ou moy pauvre innocent (vv. 1047–86)
Oh iniquitous fate! Oh unfortunate people!
Destined for such a labor!
Think, my beloved, about the misery
Of these slaves condemned to galleys.
But consider also
That my ills are greater than their pain:

. . .

That my sorrow is harsher
Than their servile condition.
Each of them is called a serf, and captive.
A serf I am, but on my own accord and not forced.

. . .

The poor people are, by slavery's hardship,
Tied at their feet, and I am in my heart,
Which is the body's noblest part.

. . .

But consider which of us feels worse,
They, the sinners, or I, the poor innocent.

Slave among the slaves, the narrator is a noble captive. His servitude, voluntary and caused by Love, is worse than the captivity of the galley slaves because it affects his heart, not only his body. Differentiating between forced captivity and voluntary servitude, La Borderie affirms the narrator's personal woes at the expense of a larger community of captives, both Christian and Muslim, who suffer physically and psychologically. Focusing on himself, the narrator begs his beloved to be kind but, using an individualistic approach to his plight, he is suspicious of both captives and "amye."

The *Discours* posits two types of infidels, the 'Turks,' who are of a different faith, and the beloved, who might not remain faithful in the narrator's absence. The woman's potential infidelity appears early in the poem: in verses 63–70, the narrator imagines that, as his travel takes him to foreign lands, his beloved will seduce another man and forget him. Such a fickle beloved recalls the opportunistic and unpredictable female protagonist of another better-known poem by La Borderie, *L'amie de court*. Published in 1542 like the *Discours*, *L'amie de court* is thought to have started the "querelle des amyes," an early sixteenth-century offshoot of the "querelle des femmes."[18] With its literary responses—Charles Fontaine's *La Contr'Amye de Court* and Antoine Héroët's *La Parfaicte Amye*—*L'amie de court* questions women's role in the private and public spheres by positing an independent and pragmatic female character who unabashedly profits from her male suitors. Like the beloved in the *Discours*, the woman in *L'amie de court* is not assuredly faithful. *L'amie de court* might have been a satirical reworking of Baldassare Castiglione's *Cortegiano*, which was translated into French in 1537, but what matters to us here is the contrast offered by the narrator in the *Discours* with the disloyal women of both poems. He claims himself to be a model of stability and recognizes

> *. . . combien vault, & profite*
> *En cueur honneste une amytié louable,*
> *Comme est la mienne, à jamais immuable.* (vv. 1458–60)
> . . . how worthy and beneficial
> In an honest heart is a praiseworthy friendship,
> Like mine, ever immutable.

Whereas Héroët's *La parfaicte amye* had opposed constancy to the *L'amie de court*'s adulteress, the *Discours*'s narrator provides his own response to the assertive female character. Comparing himself to Ariadne, the male "I" accuses his beloved of disloyalty, which he compares to Theseus' betrayal. The hero, instead of rewarding Ariadne for having delivered him from the Minotaur, abandons his savior on an island with animals:

> *. . . esquelz plus de pitié*
> *Elle trouva, qu'au trahystre d'amytie.*
> *Ò malheureux! Ò trahystre miserable!*
> *Est ce la foy promise inviolable?*
> *Qui doibt tant estre observée entre amys,*
> *Que la loy saincte ou Dieu nous a soubmis.* (vv. 1323–28)
> . . . in whom more pity
> She found than in the one who betrayed her friendship.
> Oh, unfortunate! Oh, miserable traitor!
> Is this the inviolable faith you swore?
> That which must be observed between friends
> That which is given to us by God?

The last line clearly refers to the sacrament of marriage and thus to the fictional relationship established between the poem's male protagonist and his beloved. As the narrator and his "Damoyselle Francoyse" are superimposed onto Ariadne and Theseus, the kingdom of France and the Ottoman Empire lurk behind. Indeed, La Borderie indicates that, in politics as in amorous relationships, "amytie" is essential and so is its preservation. Theseus betrayed Ariadne by not showing her the "amytie" he promised her, as the beloved could betray the narrator by not remaining faithful to her commitment. Similarly, in 1537, the Ottomans failed to keep their promise to the French. The narrator, like France, has trusted a cruel and untrustworthy partner. Lamenting his situation, the lover exclaims:

> *Que c'est grand perte, & pitié trop extreme*
> *De ceulx qui ont fondé leur loyaulté*
> *En cueur ingrat rempli de cruaulté.*
> *Et doibt on bien si amour le permect,*
> *Choisir le lieu ou c'est que lon se mect.* (vv. 1346–50)
> What a great loss and extreme pity it is
> For those who have placed their trust
> In an ungrateful heart full of cruelty.
> Thus, if Love allows it, one should
> Choose carefully the place and person one should trust.

For La Borderie, therefore, the Ottomans are the ultimate infidels. Of a different faith and untrustworthy, they are doubly infidels, religiously as well as politically. What is France to do with them when they sack Corfu instead of attacking Italy as planned? What if the Ottomans failed to honor other promises made to the French, in the Capitulations for example? What to do with them as they engage in despotism and practice slavery? What could be the place or the person to turn to? The narrator's own infidelity, his unexpected shift from "service" to "delice," provides an answer to these questions.

In verses 1367–70, the narrator states a clear preference for the king's "service" as opposed to the "delice" of staying near his beloved:

> *Pour acquitter mon humble obeissance*
> *Envers qui a me commander puissance:*
> *En preferant par debvoir le service*
> *De monseigneur, au sejour, & delice.* (vv. 1367–70)
> To fulfil my humble promise
> Toward the one who commands me,
> Choosing the dutiful service
> To my lord over staying and delight.

Ultimately for the narrator, political loyalty takes precedence over the service of love he owes his beloved.

The End of the Quest, the Beginning of Conquest: Constantinople

Whether represented as *blasons*, miniatures, or woodcuts, cities in the sixteenth century invade literary and cartographic space. Kendall Tarte has recently argued that urban centers such as Poitiers served as locales for writers as well as *foci* of scholarly attention on the part of topographers and *littérateurs*.[19] In the *Discours*, the male narrator relates a journey to the "ville famee" (v. 769) *par excellence,* Constantinople. The narrative mimics the physical voyage, across exotic islands and legendary past, before the narrator and the reader discover the Ottoman capital. Strategically placed as both the conclusion and the culmination of the poem, La Borderie's capital is an emblematic city of mythical dimensions whose rich description deserves no less than 215 verses. A multifaceted place where different religious and cultural communities coexist and collide, Constantinople is presented as a contested space. The poet suggests that the metropolis, although in Ottoman hands since 1453, remains fundamentally a Christian city. Working within and expanding the *blason* tradition, La Borderie figuratively captures the city and claims the empire for the French.

In the 1500s, the *blason* was a popular form used by French poets, particularly those who followed the *rhétoriqueurs* such as Marot, whose "disciple" La Borderie was.[20] The *blason* is a short poetic form that traditionally eulogizes, or sometimes ridicules, the fragmented female body; however, on occasion, poets also wrote *blasons* to extol the magnificence of cities. Bridging iconography and iconology, the poetic *blason des villes* echoed and reinforced the cities' emblems.[21] The *blason* as genre seeks to express the atemporality and the essence of the city it encapsulates by focusing on its most important monuments, often religious edifices. The "Blason de la noble ville et cité de Paris" by Pierre Grognet, for example, praises Paris for its ideal location among wheat fields, the river Seine, and flowering forests. The city's architecture is then carefully sketched in order to demonstrate religious and social qualities: its protective walls, towers, large churches, and the parliament indicate a place where justice, peace, and wealth encourage and are simultaneously reinforced by scientific knowledge, compassion, forgiveness, and wisdom. Nothing surprising here, claims Grognet, since the city is governed by God himself. In short, as the poet summarizes in the last two verses of his *blason*, Paris is the link between the natural and divine worlds:

> *Finalement, c'est paradis terrestre,*
> *Ne reste plus que paradis céleste.*
> In the end, it is heaven on earth,
> Only celestial heaven is of greater worth.

How does sixteenth-century Constantinople compare to Paris? To my knowledge, there is no *blason* on Constantinople. However, from the city's capture by the Ottomans and well into the seventeenth century, it attracted the attention of Western visual artists who produced numerous woodcuts and drawings.[22] As artists moved from bird's eye to more panoramic views, renditions of the city became more elongated. Constantinople lost superfluous street space and saw the leveling of its buildings. No longer represented as an enclosed space seen from above and defined by defensive walls, the city becomes more broad and open, yet also more fragmented as various elements—including people—now compete to take precedence. In contrast, the earlier bird's eye view highlighted the city's most important monuments and moral characteristics and made prints of the city reminiscent of elaborate *blasons*.

When the panorama and the human element are introduced, as in Melchior Lorcks' 1559 drawing, for example (Figure 5.1), the earlier totalizing vision gives way to a seemingly less authoritative approach. In this new perspective, the viewer no longer dominates the landscape from above; instead he is now positioned at the same level as the city and its inhabitants. Cities to be captured are transformed into cities to be read. This does not mean, however, that cities are not meant to be conquered, but now they are to be conquered by words. As details about Constantinople increase, artists and viewers alike judge the metropolis and contemplate their next move. Although appearing less openly militaristic, this new humanist orientation remains hostile since neither the artist nor the viewer have surrendered their position of superiority. In some cases, in fact, they have affirmed it. Lorcks' inclusion, in the foreground of his drawing, of the artist at work is suggestive of his approach, one shared by La Borderie. Indeed, La Borderie's Constantinople, like that of western topographers' of the early sixteenth century, posits a male narrator as domineering. The poet attempts a verbal assault on the city based on the *blason* tradition. Although La Borderie's description of Constantinople is derived from earlier sources and follows the customary mode of *descriptio civitatio*,[23] it also denotes a very up-to-date familiarity with the early sixteenth-century city. Indeed, like Lorcks' and unlike Gilles's,[24] the Constantinople of the *Discours* is resolutely "new" and Ottoman. No other space summarizes its Ottomanness better than the *sérail* which is described as superb and very useful in the poem ("superbe, & tresutile" v. 1548). Furthermore, the importance of the sultan's new palace indicates the center of a tightly organized political structure, the new seat of empire as designed by Mehmed II. Behind its doors, an assortment of horses, courtesans, pashas, and silent janissaries gather along with common people who are here to bring their grievances to the sultan.

Not far from the palace, other Ottoman buildings catch the narrator's and the reader's attention: mosques. Four of them are mentioned, all planned and commissioned by sultans who, by constructing places of worship to which they gave names, multiplied the visions of empire while anchoring it to their dominant religion, Islam. The quintessence of religious alterity for La Borderie and other early modern Christians, mosques add to the wealth and power of the Ottoman rulers, whose architects derived inspiration directly from the Byzantines and crowned their religious edifices with majestic domes (vv. 1605–6). In the *Discours*, Constantinople is a dazzling city, constantly evolving and changing in tones both political and religious. It continues to be built and aggrandized, yet not necessarily improved. After all, claims the poet, the Ottomans did demolish buildings of the old city, while leaving intact many that they converted for their own purposes. Hagia Sophia, for example, was turned into a mosque soon after the city's capture in 1453. Its mosaics were then partially covered:

Faisans autour une ronde ouverture,
Ou l'on peult veoir de pres la couverture,

Figure 5.1 Panoramic view of Constantinople. Melchior Lorck. Courtesy of Leiden University Library, BPL 1758, sheet 11.

> *De laquelle est la voulte magnifique,*
> *D'or marqueté à la vray Moysaïque:*
> *En divers lieux painte de beaux images,*
> *Dont les Turcs ont effacé les visages:*
> *Ne povans veoir, ny souffrir pourtraicture,*
> *De ce qui est produict par la Nature.* (vv. 1661–68).

The center [of Hagia Sophia] forms a round opening
Where one can see the ceiling,
A magnificent dome
Of true mosaics encrusted with gold.
In many places beautiful images are painted,
Whose faces the Turks have effaced
Unable to see and bear with portraits
Created by Nature.

As La Borderie discovers the ever-changing urban landscape, he also rediscovers the heart of Constantinople in the mosaics of Hagia Sophia as well as in the city's location and in Christian fellows living in what has now become the Ottoman capital.

The poet describes the city schematically and methodically before zooming in. Constantinople forms an inverted triangle the tip of which is surrounded by the sea (vv. 1547–50); within this triangle, one can distinguish seven "montaignes," or mountains, on which important buildings have been erected. This approach is amplified by a historical reference to Emperor Constantine, the eponymous founder of the city:

> *Constantinoble est une ville antique*
> *De Constantin excellente fabrique,*
> *Anciennement dicte Byzantion:*
> *Dont maint autheur fait mainte mention.* (vv. 1541–44)
> Constantinople is an ancient city
> Excellently built by Constantine,
> Of old called Byzantium,
> And of which many writers make mention.

Constantinople's geographical location and its history emphasize the city's nobility and Christian foundation. Constantine intended it to be the New Rome, and on three of its seven hills stand major monuments: the old palace, the quarters of the Greek Patriarch, and Hagia Sophia. The poet stresses the number three continuously. On the public square, one can see "trois grandeurs" (v. 1681), or three marvels: "le grand Palais, l'Eglise, & la grand' Mer" (v. 1682) (the old palace, the church, and the great sea). "Trois chefz," three pashas, assist the sultan (v. 1705). The tripartite divisions constantly appearing in La Borderie's poem, be they in the form of the triangle or as a numerical reference, enhance the symbolism of the Christian Trinity. Thus, for La Borderie, Constantinople remains a Christian city, not only because of its past, but also because of its sixteenth-century inhabitants. The Greek patriarch lives there (vv. 1611–20), as do Christian merchants (vv. 1573–76). In spite of the *sérail*, the mosques, the sultans, the janissaries, and the pashas, Constantinople is neither an Ottoman nor a Muslim city. For under a large Muslim presence appears a vibrant Christian community whose strong roots, like Byzantine mosaics, were not and could not have been entirely effaced by the Ottomans.

La Borderie the antiquarian unveils the New Rome with all of its Byzantine and Christian origins. The *sérail*, despite its beauty, is eclipsed by Hagia Sophia, which is positioned at the geographical centre of the city as well as the structural and epistemological heart of the poem.[25] Symbolic of a rich religious, cultural, and political past, the architectural masterpiece represents the grandeur of an era that the poet resurrects through language. Like Gilles a couple of decades later,[26] La Borderie insists on Constantinople's ancient past and Christian-Byzantine qualities that, it seems, can be detected only by French eyes. Although none of these qualities is explicitly discussed in the poem, the reader can easily deduce that they are in complete opposition to the evils that, according to some early modern accounts like the *Discours*, characterize the Constantinople as well as the Ottomans of the early sixteenth century. For La Borderie, these strong negative characteristics have temporarily disfigured Constantinople, and only the poet and his fellow country-men can restore its original properties.

Why are La Borderie and the French, more than others, apt to recover this glori-ous and ineffaceable past? Because their lineage allows them to uncover the past. Here, La Borderie hints at a genealogy popular at the beginning of the sixteenth century that claimed to trace the ancestry of the French back to the Trojans. In verse 621, the poet declares that "yssus sommes du sang de Troye" (we come from the blood of Troy) and in verses 644–46 he depicts the travelers as Aeneas' relatives. The narrator even compares himself indirectly to Aeneas: as he follows in the geographical hero's footsteps, he suffers many misfortunes like the Trojan before him (vv. 270–74). In the *Discours*, the origins of the Ottomans are not Scythian as the majority of Italian humanists argued in the late fifteenth and early sixteenth centuries.[27] La Borderie in fact does not seem to care about the origins of the 'Turks.' What is stressed in the poem is the lineage of the French, for it is perceived as being crucial to their standing in the sixteenth-century world.

A halt on the island of Chios is the occasion to discover additional ties between the French and the Ancients. The parallel established in the poem between the French travelers and the inhabitants of Chios solidifies the uniqueness of the French and at the same time further anchors their roots in classical antiquity. The people of Chios, despite living among the 'Turks' and having to pay them a tribute, enjoy the liberty of living in their own "republique" (v. 1206). Couldn't this miracle, suggests the poet, also apply to the French in their new relation with the Ottomans? In the poem, La Borderie insists on the resemblance between the French and the people of Chios. As both meet, their mutual recognition suggests a close identification. The inhabitants of Chios

> *S'esbahissant d'ouyr nostre langage:*
> *Des habitz courtz dont nous sommes couvertz,*
> *Qu'ilz trouvent tant estranges, & divers,*
> *Comme trouvons diverses leurs facons,*
> *Et d'eulx aussi nous nous esbahissons.* (vv. 1246–50)
> Are astonished to hear our language,
> To see the short clothes covering us,
> And which they find so strange and different,
> Just as we find different their own customs
> And are astonished by them.

The symmetry of these lines is striking. "Comme" is the chiasmatic axis around which the adjective "divers" and the verb "s'esbahir" rotate, illustrating a recipro-cal reaction on the part of both the inhabitants of Chios and the French. Despite linguistic and fashion variances, both parties quickly recognize and respect each other as "amys," friends (vv. 1220 and 1233–34). Through a syntactic equilibrium, the difference between the two groups disappears to privilege resemblance and equality in their uniqueness. Whereas the French and the Ottomans were on equal footing in Jean de Vega's account, the French are synonymous with the islanders of Chios in La Borderie's poem. If Chios has succeeded in retaining its past and its cultural characteristics in spite of being under Ottoman rule, La Borderie asks, why couldn't the French? An early call for the recognition of French exceptionalism among its western neighbors, this passage propels the French to the forefront.

As La Borderie rediscovers French lineage and France's special position in the world, he unearths Constantinople's ancient past and appropriates its present if not for himself, then certainly for his king and the kingdom. The French are heirs to the empire, claims the poet in his own understanding of the *translatio imperii*; as such, they are a looming presence in the *Discours*. Indeed, sixteenth-century Constantinople, ancient and beautiful as it may be, is not equal to Paris, the new center of empire. Although comparable to the French city in terms of size, the Ottoman capital is lacking in other ways:

> *Au grand Paris egal en quantité,*
> *Mais non si bien basti, & habité.* (vv. 1599–1600)
> Equal to the great Paris in quantity,
> But neither built nor inhabited with like quality.

Cairo was Thenaud's capital.[28] Here, as in Grognet's *blason*, Paris surpasses other cities. It reflects the innate and undeniable superiority of all things French, a point reiterated on several occasions by the poet. At the opening of the *Discours* for example, La Borderie makes clear that France is "à nulle aultre seconde,/La plus fertile, & fameuse du monde" (vv. 1–2) (second to no other,/the most fertile and famous in the world). Later, he insists that the *fleur de lys* is feared and honored "en tous climatz de ce siecle doré" (vv. 1223–6) (in all latitudes of this golden era). If Constantinople is rich, France is opulent and no one can truly appreciate its grandeur unless one has traveled and compared it to others:

> *Vous jugerez que de France opulente*
> *Nul ne congnoist la richesse excellente,*
> *Les grands tresors, les delectations*
> *Qui n'a point veu estranges nations* (vv. 1495–98).
> You will judge whether one knows
> Opulent France's excellent richness,
> Its great treasures and delectations,
> If one has never seen foreign nations.

Similarly the *Discours*'s printer, Pierre de Tours, emphasizes France's grandeur in his allographic introduction and links the status of the kingdom in the sixteenth century to its king, Francis, and the French language:

> *Tu trouveras une facilité, & felicité bien grande de nostre langue Fran-*
> *çoyse, une doulceur, & proprieté moderne, au lieu d'une rudesse, & barbarie*
> *antique avec ses equivoques contraintz. Sur quoy (lecteur) t'esmerveillant*
> *avec moy loueras Dieu, qui t'a faict la grace d'estre de ce temps, qu'on peult*

à bon droict nommer Siecle doré, pour les sciences tant esclarcies, & advan-
sees de jour en jour, & les bons esprits, que Dieu de sa grace a resveillez, &
illuminez par tout, & en si grand nombre, mesmement de nostre France, &
langage françoys, que tous les jours on enrichit, & ennoblit, en toute sorte,
par nouvelles oeuvres, & traductions, à quoy nous a ouvert la voye, & donné
courage nostre bon & vertueux Roy Françoys, la noblesse duquel Dieu
accroisse autant en conqueste & acquisition de pays, qu'en augmentation de
lettres. (59–60)

You will find easiness and a great felicity to our French language, sweet-
ness and modernity instead of roughness and barbarity with their forced ambi-
guities. Therefore, reader, while marveling at this, praise the Lord with me,
He who has granted you to be born in these days that can be rightfully called
the Golden Century thanks to its sciences so clear and advancing day by
day, and within the virtuous souls awakening and illumined by God's grace
everywhere in great numbers, and likewise with our France and our French
language that is enriched and ennobled daily in all manner by new works and
translations revealed to us by our kind and virtuous King Francis who has
shown us the way and given us courage and whose nobility may God increase
through conquests and acquisition of lands as enrichment of learning.

As in the 1542 preface to *L'amie de court* where Étienne Dolet explains that
the reader will find eloquence in the French language—"l'eloquence de nostre
langue"—in his introduction to the *Discours*, Pierre de Tours stresses the special
qualities of 'le français.' Dolet too finds 'Les Français' quite special; he adds, "Le
Francoys n'est plus barbare en parler, ny plus lourd en inventions d'esprit, que
toute autre nation"[29] (the French are neither more barbaric nor more inept with
literary creations than any other nation). De Tours equally posits France and the
French language side by side—"France, & langage francoys"—soon followed
by King Francis—"nostre bon & vertueux Roy Francoys." Anticipating Joachim
Du Bellay's *La deffence et illustration de la langue françoyse* (1549),[30] language
and nation here are closely intertwined. La Borderie, Dolet, and de Tours used the
homophony of 'le français, les Français, François' to link fiction and historical
reality, 'nation' and individual.[31]

La Borderie, seconded by Pierre de Tours, calls for French literary and military triumph by stating that language and territorial conquests go hand in hand.
His poem implies that Constantinople and its glorious past deserve better people,
more precisely the French whose conquest of the Ottoman capital the *Discours*
initiates. By circumscribing the city as an elaborate poetic equivalent of a woodcut, drawing, or *blason*, the poet contributes to the taking of this legendary city
and with it the empire of which it was once the seat.

In *La défense et illustration de la langue française*, the French language's vir-
tues are extolled by comparison to Italian. In the *Discours*, the empire of France
will happen not at the expense of the Ottomans, but over Italian powers, more
specifically the Venetians and the Sicilians. Directly named in the *Discours*, both
are accused of treason. In Corfu, the Venetians decline to offer water and food to

the French, which prompts the narrator to wish that they be turned into frogs like the peasants of Lycie (vv. 195–214). Additionally, in Venice's mistreatment of Egina, the Serenissime shows no more respect than the sultan towards its possessions. Egina was once

> *. . . superbe Athenienne,*
> *Et de present pauvre Venicienne.*
> *Ayant changé sa premiere puissance*
> *Au dernier faix de serve obeissance.*
> *L'horreur en moy, & la pitié domine,*
> *Voyant à l'œil celle triste ruyne.* (vv. 951–56)
> A . . . superb Athenian
> And now a poor Venetian,
> Having exchanged its original power
> For servile obedience.
> Inside I feel horror and pity,
> Seeing this sad ruin.

As for the Sicilians, they have inflicted terrible pain on the French by befriending and collaborating with Charles V (vv. 131–44). Venetians and Sicilians also oppose France by showing total indifference to friends and cruelty to conquered people. Whereas in earlier texts like Lemaire's *Traicté* the enemy was the pope, here, in addition to the Ottoman Sultan, it is Charles V, who is indirectly designated as the cause of all problems for France through his allies, the Venetians and the Sicilians. Less poetically than La Borderie, Francis I himself openly admitted to Venetian Ambassador Marino Giustiniano in 1535 that his enemy was Charles V: "Monsieur l'ambassadeur, je ne puis pas nier que je désire vivement voir le Turc très-puissant et prêt à la guerre, non pas pour lui, car c'est un infidèle, et nous autres nous sommes chrétiens ; mais pour affaiblir la puissance de l'empereur"[32] (Mister Ambassador, I cannot deny that I keenly wish to see the Turk become more powerful and ready for war, not for his own sake, for he is an infidel and we are Christian, but rather to weaken the Emperor's power).

In the *Discours*, La Borderie answers the detractors of the Franco-Ottoman alliance that Francis I instigated in the mid-1530s by naming La Forest as permanent ambassador to Constantinople and drafting the Capitulations. La Borderie situates his poem and France's past in Ancient Greece in order to assert a new political influence for the French kingdom of the early sixteenth century. However, the goal of an alliance with a Muslim power, never unequivocally condoned in La Borderie's poem, is only to gain visibility and force within Christendom. One cannot help but see a disinterest in, almost a blindness toward the military strength of the Ottomans and more generally toward their Empire. Fighting Islam is a rhetorical goal and the Ottomans' very real presence in the Mediterranean is understated, almost ignored in La Borderie's *Discours* while the ancestry of the French and their glorious future are highlighted.

Notes

1 Bertrand de La Borderie, *Le discours du voyage de constantinoble*, ed. Danielle Trudeau (Paris: Champion, 2003).

2 See Introduction.

3 On La Forest and his Ottoman missions, see: Rouillard, *The Turk*, 111–passim; Victor-Louis Bourrilly, "L'ambassade de La Forest et de Marillac à Constantinople," *Revue Historique* 76 (1901): 297–328; and Charrière, *Négociations*, 246–420.

4 See Chapter 3.

5 The *Discours* was published again in 1546 by G. Corrozet, in 1547 by J. de Tournes in his *Opuscules d'amour*, and again in 1548 in an anthology titled *Livre de plusieurs pièces*.

6 But it is not unique. Indeed, Jeannine Guérin-Dalle Mese mentions *Il Dittamondo*, a long poem by Fazio degli Uberti describing an imaginary travel to Egypt in *Égypte, la mémoire et le rêve: Itinéraires d'un voyage. 1320–1601* (Florence: Olschki, 1991), 15.

7 Bourrilly speaks of a "*versificateur à l'esprit encombré de souvenirs de l'antiquité classique et obnubilé par la poésie amoureuse à la mode,*" "Borderie," 186.

8 La Borderie, *Amie*, xii.

9 The "service" in line 4 and the "charge" in line 332 are confirmed by an entry in the *Catalogue des Actes de François Ier* showing La Borderie's participation in the venture (La Borderie, *Amie*, xii).

10 Jean de Vega's account, published partially by Charrière, *Négociations*, 340–53 and 371–83, corroborates their presence.

11 See Introduction.

12 See Chapters 1 and 2.

13 Jean de Vega's account is much more prosaic. Of course de Vega's version also contains inadequacies, but contrary to the poem, it stresses a civil encounter in which Ottomans and French spontaneously exchange simultaneous greetings. As for the sultan's boat, it is described as beautiful, well built, golden and painted, made of figtree wood (Charrière, *Négociations*, 1: 345).

14 For example, the narrator talks about "*maint lieu, & mainte isle souvent/Estrange à nous, & de nom incongneue*" (vv. 964–65) (many places and many islands/Foreign to us and of unknown names). See also vv. 1405–6 and v. 1185.

15 See my article on Bounin's *La Soltane*, a play that comments on the French political instability of the 1560s.

16 Houses are small, "*basses, à simple estage*" (v. 1511) (low, one-story high); there are no beds and one sleeps fully clothed (vv. 1499–1502). There are no linens and no tables either (v. 1533); as for food, it is rarer still because the people are "*Tant oppressé de tyrannie inique,/Qu'il n'a povoir les beaux champs cultiver*" (vv. 1508–9) (so oppressed with unjust tyranny/That they cannot cultivate the beautiful fields).

17 Eventually, Death strikes the Ottoman camp as cruelly and indiscriminately as the sultan who oppresses his people later in the poem.

18 The stories in Marguerite de Navarre's *Heptaméron* and their related discussions by the ten *devisants* echo the "querelle des amyes."

19 Kendall Tarte, *Writing Places: Sixteenth-Century City Culture and the Des Roches Salon* (Newark: University of Delaware Press, 2007).

20 Charles Livingston, "Un disciple de Clément Marot: Bertrand de La Borderie," *Revue du Seizième Siècle* 16 (1929): 219–82.

21 The following comments are derived from Alain Toumayan's "The Iconology and Iconography of Paris in Pierre de Grognet's 'Blason de la noble ville et cité de Paris'," *Romanic Review* 80, no. 4 (1989): 512–20.

22 For example, Pieter Coecke van Aelst (1533); Cristoforo Buondelmonti (ca. 1470?); Schebel (1493); Vavassore (1520); Grelot (1680). On Grelot, see Michèle Longino's "Imagining the Turk in Seventeenth-Century France: Grelot's Version," working paper,

http://www.duke.edu/~michelel/projects/visions/2.html. See also Amanda Wunder, "Western Travelers, Eastern Antiquities, and the Image of the Turk in Early Modern Europe," *Journal of Early Modern History* 7, no. 1–2 (2003): 89–119.
23 The sixteenth-century poet borrows almost word for word from Robert de Clari in verses 1645–49. Verses 1545–46 provide an example of unrestrained praise.
24 Gilles, the antiquarian, sees in Constantinople a byzantine Rome. See Frédéric Tinguely, *L'écriture du Levant.*
25 The 57 verses devoted to Hagia Sophia are approximately in the middle of the description of Constantinople.
26 Tinguely, *L'écriture du Levant,* 97–112.
27 Meserve, *Empires of Islam.*
28 See Chapter 2.
29 La Borderie, *Amie,* 55–56.
30 Joachim Du Bellay demonstrates that the French language is not barbaric in Chapter 2 of *La deffense et illustration de la langue françoyse* (Geneva: Slatkine Reprints, 1972). He comments on the link between language and nation in Chapter 12 of the second book.
31 Anne-Marie Lecoq discusses linguistic games associated with these homonyms in Chapter 2 of *François Ier imaginaire* (Paris: Macula, 1987).
32 Charrière, *Négociations,* 1: 67.

6   The Peacock's Beautiful Feathers

Jean Yversen (Re)Dresses the Protestants and Himself

The influx of French scholars in and around Constantinople from the 1540s to the 1560s was a direct consequence of the Capitulations, which were reaffirmed by Henri II (r. 1547–1559) at Francis I's death.[1] Thanks to the accounts these scholars penned during or after their journeys, information about the Ottomans increased and the 'Turks' became more familiar, so familiar indeed that Frenchmen like Bertrand de La Borderie would seek to domesticate them in their writings, using them as props to envisage an embryonic French empire.[2] Meanwhile in France, tensions between Protestants and Catholics began to spread and, in the second half of the sixteenth century, the French appeared less preoccupied with the Ottomans than with domestic religious conflict and with the neighboring countries where the reform movement was thriving. This did not imply the disappearance of the 'Turks' however, for both Protestants and Catholics took to accusing each other of Ottomanization, or contamination by the 'Turks'. The Ottoman became a favorite tool of propaganda for both religious parties. At the same time, familiarity with Ottoman culture was used as a personal *faire-valoir*, a way to add a few colorful feathers to one's cap. Evoking real and imaginary Ottomans to both ends, Jean Yversen is an interesting case in point.

Born in southern France in the late 1520s or early 1530s, Jean Yversen served as France's representative in Ragusa—modern-day Dubrovnic in southern Croatia—in the late 1550s.[3] Private archives in Gaillac, Yversen's hometown, contain a 'travel journal' and unpublished letters which shed light on the diplomat's duties in the Mediterranean as well as on his subsequent local political career in France. Timothy Hampton describes early modern ambassadors as figures of suture, in other words as facilitators of contact and markers of difference.[4] Yversen is very much such a figure, maintaining relations between the French kingdom and the Islamic world in Ragusa and Constantinople on the one hand, and between Catholics and Protestants in Gaillac on the other, yet never collapsing these various religious identities into a single one.

Garrett Mattingly asserts that the biggest change in Renaissance diplomacy sprang from shifting political and religious circumstances, and the subsequent official naming of ambassadors. The ongoing physical presence of an official representative in a foreign land, used extensively by the Italians during their inner struggles in the fourteenth and fifteenth centuries, set the tone for new ways of establishing and maintaining relations between political powers.[5] The concept of the permanent ambassador, Mattingly asserts, changed how Europeans engaged in political matters and marked the beginning of modern diplomacy. I would argue that this new diplomacy did not derive only, or even primarily, from Italian practices and that the naming of permanent ambassadors abroad was of limited influence. Rather, as Yversen's case shows, early French embassies to the Orient did not put an end to old diplomatic practices. Not only had permanent French ambassadors in Constantinople trained in this tradition, but they would remain utterly dependent on a vast array of itinerant envoys like Yversen. These envoys were educated in the same fashion and would continue to play a major role in diplomatic relations for many years to come, all the while implanting the Ottomans in French soil and *mentalités* very effectively.[6] The first instances of modern diplomacy may have taken form outside of France with the naming of permanent ambassadors, but the repercussions in the French kingdom—for example, in Gaillac, a city far removed from Ragusa and Constantinople—were immediate and profound as local *bourgeois* like Yversen tried to negotiate their religious, economic, and political space by rewriting history and themselves. In addition to more sustained contacts with foreign powers, local challenges like French Protestantism contributed greatly to the development of a new diplomacy. Time, place, and personal predicament undoubtedly influenced Yversen's radical religious stance and the art he commissioned. Orientalism in the second half of the sixteenth century depended as much on global diplomacy as on its regional religious and political context.

Scripting an Ambassador: Jean Yversen's Correspondence

Recounting preparations for a delicate meeting between a French delegation and the Ottomans in 1559, Jean Yversen notes that his superior, Ambassador La Vigne, did a fair amount of rewriting prior to the reception and negotiations. La Vigne, in anticipation of the mission, had been composing a message to the sultan, but upon receiving specific orders from King Henri II, he revised his original statement in order to reflect better the monarch's wishes for this particular assignment. La Vigne set out to refashion the letter he had started: "Après que led. s^r ambassadeur eust veu ce que le Roy mandoyt à Sa Haultesse, fust constrainct de rabiller la lettre qu'il luy escripvoyt" (after the said ambassador saw what the King was asking of His Highness [the Sultan], [he] was forced to refashion the letter he was writing to him).[7] La Vigne labored over his scriptorial alteration so admirably that at the end of the encounter, the sultan, happy and satisfied, assured the French of his renewed "amytié"—his friendly intentions and support.[8]

This episode showcasing La Vigne as masterful editor and successful diplomat is included in the lengthy and undated 'travel journal' written by Jean Yversen in the later part of his life, long after his return to France. Yversen, himself a member of the French delegation that fared so well in 1559, did not merely relate the ambassador's recourse to last-minute editing and subsequent political success. Several decades after his own diplomatic services in the East, having returned to his hometown of Gaillac in southwestern France, where he was confronted with the religious wars, Yversen reproduced La Vigne's strategy and embarked on a self-fashioning mission the aim of which was to posit himself as a major political figure.[9] The 'travel journal' and a plethora of rare primary sources located in private archives in Gaillac provide insight into Yversen's diplomatic career abroad, as well as in France during the second half of the sixteenth century. Faced with the Protestant peril in his hometown, the Gaillacois shaped a new diplomacy by rewriting his own political accomplishments in the East. In 1559, Yversen played his role as diplomat well, but his was mainly a secondary role in the early modern diplomacy that La Vigne embodied, as the example above shows. Three decades later, however, the French nobleman scripted an image of himself that surpassed his superiors by recounting, and often embellishing, his past political achievements. Local religious tensions prompted Yversen to redefine himself and to claim a new socio-political status while eyeing posterity.

Yversen in the East

In the early modern world, political emissaries enjoyed a variety of names and titles. Daniela Frigo explains that in Italy "until the middle of the sixteenth century, they were typically designated by the terms 'orators' (*oratore*), 'secretaries' (*segretari*), 'gentlemen' (*gentiluomini*), and 'agents' (*agenti*)."[10] These titles were often interchangeable and their meanings slippery,[11] but they point to two important features of early modern diplomacy. First, envoys in the early modern era were involved in a wide range of negotiations that were politically as well as economically and religiously motivated. Their responsibilities, for example, included purchasing specific luxury goods, or securing a pilgrimage route in a foreign land. All diplomats, Frigo points out, were involved in "*negozio*," a generic term referring to any and all actions undertaken by envoys.[12] Second, early modern dignitaries were expected to follow a precise code of behavior and to possess specific qualities such as prudence,[13] loyalty to a superior, and reporting skills often implying oratory talent. They were trained to perform a specific role and belonged to a well-connected elite who shared similar education and values. Early modern diplomacy was not only based on canon law, customary law, and civil law, as Mattingly sees it;[14] it was, first and foremost, deeply embedded in courtly culture and it spoke the court's "grammar of life," that is to say, a common language which exposed and solidified this courtly culture.[15]

There are only a few direct traces of Yversen's missions in the East, but all point to a man who clearly understood the demands of Renaissance diplomatic culture. Jean Yversen was first posted in Ragusa, a city that in the early modern period enjoyed a special and privileged status. Granted Ottoman protection in 1481, the Republic of Ragusa was after that expected to pay an annual tribute to the sultan but was otherwise left free to function independently. An open competitor to Venice, Ragusa enjoyed a commercial influence that was crucial for Ottomans as well as for Europeans. Its geopolitical situation was equally important for the entire diplomatic corps, as Yversen's outpost in the Mediterranean was at the crossroads of France, the republics of Genoa and Venice, the kingdom of Hungary and Transylvania, and the Ottoman Empire. In Ragusa, the French diplomat was necessarily exposed to a wide variety of peoples as well as religious and cultural traditions. Barely in his thirties when he took his post, Yversen must have relied on a solid humanist training to carry out his missions, several of which took him as far as Constantinople. While in faraway lands, the Frenchman quickly learned to negotiate between his fellow countrymen, Ottomans, Venetians, and diplomats working for the Habsburgs.

In a piece of correspondence dated November 26, 1558, Yversen identified himself as "agent pour le roy" (the king's agent).[16] At about the same time, La Vigne, the French ambassador in Constantinople between 1556 and 1559, refers to him as "homme exprès" (special envoy) in a letter addressed to Henri II.[17] As a political emissary, Yversen carried different titles that shed light on his various responsibilities, some of which were long-term and prestigious, others improvised and temporary. The diverse terminology also indicates a hierarchy among French dignitaries: in Ragusa in 1558–1559, Yversen was the topmost French authority, whereas in Constantinople he was only a subaltern to the ambassador. In both cases nevertheless, Yversen was at the service of the king of France, and his correspondence reflects his acute awareness of the often ephemeral missions and the ambiguous posts held by political representatives, as well as his careful positioning within the larger diplomatic corps.

Private archives in Gaillac contain three pieces of correspondence that bear Yversen's 'signature.' The first of these documents is a long note which begins by identifying the author of the correspondence (Figure 6.1). "Estat des pacquets addresses par moy jehan yversen" (state of the correspondence written by me, Jean Yversen) describes in detail the exchange of messages received, passed on, and sent by Yversen in Ragusa from March to October 1558, along with a careful record of monetary transactions associated with various diplomatic communications and missions. The note is factual, detailed, and organized in a series of easily identifiable daily entries. It shows careful diligence in recording and reporting dealings crucial to the proper and swift exchange of information necessary to France's international affairs.

Not only does this letter, along with the rest of the correspondence preserved in Gaillac, show Yversen as an apt secretary, it also points to the agent's connection to a complex web of French political figures and emissaries based throughout the Mediterranean, along with their allies: Pierre de Martines, "conseiller du roy et son Ambassadeur vers ledit roy et royaume de hongrie et estat de Transilvanie" (counselor to the king and Ambassador to the kingdom of Hungary and the state of Transylvania); Ambassadors Codignac and La Vigne in Constantinople; François de Noailles, bishop of Dax and French representative in Venice;[18] Queen Isabella of Hungary; Diane de Poitiers;[19] and even Sultan Süleyman whose *laissez-passer* Yversen brought back to Gaillac (Figure 6.2). These personages reveal a highly complex society in which diplomats like Yversen were asked to move rapidly but carefully, always respectful of hierarchy and codes of conduct.

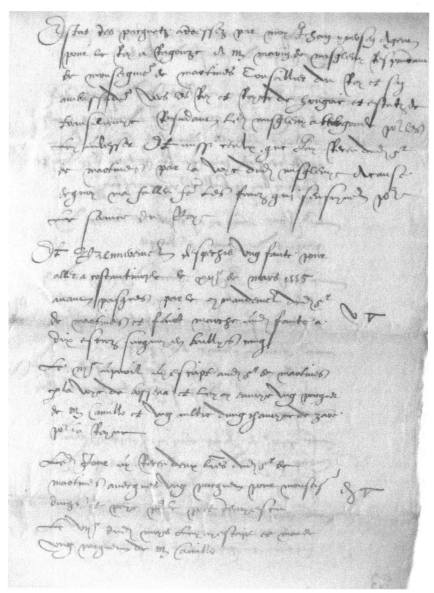

Figure 6.1 "Estat des pacquets." Jean Yversen's correspondence in Ragusa. Private archive.

The fact that peace was Renaissance diplomacy's main objective,[20] at least publicly if not always privately, further complicated political operations with foreign nations or representatives. A second holding in the Gaillac archive makes this clear. A one-page letter dated June 6, 1559 and signed by Yversen and his superior, La Vigne, attests to their arrival in Constantinople in preparation for the delicate

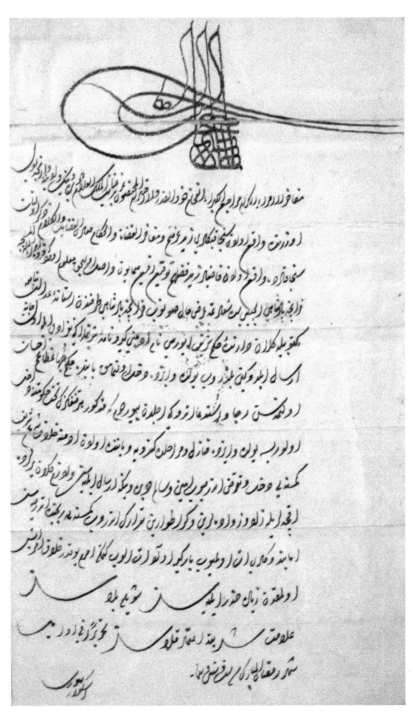

Figure 6.2 Yversen's *laissez-passer* with Sultan Süleyman's tughrā on top. Private archive.

task of informing the Ottomans of the signature of the treaty of Cateau-Cambrésis by Henri II of France and Philip II of Spain on March 3, 1559 (Figure 6.3).
This particular mission seems to have been unexpected for Yversen. Its difficulty
resided in the fact that, as the Cateau-Cambrésis treaty brought the Valois and the
Habsburgs closer by putting an end to their wars waged in Italy, Sultan Süleyman
could envision severing his two-decade long alliance with the French, thereby
potentially depriving the French king of a powerful ally.

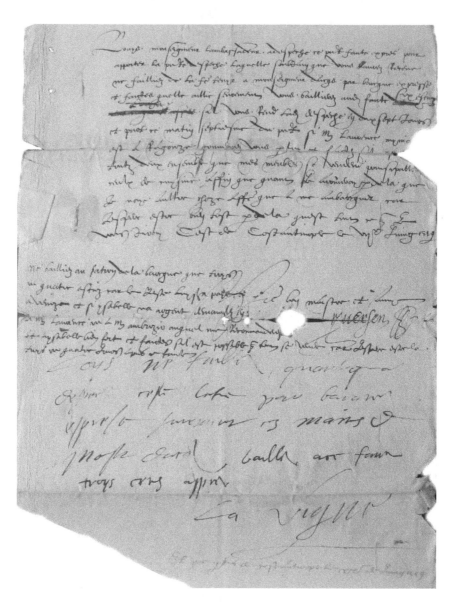

Figure 6.3 Letter cosigned by Yversen and La Vigne, dated June 6, 1559. Private archive.

The presence of Yversen within the co-written and co-signed letter reflects the diplomat's political standing during this particular mission. Yversen's contribution and signature are dwarfed, and almost eclipsed, by La Vigne's oversized inscription superimposed on the piece of correspondence. Compared to La Vigne, Yversen's words occupy a larger yet negated place on the page. The page then mirrors his inferior status in Constantinople in 1559.

Four years earlier, however, Yversen's position in the Ottoman capital was altogether different. In a letter dated August 26, 1555, Yversen displays his proud *appartenance* and adherence to early modern diplomatic culture (Figure 6.4). This document, one of the earliest indications of Yversen's familiarity with complicated diplomatic activity in the East, also reveals a shrewd and highly competent diplomat. In a long and detailed dispatch written from Constantinople and addressed to François de Noailles, Yversen gives his official report on a failed mission that was meant to convince the Ottomans to keep their fleet in a French port for the winter, and possibly to embark on a joint military operation. A decade earlier, in 1543–1544, the Ottomans had stayed in Toulon for several months and the offer that Yversen presented in 1555 was not as bold as it might seem.[21] Pierre de Martines and Yversen proposed the deal to the pasha directly, thus addressing an Ottoman military commander and high statesman and somewhat bypassing Ambassador Codignac.

In his report to Noailles, Yversen depicts himself as the perfect diplomat. He follows many of the precepts put forth by Bernard de Rosier in his 1435 *Ambaxiator Brevilogus*:[22] he is loyal to the king, whom he represents, and faithful to his immediate superior, Noailles, to whom he reports; he is able to improvise and adapt during tense negotiations, thereby showing a certain degree of good judgment and independence. The report stresses Yversen's patience, perseverance, flexibility, and especially his diligence, a word the Frenchman does not hesitate to use to describe his work and which recalls the quality of *prudenza* highly valued among Italian diplomats. Yversen also deplores the countless difficulties encountered by diplomats—some of which are due to the time it takes to travel from one place to the next, and others of which one's interlocutors bring about. Having to report on a failed mission was certainly one of the more trying difficulties diplomats faced. Although the French negotiators almost managed to convince the pasha, the Ottomans ultimately refused the offer of "hivernement," and Yversen had to communicate their negative response and his disappointment to Noailles: ". . . je suis fort marry de navoir peu tirer ce quon mavait donne en charge . . ." (I am quite disappointed to not have been able to accomplish what I was charged to do). In the end though, Yversen insists that no one else could have done more— "ung aultre ny eut pu faire dadvantaige"—while underscoring a very positive outcome: the sultan had once again expressed his "amytie" for his European allies and promised to make his fleet available to the French during the summer if they so wished:

> . . . *si on eut propose a temps cest hyvernement il ne leut refuse estant son intention de fere tout office de bon amy tel quil entendait estre toujours tellement que si sa majesté avait besoing cest este de son armee il la lui concedroit*

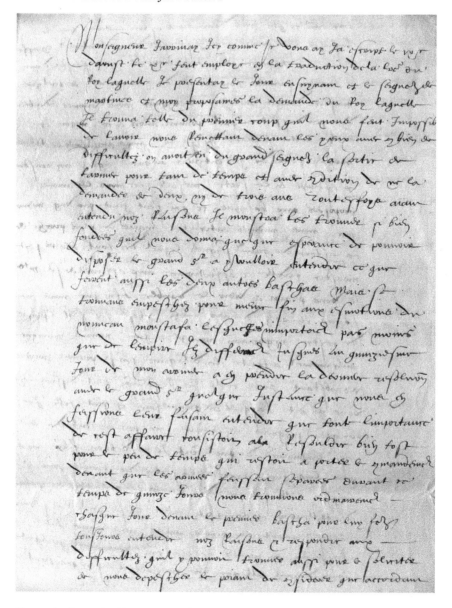

Figure 6.4 Letter by Yversen, sent from Constantinople to François de Noailles, dated August 26, 1555. Private archive.

fort voluntiers dequoy il nous donnait charge den adviser le roy expressement et voila au moins quelque bon fruict que nous avons tire de ceste negociation naiant peu obtenir le principal de ce que nous demandions.

    . . . if we had made this offer on time, he [the Sultan] would not have refused, his intention to behave as a good friend should, and wishing to remain one—so much so that, if his majesty were in need of his army, he would most willingly lend it to him. Of this, he asked that we inform the king quickly. Here is some good result that we have gotten from this negotiation, the main objective of which we could not obtain.

Yversen's missions in Ragusa and Constantinople were extremely diverse, at times predictable, at times particularly intricate and unexpected.[23] Contemporary documents from the period show Yversen as a dexterous and independent envoy always aware of his ever-changing charges and positions. Some missions were marked by success, and others by less positive results, but all were perfectly executed by a man who understood well his position vis-à-vis his superiors. They undeniably equipped Yversen with skills that would be valuable after his return to his native land in the early 1560s.

Yversen in Gaillac

By the time Yversen returned to his hometown of Gaillac, religious tensions between Protestants and Catholics had reshaped the political landscape of southwestern France. Contemporary sources reveal that, from 1560 onward, Gaillac witnessed considerable hostility between local Catholics and Protestants, each group vying for religious space and power.[24] Freshly returned from the East, Yversen was in Gaillac in 1562 when Protestants forcefully occupied the church of Saint Pierre and led a religious service.[25] This first case of Protestant bravado led to a severe Catholic retaliation in which many Reformers were killed. Three years later, two outspoken Protestants from the town, Jacques Sabuc and Pierre Pasquet, were arrested, judged by Henri de Montmorency, Seigneur de Damville, then Governor of Languedoc, and subsequently hanged.[26]

Catholics too came under attack, especially in 1568 when Gaillac fell into the hands of Protestants.[27] We know from the Gaillac archive that Yversen himself was imprisoned for a certain time, his home destroyed, and his *capitainerie* claimed by an opportunist named Villeneuve.[28] Much as in Ragusa and Constantinople, connections in Gaillac were vital to one's political and personal survival. Thanks to his diplomatic experience Yversen knew how to win the help of influential figures. Born into a well-known and politically active family,[29] Yversen was elected *consul* in Gaillac on several occasions. During and after his captivity, he contacted influential people who worked to protect his property, as well as his wife and young children. Two letters underscore Yversen's plight. They are addressed by dignitaries who intervened in Yversen's favor in 1570. Audrand, a locally influential cleric,[30] sought to protect the Gaillacois's family financially by emphasizing his friendship with Yversen: "je ne veuls quitter l'amytye que je luy ay portee" (I do not wish to abandon the friendship I have had for him).[31] An even more prominent person came to Yversen's help on August 22, when Cardinal de Bourbon asked Damville to see to it that Captain Villeneuve, Joyeuse's lieutenant and governor of Albi, return the *capitainerie* of Couffouleux to Yversen, its legitimate owner.[32]

Yversen did not merely count on others to help him recuperate his goods and reputation; he took matters into his own hands. He first fought his own sister,

Jeanne, who in his absence had allegedly stolen some of his wheat and wine sup-
plies, which might raise the question of her religious affiliation.[33] As for Yversen's
own religious allegiance, he had taken up the Catholic cause, of which he became
a noted representative as early as 1565. In a verbal joust, he once defended the
local Catholics against Thoery, the Protestants' spokesperson. This speech does
not survive and may have never been written down. Testimonies of Yversen's
oratory prowess exist, however. Mathieu Blouin, the author of a chronicle in
Occitan describing the religious troubles in Gaillac between 1559 and 1572,
recalls Yversen as "ung bourges appelat noble Jean d'Ibercen, / fort selat cathou-
lic, boun parlie, ben disen" (a *bourgeois* called noble Jean d'Iversen, / a zealous
Catholic, great speaker and good orator).[34] Thus, Yversen demonstrated in France
the same effective rhetorical and diplomatic skills he had used in his earlier Ottoman missions.

Yversen on the East

As troubles in Gaillac subsided in the 1570s, Yversen went much further than
using a competence acquired abroad: he embarked on a vast program of self-
refashioning. Two works, one sculpted and the other written, exemplify his
attempt at spelling out, and at times redefining, his political stature and his own
diplomatic services in the East. The first is a large sculpted wood panel dated
1584 which most likely was commissioned by Yversen to decorate the mantel of
a fireplace (Figure 6.5). This *boiserie*, still visible in the house that the diplomat's
descendants occupy today in Gaillac, depicts Yversen's embassy to Constantinople and culminates with his personal encounter with the sultan. One striking detail
is Yversen's spatial, as well as political, preponderance in the *boiserie*, emphasized by the marked absence of other Europeans. Additionally, even though the
Ottomans are clearly the central focus of the piece, the wars of religion are a powerful undercurrent here and may have been the main reason for the creation of the
sculpture. This interpretation is reinforced by a painting subsequently inserted in
the center of the *boiserie* which depicts, perhaps, Yversen himself (Figure 6.6).[35]

   A second artifact reinforces the importance Yversen claims for himself to the
exclusion of other Europeans, emphasizing the narrative of assertion by occul-
tation that is visible in the *boiserie*. It is Yversen's report of his 1559 mission
to Constantinople with which this chapter began. The eight-page document is
neither dated nor signed, but is written in the first person, and the handwriting
matches that of the three pieces of correspondence from Yversen mentioned earlier (Figure 6.7). Marie-Thérèse de Martel, who transcribed and published most of
this text, refers to it as Yversen's travel journal in spite of the fact that it is neither
a diary nor a 'relation,'[36] but rather a report written after the mission. No daily
entries are visible in this document; instead, a coherent and overarching narrative
indicates a physical and textual purpose that would be uncharacteristic of a travel
journal. Although it is impossible to date the document with precision—unlike
the *boiserie*—it is clear that Yversen's text was written later in order to assert and
strengthen a socio-political status that had been partially eroded during the wars

Figure 6.5 Late sixteenth-century *boiserie* representing Jean Yversen and his diplomatic encounters with the Ottomans in the 1550s. Photo by the Archives départementales du Tarn.

Figure 6.6 Portrait of Yversen. *Boiserie*, detail. Photo by the Archives départementales du Tarn.

of religion. To all appearances, the text does not echo, or even refer to, the various scenes in the *boiserie*. In fact, the geographical, architectural, and cultural details visible in the sculpture are totally absent from the report, with the notable exception of the meeting between the European envoy and Sultan Süleyman. But what is particularly remarkable is the effacement of La Vigne in both the *boiserie* and the report, both of which, I argue, operate in parallel. Yversen's unofficial report, like the *boiserie* he commissioned, effectively eclipses La Vigne from the narration and the 1559 diplomatic mission altogether.

The report alleges to describe events of the Cateau-Cambrésis mission as they occurred chronologically. However, after an introductory paragraph that ambiguously portrays Yversen as a welcome guest at the sultan's court,[37] it becomes a straightforward condemnation of La Vigne's short-tempered character.

> *Monseigneur de la vigne na este guyere contens de ce que le roy na escript a sa haultesse de luy donner congé pour le venir trouver sans mander aultrement aulcung en sa place dont il l avoict adverty sa majeste que si luy feust faict ainsy come il lavoyt escript les affaires de sa dite majeste . . . a la porte sen feussent beaucoup mieux porte.*
>
> Ambassador La Vigne was not at all pleased that the king omitted to write the sultan to ask that he allow [La Vigne] to come to his highness without calling on someone else to replace him, regarding which [La Vigne] had warned his majesty that if it had been done the way he had suggested his majesty's business . . . in Constantinople would have fared much better.

Yversen asserts his authority by suggesting that La Vigne did not behave as a diplomat should. In his report, the Gaillacois claims that he had anticipated his superior's negative reaction and that he had even warned the king of potential negative repercussions to the mission itself. Thus, in the 'travel journal,' Yversen—and not La Vigne—is seen closely advising the king on diplomatic affairs.

The narration continues to emphasize Yversen's presence until the end of the document. The meeting to announce the Cateau-Cambrésis treaty begins by staging a first encounter between Ottomans and French diplomats, among whom we find La Vigne and Yversen. It shows the Gaillacois following the ambassador to the sultan's camp and sitting next to the French diplomat:

> *. . . le Bassa manda aud. s^r ambassadeur qu'il s'en vint baiser la main au Seigneur, lequel [La Vigne], soubdain, monta à cheval avec toutz ses gens et s'en alla dessendre au devant du pavyllon, là où les bassas font leur dyvan, et entra dedans et me fict assouer auprès de luy.*
>
> . . . the Pasha asked the ambassador to come and kiss the Sultan's hand, whereupon La Vigne, accompanied by all his men to the pavilion where the pashas meet, entered, and bade me sit beside him.

At this point in the narration, La Vigne is clearly the main dignitary who is received by the sultan; Yversen simply accompanies him. As the meeting progresses,

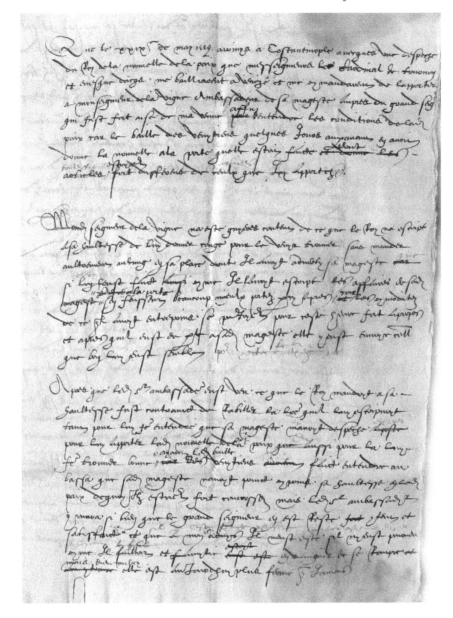

Figure 6.7 First page of Yversen's "travel journal." Private archive.

however, the text raises Yversen to a position of equality with La Vigne. Together, they reach the sultan's pavilion: "Incontinant après, les bassas se levarent de leurs sièges et entrarent dans le pavyllon du Grand Seigneur, ensemble led. s^r ambassadeur et moy" (Soon afterwards, the pashas got up from their seats and entered the

Sultan's pavillion with the said ambassador and myself). The ceremony continues as La Vigne, then Yversen, once again appearing *after* his ambassador, salute the sultan. La Vigne proceeds to speak as Yversen remains silent, and the meeting ends with the French ambassador kissing the sultan's hand, a gesture repeated by Yversen as well. The two foreign delegates leave the tent side by side, just as they had entered it.[38] The description of this first visit to the sultan is thus a delicate balancing act between the two French diplomats whose roles are slowly being redefined by Yversen. The Gaillacois has not yet surpassed his superior, but as the report unfolds, he slowly effaces La Vigne from the narrative—and diplomatic history.

Indeed, what follows are several missions carried out by Yversen himself, without the supervision or the assistance of La Vigne. One of them implies the liberation of Christian prisoners. Undoubtedly this required a high degree of secrecy, which could explain why Yversen did not treat it explicitly in his correspondence at the time. These missions do appear in La Vigne's letters however, suggesting that it was not the Gaillacois' place to report on such sensitive issues in the 1550s. Three decades later, after La Vigne had died, mentioning such operations became not only a possibility for Yversen; it was a golden opportunity.

To accomplish his mission of liberation, Yversen claims that he met personally with the Venetian *bailo*, the "belierbey de la mer" (the commander of the Ottoman fleet), and the pasha. Here, Yversen shines as a seasoned diplomat. A verbal joust between the French emissary and the pasha illustrates Yversen's oratory talents. I abbreviate the following quotation in order to highlight its most salient characteristics:

> *Et arrivé que je feuz devant led. bassa,* luy dictz que *monseigneur l'ambassadeur m'avoyt commandé de venyr prendre congé de luy et sçavoir s'il me voulloit rien commander que je disse à Sa Magesté.*
>
> Me respondit que *c'estoyt une belle amytié que le Roy pourtoyt au Grand Seigneur, veu qu'il comportoyt que leur hennemy eust envoyé vingt et deux galleres à soixante mil de là d'Argier, que avoyent sacquaigé troys ou quatre villaiges et, après, s'estoient retirez et faisoient l'amasse à Messina et que les soldatz de Naples s'embarquoient sus les galleres qu'estoient au nombre de septante.*
>
> Je luy respondys que *monseigneur l'ambassadeur avoyt esté adverty de sa part par ses dragomans de touttes ses nuvelles qu'il ne croyoit entièrement; touttefoys, il [La Vigne] m'avoyt commandé de luy présenter [au Pascha] ung escript qu'il luy envoyoit.*
>
>   . . .
> Il dict que . . .
> Je luy respondys que . . .
>
>   . . .
> Il dict: *Or. . .*
> Respondu que *le Roy n'avoyt poinct faict peu que d'estre demeuré amy de Sa Haultesse et que, pour conserver ceste amytié, il avoyt beaucoup mieulx*

aymé rendre une infinyté de places que de la perdre, faisant le Roy Philippe tout ce qu'il pouvoyt que Sa Majesté ne comprint Sa Haultesse en la paix et que si le beglierbey de la mer n'eust poinct faict l'erreur qu'il fict l'esté passé, la paix se fust faicte beaucoup plus à l'honneur et advantaige du Roy et de Sa Haultesse.

Luy respondys. . .

Dict qu'. . .

. . .

Je luy dictz. . .

Il respondit que. . . [39]

Having arrived in front of the said pasha, *I told him* that my lord the ambassador had ordered me to wish him goodbye and to inquire whether there was anything he wanted me to say to His Majesty.

He answered that the King shared a fine friendship with the Great Sultan given that it meant that their enemy had sent twenty-two galleys sixty miles from Algers that had pillaged three or four villages and had thereafter retreated to Messina and that the soldiers in Naples were boarding on some seventy galleys.

I replied that my lord the ambassador had been warned of all this by the dragoman [official translator] and that he did not believe the news entirely; nevertheless he had ordered me to present a message which he was sending him. . .

He said that. . .

I answered that . . .

. . .

He said: However. . .

[I] answered that the King had done much to remain friends with His Highness and that, in order to maintain this friendship, he had prefered to give countless places instead of losing it, whereas King Philip had done what he could so that His Majesty did not include His Highness [the sultan] in the peace negotiations and that if the commander of the sea had not made the mistake he made last year, peace would have been more advantageous to both the King and His Highness.

[I] responded that . . .

[He] said that. . .

. . .

I told him. . .

He answered that. . .

The dialogue is written in indirect discourse but the replies are fast-paced and lively. Having built his confidence with this vivacious exchange, Yversen even dares to accuse the Ottomans of an unspecified mistake: "si le beglierbey de la mer n'eust poinct faict l'erreur qu'il fict l'esté passé, la paix se fust faicte beaucoup plus à l'honneur et advantaige du Roy et de sa Haultesse" (if the commander of the sea had not made the mistake he made last year, peace would have been more beneficial to both the King and His Highness, the sultan). One may wonder whether this very direct charge was ever communicated orally, but its presence in the report shows Yversen as a major diplomat capable of evaluating events critically—if only after the fact—and also of rearranging the political hierarchy by relating historical events the better to showcase his own performance.

Similarly, later in the report, Yversen offers a personal commentary on the *bailo* and the Venetians' efforts to discredit the French: "([le baille] *à mon advyz* ne les avoyt faict dire sinon que pour le faschier)" ([the *bailo*] *in my opinion* had spread the rumor only to create troubles for [the French king]). Yversen's opinion appears in parentheses in the text, which calls attention to his interpretation of events. This episode indicates overt contention and competition among Christians in Constantinople, a reality confirmed when Yversen mentions that the French embassy had stayed close to the emperor's delegate and managed to meet the sultan ahead of Ogier de Busbecq. Yversen's parenthetical commentary makes clear that the Franco-Venetian rivalry in the Ottoman capital of the late 1550s was fierce; so was, obviously, the antagonism between Henri II and Philip II, despite the signature of the peace treaty in Cateau-Cambrésis. More to the point, in the relation he gives of these events years later, Yversen suggests that frictions among Christians in Constantinople were but a prelude to what the diplomat would face in Gaillac upon his return from the East.

Three decades after his missions in Constantinople, Yversen, on the *boiserie* and in his report, envisions himself as a much more important political figure than his correspondence and others' suggest. He literally and figuratively redresses La Vigne and casts doubt on his superior's diplomatic skills, while portraying himself as a main political player on the international as well as the local scenes. Yversen may have learned the rhetoric and skills of diplomacy when he was in contact with French and foreign dignitaries and rulers in Ragusa and in the Ottoman capital, but he also used them widely at home during the wars of religion, before mastering them in his report and the *boiserie*, which both place the diplomat at the forefront of local and modern politics. Yversen had skilfully transfered the art of diplomacy from the East to the West.

Crusading Southwestern France

The wars of religion in France were the occasion of countless acts of cruelty and oppression perpetrated towards, as well as by, both Catholics and Protestants. Contemporaries commented extensively on the period. Montaigne and Agrippa d'Aubigné were two of the many literary voices that questioned the necessity of violence and, in the case of d'Aubigné, openly criticized Catholic atrocities such as the St. Bartholomew's massacre on August 24, 1572. As commentators offered their poetic renditions of the bloodshed or sceptical takes on this complex situation, so did visual artists in their own way capture the brutality and profound interrogations that marked the second half of the sixteenth century. One such artist was François Dubois, who painted his famous "Massacre de la Saint Barthélemy" around 1576.

Less known than Dubois's visual accusation of Catholic brutality is the *boiserie* commissioned by Yversen. In many ways a counterpoint to Dubois's painting, the Gaillac sculpture presents Yversen's personal response to the religious crisis. Both subtle and forceful in its condemnation of the Reformation, it is a highly original and rare example of sixteenth-century interior decoration. As can be seen on the *boiserie*, the Catholic Yversen chose to focus not on the Protestants but rather on the Ottomans—another, arguably more obvious enemy of Catholicism. By recalling his position as a diplomat and thereby stressing his power as an intermediary between two religiously different parties, the kingdom of France and the Ottoman Empire, Yversen puts forth the following radical idea: the way to resolve the religious crisis affecting southwestern France would be to deal with Protestants in exactly the same way the French dealt with Muslims (and by extension the Ottomans) during the crusades. What follows is an examination of the crusade ideology underlying Yversen's *boiserie*.

The commission of the *boiserie* is part of Yversen's efforts to regain his own power as well as re-establish Catholic authority in his hometown, as Gaillac itself was in the process of eliminating the Protestants' influence. The *boiserie* does not explicitly reflect his preoccupation with the Protestants. Instead, it focuses on the seemingly unrelated Ottoman world. The panel is composed of several distinct, yet blended, scenes which I will address first individually before proceeding to the overall significance of the ensemble. In the first fragment at the top left, a mosque with its minarets welcomes the faithful, one of whom is shown removing his shoes while another is busy performing his ablutions. A *muezzin* calls people to prayer and a man bends over a tomb decorated with turbans in traditional Ottoman fashion (Figure 6.8). Further down, a picnic scene adds a touch of tranquillity by stressing the simple pleasures in life (Figure 6.9). The right-hand side of the *boiserie* depicts more crowded and formal spaces. At the top, the sultan on horseback parades the streets of Constantinople (Figure 6.10). He is surrounded by his army of janissaries as well as common people, among whom a water carrier stands out (Figure 6.11). The sultan appears again, below the procession scene, this time receiving a foreign guest. Reminiscent of the woodcuts from Nicolas de Nicolay's *Navigations* and Ottoman miniatures, these four scenes appear independent of one another due to their composition and their rather loosely related subject matter. However, one should not underestimate their interconnectedness. When viewed together, these scenes form a narrative discourse of their own in which the Ottoman world is fully exposed in a disarmingly detached fashion, and in fact neutralized.

The foreign and very realistic character of the Oriental world in all its specificity exudes from the *boiserie*, which is replete with characteristic details. From clothing and headgear to landscape and architectural details, the focus is on lavish, remote, and non-threatening aspects of Ottoman culture. The picnic scene, for example, is most serene: the three participants, two Ottomans and a European, are engaged in a communion of sorts. Having gathered around food, two men sitting cross-legged are ready to partake in a meal. One of them holds a jug and seems to welcome a third guest, a foreigner, who returns his companion's gaze and slightly

Figure 6.8 Mosque, minaret and *muezzin*. *Boiserie*, detail. Photo by the Archives départementales du Tarn.

Figure 6.9 Picnic in Constantinople. *Boiserie*, detail. Photo by the Archives départementales du Tarn.

Figure 6.10 Sultan on horse. *Boiserie*, detail. Photo by the Archives départementales du Tarn.

Figure 6.11 Water carrier. *Boiserie*, detail. Photo by the Archives départementales du Tarn.

bows to him. Similarly, the parade, seen from a safe distance, is pleasing to the eye. The sultan, clearly detached from his attendants, is majestic and appears to be heading to the mosque instead of to war. It is as if the choice of pastoral, spiritual, and convivial settings serves to cast a foreign and potentially threatening culture in a friendly light. The most unfamiliar elements have been domesticated. Above all, it is the presence of a European man that renders the Ottoman world familiar and innocuous at the same time. Recognizable by his ruff and western clothes, the European character is perfectly at ease among the Ottomans, as it is made clear by the way he adopts some of their customs: he is about to sit on the ground to join and enjoy the picnic, and when he is received by the sultan, he wears a caftan on top of his western dress (Figure 6.12). The European ambassador faces the Sultan and shows him his empty hands in a gesture of peace. This scene is perhaps the culminating moment of the Ottoman presence in the *boiserie*. The sultan is certainly the most highly ranked character in the whole sculpture, and the meeting between the two men is clearly a special moment, as it is in Yversen's report. The eye of the sixteenth-century Frenchman would surely have paused upon this scene. The message is clear however: despite all its glory and ceremony, the encounter would not have happened had it not been for the inconspicuous European dignitary, a figure emblematic of early modern diplomacy. Having mastered Ottoman ways, the envoy stands out as the only European, as if he had single-handedly won the sultan's and, by extension, the Ottomans' confidence and respect.

Figure 6.12 European visitor to the Ottoman court. *Boiserie*, detail. Photo by the Archives départementales du Tarn.

The identity of the European dignitary is revealed in what lies beneath the Ottoman scenes. Two horizontal sections unite and bring depth to the Ottoman experience. Embedded in the panel itself, the first transports us to a maritime world that represents the Mediterranean (Figure 6.13). Replete with galleys and monstrous fish, the sea is depicted as a geographical and physical link between France, Ragusa, the Ottoman Empire, and, further south, Jerusalem. The sea is what allowed pilgrims on their way to the Holy Land, merchants, diplomats, and armies to circulate between seemingly different cultures that shared much in common. Danger and conflict, however, were not always absent from this aquatic bridge. Whether because of its natural elements, piracy, or open military skirmishes between Christian and Muslim forces, the Mediterranean was well known for its creative instability.

The second horizontal scene, composed of two battle scenes separated by a coat of arms held aloft by angels, forms the lintel and is distinct from the main sculpture.[40] At the same time, the lintel can be seen as a framing device to the extent that the battles represented in it echo the turbulent maritime scene directly above. Here, a battle is raging. But who precisely are the opponents? The art historian Marie Cadet interprets this scene as two separate battles. According to Cadet, the one on the left represents Christians and Muslims, in other words, a crusade, while the one on the right shows Christian fighters engaged in the wars of religion. Although supported by an analysis of each soldier's weapons and battle dress,

Figure 6.13 Galleys in the tumultuous Mediterranean. *Boiserie*, detail. Photo by the Archives départementales du Tarn.

in my opinion, this argument ignores other crucial evidence. The architectural details of the sculpted lintel, for example, point to a more complex interpretation: both an Islamic city with its minarets and a western city with its protective walls form the background of the supposed crusading scene on the left (Figure 6.14). A similar blurring of architectural identifiers occurs in the scenes where the sultan appears: Roman columns decorate the streets of Constantinople and a western throne embellishes the palace. As for the flags distinguishing each army, they both proudly display crosses (Figure 6.15). One could read these seeming inconsistencies as signs that the Islamic peril was at Europe's door, a warning often repeated in the sixteenth century, and that the inner struggles of Christianity could be seen as a phenomenon of the East. The trouble is that while on the one hand, Western Europe, and in particular France, invited the Ottomans; on the other, the Reformation had spread very much to the West as early as the 1530s, and southwestern France, including the small town of Gaillac, was particularly under the influence of the new faith in the 1560s. I interpret such apparent geographical and architectural incongruities as the depiction of a larger and more complex idea. Just as the Ottoman world of the sculpture is itself composed of individual yet interconnected scenes, so too are the lintel's battle scenes, and all participate in the same ideological movement by conflating Protestants and Ottomans. In Jean Yversen's home, a sixteenth-century Catholic would have read the *boiserie* as a particular response to the wars of religion: Protestants were to be treated as infidels and crusaded.

The metaphor of the crusade and its adaptation to what was viewed as the Protestant threat was not uncommon in Yversen's time. As Denis Crouzet and Kevin Gould have shown,[41] the crusade ideology and mode of operations were shared by many Catholics in southwestern France, particularly in Toulouse—located some forty kilometres from Gaillac—where in 1568 the Catholics formed a group they called *croisade* to defend themselves against Protestants.[42] Unlike Montauban, Castres, Réalmont, and even Gaillac, Toulouse remained a stronghold for Catholics during the wars of religion. Similarly, Albi, Agen, and Bordeaux stayed firmly in Catholic hands. Geographically located at the crossroads of Albi and Toulouse, Castres and Montauban, Gaillac was a battleground of religious ideologies, vacillating between Catholicism and Protestant Reformation. For staunch Catholics of the southwest like Yversen, the crusades were not a thing of the past, but rather a sensible and practical solution to the crisis at hand. This approach had a particular echo for Yversen since Albi, a bastion of Catholicism in the sixteenth century merely 20 kilometers east of Gaillac, was remembered as the seat of power that three centuries earlier had successfully annihilated other perceived Christian heretics, the Cathars.

That crusading the Protestants was indeed Yversen's position is made clear by a coat of arms found in the centre of the lintel (Figure 6.16). The winged deer and above it a sun surrounded by two moon crescents, such is indeed the description of Yversen's coat of arms according to Charles d'Hozier's *Armorial Général de France*.[43] It reveals the identity of the *commanditaire* of the *boiserie* as well as that of the European character who is featured twice in the above-mentioned scenes. The coat of arms also calls to mind Yversen's radical position on the Catholic-Protestant divide. Joining the two seemingly separate battle scenes,

Figure 6.14 Battle scene with western and Islamic cities in the background. *Boiserie*, detail. Photo by the Archives départementales du Tarn.

Figure 6.15 Cross against cross. *Boiserie*, detail. Private archive. Photo by Cara Welch.

Figure 6.16 Yversen's coat of arms. *Boiserie*, detail. Photo by the Archives départementales du Tarn.

Yversen's heraldic shield suggests that the diplomat was able to bridge time and
space, and consequently bring the crusade to Gaillac's new religious enemies, the
Protestants. This strong view and the only possible outcome of the battle were
once made apparent with a sculpted deer kicking an Ottoman Turk, a piece which
once stood in front of the fireplace but is now, unfortunately, lost.[44]

Yversen's commissioning of the sculpture is, therefore, an integral part of his
program of political and religious rehabilitation, both personal and collective. The
boiserie comes after years of unrest and sustained violence in Gaillac and parallels Yversen's attempts to reestablish Catholic rule. As a nobleman who fought for
his own rights, he simultaneously worked for the larger Catholic cause. Having
been elected city *consul* in 1571, Yversen was asked to request a governor for his
city. His negotiations were met with great success: soon Mons arrived in Gaillac[45]
where he would orchestrate a Saint Bartholomew's massacre a year later. In 1585
and the following years, Gaillac would continue supporting the Catholic cause,
regularly giving troops to the League.[46] In light of this context, the *boiserie* can
be seen to assert Yversen's individual power, as well as the Catholics' final victory over the Protestants in Gaillac, and it is tempting to imagine that Joyeuse, the
Catholic *Ligueur* who walked through Gaillac in 1586,[47] could have seen it.

One of the dilemmas facing French Catholics during the wars of religion was to
determine what to do with a growing, organized, and virulent religious minority.

The answers ranged from the *moyenneurs'* balanced policy, to extreme calls for violent retaliation, all of which contributed to what Crouzet has termed the "civilisation de l'angoisse." For Yversen in his native southwest, the solution was simple: Protestants had to be eliminated and the crusade was the most efficient way to achieve that result. The Gaillacois displayed his agenda in a *boiserie* that placed him at the forefront of the religious battle. The panel suggests that Yversen was particularly well-positioned to counter the new faith that had been steadily gaining ground in his native region. Experienced in the ways of religious *Others*—the Ottomans—and having delivered strong and difficult messages in the past, the Gaillacois was perfectly equipped to respond to the Protestant threat. Yversen's coat of arms and its position on the sculpture suggest a central and powerful individual, one who, both on the *boiserie* and in real life, was able to stand out and impose an assertive presence on all sides: visually on the left and on the right of the artwork, but also politically and religiously on the French and the Ottomans, and their counterparts, the Catholics and Protestants. The "machinery of persecution" put in place by Lateran IV and first aimed at Jews, lepers, homosexuals, and heretics, was now being used to crush the Protestants.[48]

Crusading Protestants would have been a powerful proposition in sixteenth-century France and yet, it was not an unusual one in southwestern France. The originality of the *boiserie* then lies in its form more than in its content. More subtle and nuanced than Catholic printed propaganda circulating at the time, Yversen's is a unique sculpture that suggests a knowledge and an understanding of the *Other*: the Ottomans, and by extension, then, of the Protestant as well. Yversen's motto graces his coat of arms and reflects the ambiguity of the Gaillacois's position regarding alterity: *fontes allii cœlum peto*, reads the *boiserie*, "from the fountain of others, I reach the sky." Ironically, his knowledge of the Ottoman world served his diplomacy but also his crusade against the Protestants.

By calling forth a not so distant historical past and by visually bringing the Ottomans to a small town in the heart of religiously torn southwestern France, Yversen firmly asserts his personal influence in Gaillac and beyond for centuries to come. Like a peacock spreading its most beautiful feathers, Yversen performs early modern diplomacy aimed at individual advancement. Adding experience in the East to literacy, he was able to satisfy his social ambition.[49] Three sonnets glorifying the diplomat and his political successes illustrate the long-lasting effects of his refashioning. Signed O. Blondeau,[50] these short pieces praise the Gaillacois' accomplishments. They tell of his later years of learning in Paris and summarize Yversen's life and devotion to France, particularly to his king, in an anagram that transforms the diplomat's name into the monarch's own: JEHAN YVERSEN—EN HENRY SA VIE (Figure 6.17). Yversen, the poem suggests, gave his life to his king as a diplomat; he also gave Henri life by fashioning a new image of his superiors, particularly Ambassador La Vigne and Sultan Suleÿman, and more importantly of himself. Significantly, sonnet 1 includes a very visible particle in the diplomat's name: "sonnet pour Estreinnes (?) à Monsr Dyversen."[51] Diplomacy enabled Jean Yversen to become noble. Jean d'Yversen was born.

Figure 6.17 Undated sonnet by O. Blondeau, glorifying Yversen. Private archive.

Notes

1 Frédéric Tinguely evaluates the works by such scholars, who include Belon, Chesneau, Gassot, Gilles, Nicolay, Postel, and Thevet. See Tinguely, *L'écriture du Levant.*
2 On La Borderie, see Chapter 5. On the rise of anthropology as a means to organize the large amount of information on the 'Turks,' see Höfert, "The Order of Things."

3 Yversen was born before 1532 and died circa 1604, the year of his testament.

4 Hampton, *Fictions of Embassy: Literature and Diplomacy in Early Modern Europe* (Ithaca, NY: Cornell University Press, 2009), 8.

5 See Garrett Mattingly, *Renaissance Diplomacy* (London: Butler and Tanner, 1955), Chapter 5, particularly 55–63.

6 Interestingly enough, diplomacy in the second half of the twentieth century and today favors, once again, the dispatch of special envoys whose understanding of a specific region and culture make their services invaluable, whereas the ambassador has become more of a bureaucrat who rarely engages in political negotiations.

7 Cited from Yversen's 'travel journal' (21), analyzed and partially transcribed by Marie-Thérèse de Martel, "La mission de Jean Yversen à la Porte du grand Seigneur," *Revue d'Histoire Diplomatique* 12 (1983): 5–53.

8 "Amityé" is a term often employed in early modern diplomacy where it describes an agreement that is both social and private, very much utilitarian in nature as well as reciprocal. Yversen reports that "... led. s^r ambassadeur y œuvra si bien que le Grand Seigneur en est resté content et satisfaict ... et l'amytié ... est aujourd'huy plus ferme que jamais" (The said ambassador worked on this so well that the Sultan felt content and satisfied ... and [that] our friendship ... today is stronger than ever), ibid., 22.

9 On self-fashioning, see Stephen Greenblatt's seminal work, *Renaissance Self-Fashioning: From More to Shakespeare* (Chicago: University of Chicago Press, 1980).

10 Daniela Frigo, "Prudence and Experience: Ambassadors and Political Culture in Early Modern Italy," *The Journal of Medieval and Early Modern Studies* 38, no. 1 (2008): 15–34, here 19.

11 Like the earlier ones described by Mattingly, *Renaissance Diplomacy*, 28–33.

12 Frigo, "Prudence and Experience," 21.

13 Frigo argues in her analysis of de Rosier that *prudenza* is one of the most important qualities for an early modern diplomat. "Prudence and Experience," 24–29.

14 Mattingly, *Renaissance Diplomacy*, 21.

15 Frigo, "Prudence and Experience," 29.

16 Yversen, "Estat des paquets," folio 1, private archive.

17 Letter dated June 21, 1559 and printed in Charrière, *Négociations*, vol. 2. The letter is on pages 582–90; the reference to Yversen and his title are on pages 582 and 583 respectively.

18 Dax was to become French ambassador in Constantinople in 1571 and remain in that position until 1575.

19 Diane de Poitiers, also known as the Duchess of Valentinois, was Francis I's mistress. A letter in Gaillac's private archive, written by La Vigne and addressed to the Duchess, identifies Yversen as the carrier. This suggests that Yversen could have been sent to the French court to report on a particular mission.

20 Hampton, *Fictions of Embassy*, 49.

21 On the 1543 "hivernement," see Isom-Verhaaren, "'Barbarossa and His Army'."

22 De Rosier was bishop of Toulouse between 1400 and 1475. For biographical information on de Rosier and on his writings, see Patrick Arabeyre, "Un prélat languedocien au milieu du XVe siècle: Bernard de Rosier, archevêque de Toulouse (1400–1475)," *Journal des Savants* no. 3–4 (1990): 291–326. On de Rosier's *Ambaxiator Brevilogus* and its importance in medieval and Renaissance diplomacy, see Mattingly, *Renaissance Diplomacy*, 34–44. Frigo insists, rightfully so, on the "role" or "office" of the diplomat delineated in de Rosier, as opposed to the institution of diplomacy which did not develop until much later. See Frigo, "Prudence and Experience," 15–16.

23 Yversen may have drafted several other documents during his diplomatic career in the East. He may have contributed, for example, to the composition of the message handed directly to the sultan in 1555. The Gaillac archive holds a piece entitled "*double de ce qui a este propose par escript au grand seigneur*," which corresponds to what Yversen

describes in his letter to Noailles as the written request given to the sultan. A second document accompanies it; this one must have been for Yversen only since it gives advice as to what to reply to the sultan's possible objections.

24 Three primary sources inform us on the wars of religion in Yversen's hometown. Mathieu Blouin, who was born in Gaillac in 1554, is the author of *Historio vertadieiro*, a rhymed chronicle in Occitan written in the 1580s, and of memoirs (in French) that detail religious troubles in Gaillac up to 1574. Both works were translated and published by Ernest Nègre in *Les troubles à Gaillac* (Toulouse: Collège d'Occitanie, 1976.) Jacques Gaches and Jean Faurin are additional contemporary observers who focus on Castres, but they also mention Gaillac. See *Mémoires de Jacques Gaches sur les guerres de religion à Castres et dans le Languedoc (1555–1610)*, ed. Charles Pradel (Geneva: Slatkine Reprints, 1970) and "Journal de Faurin sur les guerres de Castres," in recueil factice *Varia histoire locale* vol. 39 s.l., s.d., Archives départementales du Tarn, ADTarn BIB C1420, 425–702. The following nineteenth-century works, which are based on earlier sources, are also worth consulting: Elie Rossignol, *Monographies communales: Gaillac* (Toulouse: Delboy, 1864); and Cl. de Vic et J. Vaissete, *Histoire générale de Languedoc*, vol. 11 (Toulouse: Privat, 1889). The following remarks are based on these works.

25 Gaches, *Mémoires*, 24–25; Rossignol, *Monographies communales*, 5. Blouin dedicates Chapters 3 through 6 of his memoirs to the 1562 events; see Nègre, *Les troubles à Gaillac*.

26 Gaches, *Mémoires*, 53; Rossignol, *Monographies communales*, 78.

27 Gaches, *Mémoires*, 76–77. Chapters 7 and 8 in Blouin's memoirs detail the year 1568, and Chapters 9 and 10 focus on 1570; see Nègre, *Les troubles à Gaillac*.

28 Letter from Audrand dated 1570, private archive.

29 Elie Rossignol considers Yversen's family to be a respectable one: "*La famille d'Yversen, une des plus ancienne [sic] de la ville, dont plusieurs membres ont occupé les premières charges du consulat*" (The Yversen family, one of the oldest of the city, of which several members were *consuls*) See *Monographies communales*, 107.

30 Marie Cadet describes Audrand as "Chanoine de Gaillac et vicaire général du cardinal de Bourbon" in "La boiserie de cheminée de l'hôtel d'Yversen à Gaillac en 1584: Mémoire de maîtrise d'histoire de l'art dirigé par Christine Aribaud," 2006, unpublished, 84.

31 Letter from Audrand, private archive.

32 Letter from the cardinal de Bourbon addressed to Damville, mar(echal) de France, private archive.

33 "Proclamation de sentence arbitralle de noble Jehan yversen cap(itaine) de Coffoleux contre Jehanne yversenhe," private archive.

34 Nègre, *Les troubles à Gaillac*, 227. The French translation is on page 232: "un bourgeois, appelé noble Jean d'Iversen, catholique très zelé, grand parleur et bon orateur."

35 It has been impossible to date the painting and to confirm that it represents the sixteenth-century envoy and was part of the initial commission. Therefore I will not discuss it here. In these considerations, I follow Cadet's careful analysis in "La boiserie."

36 That is to say, an official report given in writing after an oral presentation to one's superior.

37 *Que le XXIXᵉ de may 1559, arrivys à costantinople avecques une despeche du Roy de la nouvelle de la paix que messeigneurs le Cardinal de Tournon et évesques dacqs me bailliarent à Venize et me commandarent de l'apporter a monseigneur de la Vigne, ambassadeur de Sa Majesté auprès de Grand Seigneur, qui fust fort aise de ma venue affin d'entendre les conditions de lad. Paix car le baille des Vénytiens, quelques jours auparavant, en avoit donné la nouvelle à la Porte quelle estoit faicte, dont les articles, toutesfois, estoyent fort differens de ceulx que j'y apportis.*

On May 29, 1559, I arrived in Constantinople with a message of peace from the King handed to me by Cardinal de Tournon and Bishop of Dax in Venice. They requested that I bring it to Sir La Vigne, her Majesty's ambassador to the Sultan, who was delighted that I came to tell the conditions of the said peace for, several days earlier, the Venetian bailo had broken the news to the Porte, the articles of the peace agreement, however, being significantly different from the ones I had brought there.

The ambiguity stems from the relative clause ("qui fust fort aise de ma venue") which follows "Grand Seigneur" instead of "la Vigne" as it should. This almost imperceptible ambiguity is quickly and astutely solved in the sentences following this quote.

38 *"Il alla baisser la main de sa Haultesse et luy présenta un rescript qu'il luy bailla de sa main, choze non accoustumée, et se retira à l'entrée dud. pavyllon et, après, l'on me mena aussi baiser la main et, ce faict, me retirois auprest dud sr ambassadeur qui parla à sa Haultesse en ceste sorte"* (23) (He went to kiss his Highness's hand, presented to him a letter which he gave to him personally, an unusual step, and moved back to the entrance of the said pavillion; afterwards, I was also brought to kiss the [sultan's] hand and, once this was done, I went back next to the ambassador who spoke to his Highness in this way).

39 Emphasis mine.

40 According to Cadet in "La boiserie," it may have been commissioned and/or made at a different period.

41 Denis Crouzet, *Les guerriers de Dieu: La violence au temps des troubles de religion (vers 1525–vers 1610)* (Seyssel: Champ Vallon, 1990) and Gould, *Catholic Activism in South-West France.*

42 Vic and Vaissete, *Histoire générale de Languedoc*, 509; Gould, *Catholic Activism in South-West France*, 137–42. Gould insists, rightfully, on southwest France's early Catholic activism and describes pre-League organizations in Bordeaux, Agen, and Toulouse set up by local powers.

43 See Louis d'Izarny-Gargas, ed., *Armorial de France: Généralité de Toulouse* (Paris: Sedopols, 1987), 34. This edition contains descriptions of blasons with abbreviations and is based on manuscripts held in the Bibliothèque Nationale de France. The *Armorial général des registres de la noblesse de France* gives the following description: "D'or, à un cerf courant ailé de gueules, ayant le bois de sable ; et un chef d'azur, chargé d'un soleil d'or et de deux croissants d'argent." See Louis-Pierre d'Hozier et Antoine-Marie d'Hozier de Sérigny, *Armorial général des registres de la noblesse de France* (Édouard de Barthélemy ed. Paris: E. Dentu, 1867), 310–11. The most complete document includes a black and white rendition of Yversen's blason, a precise listing of the six degrees of lignage linking "Noble Charles d'Yversen-de Saint Fons II. du nom né le14 juillet 1710" to his ancestor Jean, and transcriptions of original letters showing the family's nobility. It is printed and signed d'Hozier. See *Archives départementales du Tarn*, ADTarn BIB C2293[5]. Two other emblems are present on the boiserie, referring to Yversen's wives: Catherine de Reynes and Jeanne Carivenc.

44 Rossignol, *Monographies communales*, 169.

45 " . . . *mais bientôt (1572) les catholiques, sur de nouvelles agitations des protestants, firent demander par le consul Jean d'Hyversenc, une compagnie de soldats au maréchal, qui leur envoya le capitaine Mons pour gouverneur.*" (. . . but soon, the Catholics, seeing new agitation from the part of the Protestants, asked the city's representative, Jean d'Hyversenc, to request soldiers from Damville, who sent them Captain Mons as governor), ibid., 79.

46 Ibid., 80, 81.

47 Ibid., 5, 80.

48 R. I. Moore, *The Formation of a Persecuting Society: Authority and Deviance in Western Europe, 950–1250* (Oxford: Blackwell, 1987), 10.

49 Moore describes the replacement of warriors by literate clerks as agents of government, and literacy as a tool for power and influence. See Moore, *Formation*, 129.

50 The sonnets are not dated and I could not identify their author. It was perhaps the early seventeenth century *agent général du clergé* mentioned in *Dictionnaire de l'Ancien Régime*, 2nd ed. (Paris: Presses universitaires de France, 2003), 41.

51 Yversen's nobility was challenged in the nineteenth century; see Cadet, "La boiserie." Blouin, a contemporary and city-fellow of Yversen, does not question it and refers to the Gaillacois as d'Yversen, but most sixteenth-century documents do not include the particle.

Conclusion

Birds of a Feather Flock Together?

From the second half of the sixteenth century on, few French commentators remained amicable towards the Ottomans. In his *République* (1576), Jean Bodin praised the Ottoman system for its meritocracy and practice of religious tolerance and favorably compared the military organisation of the 'Turks' to those of the ancient Romans.[1] Distinguishing between three types of monarchy—'royal' monarchy, 'seigneurial' monarchy, and tyranny—he assimilated the Ottoman sultan to a 'seigneurial' monarch, much closer to a 'royal' monarch than a tyrant on his political spectrum.[2] Similarly, Montaigne applauded the discipline of the Ottomans, and Guillaume Postel, in *De la Republique des Turcs* (1560) suspended—at times—his judgment toward those with whom he lived.[3] When approaching the 'Turks,' however, thinkers of the second half of the sixteenth century were not as bold as their predecessors—Rabelais, Lemaire de Belges, and Jacques de Bourbon. Focusing on the political, their reasoned analyses remove the human, collective, and sometimes emotional response visible in previous analyses. Frank Lestringant has shown that, in their various portrayals of Süleyman, François de Belleforest and André Thevet acknowledged a certain number of positive traits while underscoring the sultan's negative characteristics.[4] The evolution of Belleforest's impression of Süleyman is most striking: between 1575 and 1583, the Ottoman sultan becomes less and less appealing in the writings of the French cosmographer.[5] The diverse sources used by Belleforest and the different genres in which he writes may account for his contrasting portraits of Süleyman. Furthermore, the religious political context of the period undoubtedly played a role in the gradual change of perspective. The passage of time must also be accounted for in this case and more generally. Süleyman died in 1566 after 40 years of rule that had generated accrued contacts with the Ottomans and wide and conflicting accounts about their origins, ways of ruling, and religious and cultural customs. By the 1560s, the Ottoman coin that was once tossed, making its two sides visible, had fallen on tails, and the French had opted for one dismal narrative over several others.[6]

La France-Turquie

A pamphlet appearing at the height of the French wars of religion exemplifies the single discourse on the 'Turks' the French would adopt in the second half of the sixteenth century, eventually extending it to all Muslims. *La France-Turquie* was published in 1575. Its complete title reveals its strong political and ideological bent: *La France-Turquie C'est-à-dire conseils et moyens tenus par les ennemis de la Couronne de France pour reduire le royaume en tel estat que la Tyrañie Turquesque* (France-Turkey, that is to say the advice and means suggested by the enemies of the French kingdom to reduce the kingdom to Turkish tyranny).[7] Coming out of the printing shop of Thibault des Murs in Orléans, the pamphlet exposes Catherine de Médicis's and the Comte de Retz's scheme to turn France into a despotic 'Turquie.' The polemical piece is divided into three sections: an introduction entitled and seemingly addressed to "A tous princes seigneurs, gentils-hommes & autres bons & legitimes François, tãt d'une que d'autre Religion" (all princes, lords, gentlemen, and other good and legitimate Frenchmen, from one religion or another), the "Preface du Florentin" forming the heart of the political diatribe, and the "Advis du traducteur" which serves as a short conclusion and additional padding to the incendiary accusation. The introductory piece narrates an unexpected and fortuitous encounter, in May 1574, between the anonymous narrator of *La France-Turquie*, a Frenchman, and an Italian from Florence. Most likely fictitious, the meeting is depicted precisely so as to give a convincingly realistic tone to the pamphlet while effectively exonerating the French narrator from potential accusations of *crime de lèse-majesté*. Returning from long travels that have left him penniless, the narrator explains how he was pleased to meet a Francophile Italian and to accept his hospitality. The Frenchman recognizes his host right away—he has seen him previously in Paris and at the French court—and insinuates that in the Italian's body a French soul took hold.[8] The traveler is eager to accept both the Italian's unconditional love for France as well as a troubling story concerning the kingdom's darker side. Indeed the Italian gentleman reveals the plot that has begun to engulf France: following an incongruous meeting between Chevalier Poncet and members of the French court of which he was a witness, the French kingdom has descended into uncontrollable religious and political violence and is about to turn into a tyrannical state. The Italian tells his French guest that he has immortalized the meeting and the gist of Poncet's speech in writing. At the end of the introductory passage, the account has been delivered both orally and in writing. Now in the French traveler-narrator's possession, it is about to be divulged to a wider audience in France. Translated into French by the narrator, the Italian's story is what forms the backbone of *La France-Turquie*.

The second and main section of *La France-Turquie* aims primarily at political reformation, or rather, in the eye of the polemicist, restoration. The religious wars are said to be Catherine de Médicis and de Retz's means to get rid of French nobility. The entire work is propelled by the St. Bartholomew's massacre and by the 'Turks,' two elements that are closely connected. The preface of the Italian gentleman begins squarely with a reference to August 24, 1572, 'la journee sainct Barthelemy' (6) when Catholics in Paris slaughtered Protestants. Those who escaped the carnage left the city, sometimes even the country. One of the exiled is the Italian gentleman who was shocked by "l'horreur des execrables plus inhumains & plus detestables massacres qui furent iamais faicts auparauant au monde" (the horror of the execrable, most inhuman, and most detestable massacres ever committed in the world). According to *La France-Turquie*, the St. Bartholomew's massacre is a direct consequence and application of the "doctrine Poncetique,"[9] a set of guidelines named after Poncet's speech to de Retz and Catherine of Médicis in which the Chevalier presented what he considered the ideal political reform for France.

The pamphlet details the Ottoman tyranny from which springs the narrative and the argument, anchoring Orientalist thought in France. The description of the Ottomans is based, according to the narrative, on Poncet's travel experience in 'Turquie.' The Chevalier claims that the power of the sultan, one that the French royal house should strive to emulate, is based on the absence of nobility and of religious pluralism. In 'Turquie', there is neither prince nor lord, but janissaries who are raised by the sultan and trained to obey him unconditionally from a very young age, Poncet declares. Additionally, there is no religious debate, but only one religion, that of the sultan.[10] As a result, everything belongs to the sultan and everyone obeys him. In this passage, the image of the 'Turks' is an implacable and unidimensional one. Simplified to the extreme, tyrannical 'Turquie' serves as a potential mirror for France as it grapples with religious wars and as a political foil for the author of *La France-Turquie*, who blames the 'Turks' as much as Poncet's discourse for causing the St. Bartholomew's massacre. In the final segment of *La France-Turquie*, the reader returns to the French traveler who concludes by summarizing what he has learned from his Italian host: the French kingdom is in imminent danger and its future at stake because of the actions of Catherine de Médicis and de Retz; Frenchmen must react.

The Bayerische Staatsbibliothek München's copy of *La France-Turquie* includes two additional documents that reinforce the message of the pamphlet.[11] The first of these pieces is entitled "L'antipharmaque du Chevalier Poncet" (Poncet's antidote). Signed by the Chevalier himself, it is the official rebuttal to *La France-Turquie*. Published in Paris by Federic Morel in 1575, it gives credence to the pseudo-objectivity of the published volume by including Poncet's own counter-opinion and thereby giving the illusion of a balanced and healthy societal debate. In this segment, Poncet responds vehemently to the accusations made in *La France-Turquie*. He spent over three years in 'Turquie' and not seven or eight as alleged by the Frenchman in Italian clothes, whom he accuses of being a fugitive seeking to agitate France through his rare apparitions in public, which remind Poncet of none other than the invisible and controlling Ottoman sultan. Everyone then is accused of being a 'Turk' in *La France-Turquie*—Catherine de Médicis, Poncet, and also the anonymous author of the pamphlet. Protestants have become *têtes de turc* for Catholics, and vice versa.

The closing section reiterates the danger that Poncet and his ideas represent for France. It is wryly titled "Lunettes de cristal de roche, par lesquelles on veoyt clairement le chemin tenu pour subiuguer la France, à mesme obeissance que la Turquie: adressees à tous Princes, Seigneurs, Gentils hommes, & autres d'une & d'autre Religion, bons & legitimes Françoys. Pour servir aussi de Contre-poison à l'Antipharmaque, du Chevalier Poncet" (Crystal-clear glasses, used to see plainly the path followed to subjugate France to the same obedience as Turkey, addressed to all princes, lords, gentlemen and others of one religion or another, good and legitimate Frenchmen. To serve as counter-poison to Poncet's counter-poison). This is the feather that broke the camel's back. In this section, the anonymous author of *La France-Turquie* responds to Poncet, whom he compares to a "maquerelle" (a female pimp). He vividly stresses the horrifying acts seen during the wars of religion—rapes, thefts of goods and cattle, acts of cannibalism on young children, famine—before proposing a concrete plan of action. First, the Queen, having shown herself to be a poor administrator for the kingdom, must be prevented from having any further political role in France and, given her age, safely locked up in a convent. A close advisor to Catherine de Médicis and one of the first propagandists of the St. Bartholomew's massacre, the *Chancelier* is a pompous man unaware of the French laws; as such, he is to be sacked and declared politically incompetent. Similarly, all counsellors must remove themselves from their responsibilities. Last but not least, foreigners and illegitimate Frenchmen ("les estrangiers & ceux qui ne seront naturels & legitimes François") must be expelled from office. As a result, the French kingdom will unite behind new representatives. Once these measures are taken, claims the anonymous author of *La France-Turquie*, peace, order, and safety will prevail in the French kingdom.

Despite three decades of a tolerated and sometimes openly supported alliance between Ottoman and French, the contamination of 'Turquie' over the French kingdom never felt as real as in 1575. Never mind that the French, more than other peoples, are "naturellement traitable par douceur & amitié, & nullement flexible par cruauté & excessive rigueur" (by nature responsive to being treated [politically] with kindness and friendship, and never moved by cruelty and excessive rigor), everyone in France, every political and religious opponent, is now a 'Turk.' The pamphlet, therefore, erases 30 years of both covert and public collaboration between Ottomans and French and puts an end to alternate views of eastern neighbors at the risk of anchoring Ottoman Turks as irreducible enemies who aim at denaturalizing France. In one of the last appearances of the Ottomans in the text, the 'Turks' are animals, not men. In turn dogs, ants, and flies, the 'Turks' are "bestes brutes qui n'endurent jamais le semblable"[12] (brutal beasts that never can stand their like) unable to work together. Molinet's apocalyptic yet inclusive brush has been replaced by the polemicist's image of the 'Turk' as a brutal barbarian, an ireductible and incommensurate foe. The urgent tone of the pamphlet reminds us of Molinet's "Complainte de Grèce." However, *La France-Turquie* does not stage allegorical queens; rather, it presents the reader with one very real Queen Mother who is being held responsible for France's woes. Furthermore, the viewpoint is radically different from the *rhétoriqueur*'s poem. Whereas Molinet was looking outward to France, Greece, and 'Turquie,' the anonymous author of *La France-Turquie* pushes back at foreign influence, closing the door to the Italians and, above all, the 'Turks' by looking inward to French Protestants and Catholics. The pamphlet shows that during the course of the sixteenth century the crusade against Islam transformed into a crusade against a much closer enemy, Protestants—for whom Catholics were the principal enemies.[13] *La France-Turquie* denounces and rejects possibilities, particularly the option of "turning Turk," that is to say the option of considering and potentially adopting unorthodox ideas and beliefs.

La France-Turquie of 1575, which coincides roughly with the publication of Jean Bodin's *République*, marks the conclusion of a rich reflection on the Ottomans. It also marks the end of an era based on communal understanding, according to which many shared responsibilities, duties, and rights in a society that was highly codified to the exclusion of some but still allowed for a plurality of opinions regarding the *Other*. The pamphlet seals the beginning of an early modern Orientalist mode of operation in France. Carefully framed, the work does not make possible any alternative vision of either mid-sixteenth-century France's political reality or the Ottomans. Despite—or perhaps because of—the Ottoman defeat by Christian naval forces at Lepanto in 1571, experiencing the Orient becomes harmful, and the tyrannical Orient is now a *topos* that will be difficult to extirpate when dealing with other peoples of the East—such as the Persians and the Mughals in the seventeenth century, or the North Africans in the nineteenth, twentieth, and twenty-first centuries before, during, and after France's colonial empire.

A New Kind of Flock

Despite increased information stemming from scholars returning from Constantinople and the Levant, French knowledge and understanding of the Ottomans remained limited in the sixteenth century. Nevertheless, all the authors studied in this book sensed enough commonalities with their Eastern neighbors to be able to also detect particularities—a different pattern of social promotion, or a certain degree of religious toleration, for example. Attempting to decipher Ottoman specificities—*singularités*—Frenchmen first explored the Ottoman Empire and the Islamic world at large, formulating ideas about new forms of government for themselves. Soon, however, their *esprit de curiosité* was hampered by religious issues closer to home and gave way to a more pragmatic and reductive mode of thinking. French knowledge and understanding of the Ottomans became limiting as concepts of the individual and of empire evolved and strengthened in France. It is not far-fetched to talk about a rapid "rétrécissement de la pensée," a shrinking of discernment in the second half of the century for, between 1510 and 1560, the conic view of the Ottomans narrowed until one image only, that of the cruel 'Turk,' dominated more tolerant others. The time for encounters had ended.

This book has told the story of the rise and fall of the Ottomans in Renaissance France. Religious heterogeneity and consolidation of absolutism coincided with a rapidly evolving French society marked by the coming of a new individual and the transforming of a communal age. As the world became wider, more easily explorable, and debated, the budding nation of France dreamt of empire. The Ottomans were the perfect instrument with which to gauge the deep systemic changes that were taking place in the first half of the sixteenth century. Far from being mere tools, they were acknowledged as being prominent players in the great Mediterranean political arena and were also envisioned as active participants in the societal debates that raged in France between 1510 and 1560. In spite of misconceptions and simplifications about France's new political allies, the multitude of positions regarding the 'Turks'—including the audaciousness and the symbiosis in texts such as Lemaire's *Traicté* or Rabelais's *Pantagruel*—attests to a vibrant culture of openness towards an Islamic *Other*. The end of the romance arrived quickly though, and the French did not remain Ottoman for very long. Signs were already present in the 1540s when La Borderie evoked empire longingly. The confessionalization of the kingdom and the wars of religion precipitated the ossification of the 'Turks.' In the 1570s their stigmatization was firmly engaged, sealed as it were by the publication of an incendiary pamphlet.

It is worth recalling, however, that in the early sixteenth century and particularly up until the 1530s, even though looking to the East might have been a reaction sometimes triggered by angst, it did not produce systematic anxieties in the West. On the contrary, authors like Rabelais were able to create utopian universes out of imagined and real encounters. More interdisciplinary work is needed to uncover early modern Orientalism and the sixteenth-century Franco-Ottoman alliance fully, its immediate repercussions, and its lasting effects. Its "absent existence" should be prompting historians and literary critics, art historians, archaeologists—birds of a different feather as it were—to collaborate and embark on common projects. Scholars of all national origins and ethnicities, all manner of religious upbringing and academic training, medievalists and modernists ought to join forces in order to create a fuller picture of the Franco-Ottoman alliance, the global sixteenth-century world and its relevance for us today. Examining artistic collaboration between sixteenth-century French and Ottomans could yield surprising results. Similarly, records of trade might indicate stronger and more intricate economic ties and competition between the two allies. Research in the Catholic Church's archives might also shed light on early missions to the Ottoman lands. This book, thus, invites further dialogue between historians and critics of literature. It calls for further studies on the perceptions of France by early modern Ottomans and on the connections that characterized the early modern era.

The sixteenth century in France was a period of deep change when empire began to occupy center stage. Toying with the idea of allying with empire, France ended up becoming one herself, albeit several decades later and in other geographical places. With the centralization of political power and the hardening of religious lines, the diversity of voices disappeared and the individual lost the freedom to exist collectively. This book has tried to give a voice to lesser-known texts and ideas as well as competing discourses that coexisted until French society became more homogenized due to internal religious pressures combined with the emergence of a nation-state. It has highlighted a period when religion was sacrosanct and permeated every work and yet did not warrant a full-fledged policy of conversion, until the 1570s. It is time to rediscover and reclaim the many paths of intellectual and political curiosity that defined the early sixteenth century.

Notes

1 Noel Malcolm, "Positive Views of Islam and of Ottoman Rule in the Sixteenth Century: The Case of Jean Bodin," in *The Renaissance and the Ottoman World*, ed. Anna Contadini and Claire Norton (Burlington, VT: Ashgate, 2013), 197–217, here 201–2.

Malcolm expands on Frank Lestringant, "La monarchie française au miroir ottoman: Le portrait de Soliman le Magnifique, de Charles XII à Henri III," in Veinstein, ed., *Soliman le Magnifique et son temps*, 51–68, here 54–56.

2 Malcolm, "Positive Views of Islam," 204–10. Here Malcolm focuses on Bodin's *Colloquium heptaplomeres*, written in the 1590s.

3 Tinguely, *L'écriture du Levant*.

4 Lestringant, "La monarchie française."

5 Ibid., 57–59.

6 After the initial shock and mobilization, the French vision of the Ottomans, therefore, was not as balanced as Andrei Pippidi would have it. See Pippidi, *Visions of the Ottoman Empire*.

7 *La France-Turquie, C'est à dire, conseils et moyens tenus par les ennemis de la Couronne de France, pour reduire le royaume en tel estat que la Tyrãnie Turquesque* (Orléans: Thibault des Murs, 1576).

8 "*Si l'oppiniõ de Pytagoras estoit autant veritable comme elle est faulse, i'aurois occasion de penser que l'ame de quelque François du temps passé, sentant encores son Adam, s'estoit logee dans le corps de cest homme lors du poinct de sa naissance*" (*La France-Turquie*, 4) (If Pythagoras's opinion were true as much as it is false, I would have thought that the soul of some Frenchman from the past, still close to Adam, had found a home in the body of this man as he was being born).

9 *La France-Turquie*, 57.

10 Poncet, however, concedes that recently captured territories remain, for an undetermined amount of time, more religiously diverse.

11 Available online. Last accessed June 29, 2015.

12 *La France-Turquie*, 54.

13 Michael J. Heath, *Crusading Commonplaces: La Noue, Lucinge and Rhetoric against the Turks* (Geneva: Droz, 1986).

Bibliography

Abélard, Jacques. "Les *Illustrations de Gaule* de Jean Lemaire de Belges—Quelle Gaule? Quelle France? Quelle nation?" *Nouvelle Revue du Seizième Siècle* 13, no. 1 (1995): 7–27.

Abulafia, David. *The Great Sea: A Human History of the Mediterranean*. Oxford: Oxford University Press, 2011.

Agamben, Giorgio. *Profanations*. Translated by Jeff Fort. New York: Zone Books, 2007.

———. *Profanations*. Translated by Martin Rueff. Paris: Payot et Rivages, 2005.

Akşit, Ilhan. *Treasures of Istanbul*. Istanbul: Haset Kitabevi Tünel, 1982.

Andrews, Walter G. and Mehmet Kalpaklı, *The Age of Beloveds: Love and the Beloved in Early-Modern Ottoman and European Culture and Society* (Durham, Duke University Press, 2005).

Apologie, faicte par un serviteur du roy, contre les calomnies des imperiaulx: sur la descente du Turc. Paris: Charles Étienne, 1552.

App, Urs. *The Birth of Orientalism*. Philadelphia, PA: University of Pennsylvania Press, 2010.

Arabeyre, Patrick. "Un prélat languedocien au milieu du XVe siècle: Bernard de Rosier, archevêque de Toulouse (1400–1475)." *Journal des Savants* no. 3–4 (1990): 291–326.

Atıl, Esin. *The Age of Sultan Süleyman the Magnificent*. Washington, DC: National Gallery of Art, 1987.

———. *Turkish Art*. Washington, DC: Smithsonian Institution Press, 1980.

Attar, Farid ud-Din. *The Conference of the Birds*. 1177. Translated by Afkham Darbandi and Dick Davis. Harmondsworth, UK: Penguin Books, 1984.

———. *La conférence des oiseaux*. Adapted by Henri Gougaud from the translation by Manijeh Nouri-Ortega. Paris: Points, 2010.

Auerbach, Erich. *Mimesis: The Representation of Reality in Western Literature*. Translated by Willard R. Trask. Princeton: Princeton University Press, 1953.

Aubigné, Agrippa d'. *Les Tragiques*. 1616. Edited by Frank Lestringant. Paris: Gallimard, 1995.

Baghdiantz McCabe, Ina. *Orientalism in Early Modern France: Eurasian Trade, Exoticism and the* Ancien Régime. Oxford: Berg, 2008.

Balibar, Étienne. *Droit de cité*. Paris: Presses universitaires de France, 2002.

Barthe, Pascale. "Oriens Theatralis: La France dans le miroir de *La Soltane* de Gabriel Bounin." *EMF: Studies in Early Modern France* 13 (2010): 107–20.

———. " 'Paroles scellées': nature et langage en Turquie dans les *Observations* de Pierre Belon. *L'Esprit Créateur* 53, no. 4 (2013): 21–33.

————. "Du Turc au traître: Les chevaliers de Saint-Jean-de-Jérusalem, les Ottomans et la France de François Ier dans *L'oppugnation* de Jacques de Bourbon." *French Historical Studies* 30, no. 3 (2007): 427–49.

Beaune, Colette. *Naissance de la nation France*. Paris: Gallimard, 1985.

Belon, Pierre. *Les observations de plusieurs singularitez et choses memorables, trouvées en Grece, Asie, Judée, Arabie, et autres pays estranges*. Paris: Guillaume Cavellat et Gilles Corrozet, 1553.

————. *Voyage au Levant (1553): Les observations de Pierre Belon du Mans de plusieurs singularités & choses mémorables, trouvées en Grèce, Turquie, Judée, Égypte, Arabie et autres pays étranges (1553)*. Edited by Alexandra Merle. Paris: Chandeigne, 2001.

Bély, Lucien, ed. *Dictionnaire de l'Ancien Régime*. 2nd ed. Paris: Presses universitaires de France, 2003.

Bennassar, Bartolomé, and Lucile Bennassar. *Les chrétiens d'Allah: L'histoire extraordinaire des renégats, XVIe et XVIIe siècles*. Paris: Perrin, 1989.

Ben-Zaken, Avner. *Cross-Cultural Scientific Exchanges in the Eastern Mediterranean, 1560–1660*. Baltimore: Johns Hopkins University Press, 2010.

Bhabha, Homi. *The Location of Culture*. London: Routledge, 1994.

Blanchard, Pascal, Naïma Yahi, Yvan Gastaut, and Nicolas Bancel. *La France arabo-orientale: Treize siècles de présences du Maghreb, de la Turquie, d'Égypte, du Moyen-Orient et du Proche-Orient*. Paris: La Découverte, 2013.

Bounin, Gabriel. *La Soltane*. 1561. Edited by Michael Heath. Exeter: University of Exeter, 1977.

Bourbon, Jacques de. *La grande et merueilleuse et trescruelle oppugnation de la noble cite de Rhodes prinse naguieres par Sultan Seliman a present grand Turcq ennemy de la tressaincte foy Catholicque*. Paris, 1525.

Bourrilly, Victor-Louis. "L'ambassade de La Forest et de Marillac à Constantinople." *Revue Historique* 76 (1901): 297–328.

————. "Un ambassadeur turc à Marseille en octobre 1534," *Revue Historique de Provence* 1 (1901): 463–69.

————. "Bertrand de La Borderie et 'Le discours du voyage de Constantinople.'" *Revue des Études Rabelaisiennes* 9 (1911): 183–220.

————, ed. *Histoire journalière d'Honorat de Valbelle*. See Valbelle, Honorat de.

Braudel, Fernand. *La Méditerranée et le monde méditerranéen à l'époque de Philippe II*. 1949; rev. ed., Paris: Armand Colin, 1966.

Britnell, Jennifer. "The Antipapalism of Jean Lemaire de Belges' *Traité de la Difference des Schismes et des Conciles*." *Sixteenth Century Journal* 24, no. 4 (1993): 783–800.

————. "Jean Lemaire de Belges and Prophecy." *Journal of the Warburg and Courtauld Institutes* 42 (1979): 144–66.

Brockman, Eric. *The Two Sieges of Rhodes, 1480–1522*. London: Cox and Wyman, 1969.

Brotton, Jerry. *The Renaissance Bazaar: From the Silk Road to Michelangelo*. Oxford: Oxford University Press, 2002.

Brown, Cynthia. "The Rise of Literary Consciousness in Late Medieval France: Jean Lemaire de Belges and the *Rhétoriqueur* Tradition." *Journal of Medieval and Renaissance Studies* 13, no. 1 (1983): 51–74.

Brown, Patricia Fortini. *Venice and Antiquity: The Venetian Sense of the Past*. New Haven, CT: Yale University Press, 1996.

Brummett, Palmira. "The Overrated Adversary: Rhodes and Ottoman Naval Power." *The Historical Journal* 36, no. 3 (1993): 517–41.

Bulliet. Richard W. *The Case for Islamo-Christian Civilization.* New York: Columbia University Press, 2004.

Burke, Peter. "The Renaissance Translator as Go-Between." In *Renaissance Go-Betweens: Cultural Exchange in Early Modern Europe*, edited by Andreas Höfele and Werner von Koppenfels, 17–31. Berlin: Walter de Gruyter, 2005.

Bushnell, Amy Turner, and Jack P. Greene. "Peripheries, Centers, and the Construction of Early American Empires." In *Negotiated Empires: Centers and Peripheries in the Americas, 1500–1820*, edited by Christine Daniels and Michael Kennedy, 1–14. New York: Routledge, 2002.

Cadet, Marie. "La boiserie de cheminée de l'hôtel d'Yversen à Gaillac en 1584: Mémoire de maîtrise d'histoire de l'art dirigé par Christine Aribaud." Université de Toulouse II, 2006, unpublished.

Casale, Giancarlo. *The Ottoman Age of Exploration.* Oxford: Oxford University Press, 2010.

Cave, Terence. "Travelers and Others: Cultural Connections in the Works of Rabelais." In *François Rabelais: Critical Assessments*, edited by Jean-Claude Carron, 39–56. Baltimore: Johns Hopkins University Press, 1995.

Certeau, Michel de. *L'écriture de l'histoire.* Paris: Gallimard, 1975.

Charrière, Ernest. *Négociations de la France dans le Levant.* 1848. 4 vols. New York: B. Franklin, 1964.

Chattopadhyaya, D. P. "Itihasa, History and Historiography of Civilization." In *Cultural Otherness and Beyond*, edited by Chhanda Gupta and D. P. Chattopadhyaya, 43–74. Leiden: Brill, 1998.

Clari, Robert de. *La conquête de Constantinople.* Edited by Jean Dufournet. Paris: Champion, 2004.

Clot, André. *Soliman le Magnifique.* Paris: Fayard, 1983.

Contadini, Anna, and Claire Norton, eds. *The Renaissance and the Ottoman World.* Farnham, UK: Ashgate, 2013.

Cooper, Richard. *Rabelais et l'Italie.* Geneva: Droz, 1991.

Crouzet, Denis. *Les guerriers de Dieu: La violence au temps des troubles de religion (vers 1525–vers 1610).* Seyssel: Champ Vallon, 1990.

Dakhlia, Jocelyne. "Musulmans en France et en Grande-Bretagne à l'époque moderne: Exemplaires et invisibles." In Dakhlia and Vincent, *Les musulmans dans l'histoire de l'Europe*, 1: 231–413.

Dakhlia, Jocelyne, and Wolfgang Kaiser, eds. *Les musulmans dans l'histoire de l'Europe.* Vol. 2. Paris: Albin Michel, 2013.

Dakhlia, Jocelyne, and Bernard Vincent, eds. *Les musulmans dans l'histoire de l'Europe.* Vol. 1. Paris: Albin Michel, 2011.

Daniel, Norman. *Islam and the West: The Making of an Image.* Oxford: Oneworld, 1997. First published 1960 by Edinburgh University Press.

Davis, Natalie Zemon. *Trickster Travels: A Sixteenth-Century Muslim between Worlds.* New York: Hill and Wang, 2006.

Devaux, Jean. *Jean Molinet, indiciaire bourguignon.* Paris: Champion, 1996.

Dew, Nicholas. *Orientalism in Louis XIV's France.* Oxford: Oxford University Press, 2009.

Du Bellay, Joachim. *La deffence et illustration de la langue françoyse.* 1549. Reprinted Geneva: Slatkine Reprints, 1972.

Dumont, Jonathan. *Lilia Florent: L'imaginaire politique et social à la cour de France durant les premières guerres d'Italie (1494–1525).* Paris: Champion, 2013.

Dursteler, Eric. *Venetians in Constantinople: Nation, Identity, and Coexistence in the Early Modern Mediterranean.* Baltimore: Johns Hopkins University Press, 2006.

———. "On Bazaars and Battlefields: Recent Scholarship on Mediterranean Cultural Contacts." *Journal of Early Modern History* 15, no. 5 (2011): 413–34.

Engels, J. "Notice sur Jean Thenaud." *Vivarium* 8 (1970): 99–122.

Favret, René. "Il y a cinq cents ans, la dernière croisade ou Panurge à Metelin." *Bulletin des Amis de Rabelais et de la Devinière* 5, no. 10 (2001): 663–79.

Febvre, Lucien. *Le problème de l'incroyance au XVIᵉ siècle: La religion de Rabelais.* Paris: Albin Michel, 1968.

Fenoglio-Abd El Aal, Irène, and Marie-Claude Burgat, eds. *D'un Orient l'autre: Les métamorphoses successives des perceptions et connaissances.* Vol. 1. Paris: Centre national de la recherche scientifique, 1991.

Fleischer, Cornell. "The Lawgiver as Messiah: The Making of the Imperial Image in the Reign of Süleymân." In Veinstein, *Soliman le Magnifique et son temps,* 160–74.

———. "Shadows of Shadows: Prophecy in Politics in 1530s Istanbul." *International Journal of Turkish Studies* 13 (2007): 51–62.

Frame, Donald. *The Complete Works of François Rabelais.* Berkeley: University of California Press, 1991.

La France-Turquie, C'est à dire, conseils et moyens tenus par les ennemis de la Couronne de France, pour reduire le royaume en tel estat que la Tyrãnie Turquesque. Orléans: Thibault des Murs, 1575.

Frigo, Daniela. "Prudence and Experience: Ambassadors and Political Culture in Early Modern Italy." *The Journal of Medieval and Early Modern Studies* 38, no. 1 (2008): 15–34.

Frisch, Andrea. *The Invention of the Eyewitness: Witnessing and Testimony in Early Modern France.* Chapel Hill: University of North Carolina Press, 2004.

Gaches, Jacques. *Mémoires de Jacques Gaches sur les guerres de religion à Castres et dans le Languedoc (1555–1610).* Edited by Charles Pradel. Geneva: Slatkine Reprints, 1970.

Garnier, Édith. *L'alliance impie: François Ier et Soliman le Magnifique contre Charles Quint (1529–1547).* Paris: Le Félin, 2008.

Garnier, François, ed. *Thesaurus iconographique.* Paris: Le léopard d'or, 1984.

Gaspard, Françoise, and Farhad Khosrokhavar. "The Headscarf and the Republic." In *Beyond French Feminisms: Debates on Women, Politics, and Culture in France, 1981–2001,* edited by Roger Célestin, Eliane DalMolin, and Isabelle de Courtivron, 61–68. New York: Palgrave Macmillan, 2003.

Geisberg, Max. *The German Single-Leaf Woodcut, 1500–1550.* Revised and edited by Walter L. Strauss. 4 vols. New York: Hacker Art Books, 1974.

Genette, Gérard. *Seuils.* Paris: Seuil, 1987.

Gilles, Pierre. *Petri Gyllii de Bosporo Thracio libri III.* Lyon: Guillaume Rouillé, 1561.

Glidden, Hope. "Digression, diversion, et allusion dans l'œuvre de Rabelais." *Revue des Amis de Ronsard* 12 (1999): 83–96.

Göçek, Fatma Müge. *East Encounters West: France and the Ottoman Empire in the Eighteenth Century.* New York: Oxford University Press, 1987.

Gould, Kevin. *Catholic Activism in South-West France, 1540–1570.* Aldershot, UK: Ashgate, 2006.

Greenblatt, Stephen. *Renaissance Self-Fashioning: From More to Shakespeare.* Chicago: University of Chicago Press, 1980.

Greene, Molly. *A Shared World: Christians and Muslims in the Early Modern Mediter-ranean*. Princeton, NJ: Princeton University Press, 2000.

Green-Mercado, Marya. "The Mahdī in Valencia: Messianism, Apocalypticism, and Morisco Rebellions in Late Sixteenth-Century Spain." *Medieval Encounters* 19 (2013): 193–220.

Grosrichard, Alain. *Structure du Sérail*. Paris: Seuil, 1979.

Gruzinski, Serge. *Quelle heure est-il là-bas? Amérique et islam à l'orée des temps mod-ernes*. Paris: Seuil, 2008.

Guérin-Dalle Mese, Jeannine. *Égypte, la mémoire et le rêve: Itinéraires d'un voyage, 1320–1601*. Florence: Olschki, 1991.

La haine, directed by Mathieu Kassovitz (1995; Paris: Studio Canal+, 1996), VHS.

Hale, John. *The Civilization of Europe in the Renaissance*. New York: Atheneum, 1994.

Hampton, Timothy. *Fictions of Embassy: Literature and Diplomacy in Early Modern Europe*. Ithaca, NY: Cornell University Press, 2009.

———. *Literature and Nation in the Sixteenth Century*. Ithaca, NY: Cornell University Press, 2001.

———. " 'Turkish Dogs': Rabelais, Erasmus, and the Rhetoric of Alterity." *Representa-tions* 41 (1993): 58–82.

Harle, Vihlo. "On the Concept of the 'Other' and the 'Enemy.'" *History of European Ideas* 19 (1994): 27–44.

Harper, James G., ed. *The Turk and Islam in the Western Eye, 1450–1750: Visual Imagery before Orientalism*. Farnham, UK: Ashgate, 2011.

Harris, Steven J. "Mapping Jesuit Science: The Role of Travel in the Geography of Knowledge." In *The Jesuits: Cultures, Sciences, and the Arts, 1540–1773*, edited by John W. O'Malley, Gauvain Alexander Bailey, Steven J. Harris, and T. Frank Kenney, 212–40. Toronto: University of Toronto Press, 1999.

Hartog, François. *Le miroir d'Hérodote: Essai sur la représentation de l'autre*. Paris: Gallimard, 1980.

Heath, Michael J. *Crusading Commonplaces: La Noue, Lucinge and Rhetoric against the Turks*. Geneva: Droz, 1986.

———. "Unholy Alliances: Valois and Ottomans." *Renaissance Studies* 3, no. 3 (1989): 303–15.

Heitsch, Dorothea. "Death, Resurrection, and the Anatomy of Epistemon in François Rab-elais's *Pantagruel*." Paper, annual meeting of the Modern Language Association, Seat-tle, Jan. 6–8, 2012.

Héroet, Antoine. *Opuscules d'amour*. Lyon: Jean de Tournes, 1547.

Hitzel, Frédérick. "Turcs et turqueries à la cour de Catherine de Médicis." In Dakhlia and Vincent, *Les musulmans dans l'histoire de l'Europe*, 1:33–54.

Höfert, Almut. " 'Europe' and 'Religion' in the Framework of Sixteenth-Century Relations between Christian Powers and the Ottoman Empire." In *Reflections on Europe: Defining a Political Order in Time and Space*, eds. Hans-Ake Persson and Bo Strath (Brussels: P.I.E. Peter Lang, 2007) 211–30.

———. "The Order of Things and the Discourse of the Turkish Threat: The Conceptual-ization of Islam in the Rise of Occidental Anthropology in the Fifteenth and Sixteenth Centuries." In *Between Europe and Islam: Shaping Modernity in a Transcultural Space*, ed. Almut Höfert and Armando Salvatore (Brussels: P.I.E. Peter Lang, 2000): 39–69

Holban, Marie. "Autour de Jean Thenaud et de Frère Jean des Entonneurs." *Études Rab-elaisiennes* 9 (1971): 49–65.

Horden, Peregrine, and Nicholas Purcell. *The Corrupting Sea: A Study of Mediterranean History*. Oxford: Blackwell, 2000.

Housley, Norman. "A Necessary Evil? Erasmus, the Crusade, and War against the Turks." In *Crusading and Warfare in Medieval and Renaissance Europe*, 259–79. Burlington, VT: Ashgate, 2001.

———, ed. *Crusading in the Fifteenth Century: Message and Impact*. Basingstoke: Palgrave Macmillan, 2004.

Howard, Deborah. *Venice and the East: The Impact of the Islamic World on Venetian Architecture, 1100–1500*. New Haven, CT: Yale University Press, 2000.

Hozier, Louis-Pierre d', and Antoine-Marie d'Hozier de Sérigny. *Armorial général des registres de la noblesse de France*. Edited by Édouard de Barthélemy. Paris: E. Dentu, 1867.

Huguet, Edmond. *Dictionnaire de la langue française du seizième siècle*. 7 vols. Paris: Champion, 1925–73.

Huntington, Samuel. "The Clash of Civilization?" *Foreign Affairs* 72, no. 3 (1993): 22–49.

Inalcık, Halil, and Cemal Kafadar, eds. *Süleyman the Second and His Time*. Istanbul: Isis Press, 1993.

Isom-Verhaaren, Christine. *Allies with the Infidel: The Ottoman and French Alliance in the Sixteenth Century*. New York: I. B. Tauris, 2011.

———. "'Barbarossa and His Army Who Came to Succor All of Us': Ottoman and French Views of Their Joint Campaign of 1543–1544." *French Historical Studies* 30, no. 3 (2007): 395–425.

Izarny-Gargas, Louis d', ed., *Armorial de France: Généralité de Toulouse*. Paris: Sedopols, 1987.

Jardine, Lisa. *Worldly Goods: A New History of the Renaissance*. New York: Nan A. Talese, 1996.

Jodogne, Pierre. *Jean Lemaire de Belges, écrivain franco-bourguignon*. Bruxelles: Palais des Académies, 1972.

Jones-Davies, M. T., ed. *L'étranger: Identité et altérité au temps de la Renaissance*. Paris: Klincksieck, 1996.

Jouanna, Arlette. *La France du XVIe siècle, 1483–1598*. Paris: Presses universitaires de France, 1996.

Juall, Scott. "'Beaucoup plus barbares que les Sauvages mesmes': Cannibalism, Savagery, and Religious Alterity in Jean de Léry's *Histoire d'un voyage fait en la terre du Brésil* (1599–1600)." *L'Esprit Créateur* 48, no. 1 (2008): 58–71.

———. "Early Modern Franco-Ottoman Relations: Utopian Mapping of Imperialist Encounters in François Rabelais's *Pantagruel*." *Études Rabelaisiennes* 44, no. 417 (2006), 79–110.

Keller, Marcus. "Nicolas de Nicolay's *Navigations* and the Domestic Politics of Travel Writing." *L'Esprit Créateur* 48, no. 1 (2008): 18–31.

———, ed. "The Turk of Early Modern France." Special issue, *L'Esprit Créateur* 53, no. 4 (2013).

Kilgour, Maggie. *From Communion to Cannibalism: An Anatomy of Metaphors of Incorporation*. Princeton, NJ: Princeton University Press, 1990.

Knecht, R. J. *Renaissance Warrior and Patron: The Reign of Francis I*. Cambridge: Cambridge University Press, 1994.

La Borderie, Bertrand de. *L'amie de court*. 1542. Edited by Danielle Trudeau. Paris: Champion, 1997.

———. *Le discours du voyage de constantinoble*. 1542. Edited by Danielle Trudeau. Paris: Champion, 2003.

La Broquère, Bertrandon de. *Le voyage d'Orient*. Edited by Hélène Basso and Jacques Paviot. Toulouse: Anacharsis, 2010.

Lalanne, Ludovic, ed. *Journal d'un bourgeois de Paris sous le règne de François Premier (1515–1536)*. Paris: Renouard, 1854. Reprinted New York: Johnson, 1965.

La Roncière, Charles de. *Histoire de la marine française*. Paris: Plon, 1906.

Laurence, Jonathan, and Justin Vaïsse. *Integrating Islam: Political and Religious Challenges in Contemporary France*. Washington, DC: Brookings Institution Press, 2006.

La Vigne, André de. *La ressource de la chrestienté*. Edited by Cynthia J. Brown. Montreal: CERES, 1989.

Le Barre, Pasquier de. *Le journal d'un bourgeois de Tournai: Le second livre des chroniques de Pasquier de le Barre (1500–1565)*. Edited by Gérard Moreau. Bruxelles: Palais des Académies, 1975.

Lecoq, Anne-Marie. *François Ier imaginaire*. Paris: Macula, 1987.

Le Cornec, Cécile. "Les vertus diététiques attribuées aux poissons de mer." In *Mondes marins du Moyen-Âge: Actes du 30e Colloque du CUER MA, 3, 4 et 5 mars 2005*, edited by Chantal Connochie-Bourgne, 273–83. Aix-en-Provence: Université de Provence, 2006.

Lemaire de Belges, Jean. *La Concorde des deux langages*. 1508. Edited by Jean Frappier. Paris: Droz, 1947.

———. *La Concorde du genre humain*. 1509. Edited by Pierre Jodogne. Brussels: Palais des Académies, 1964.

———. *Traicté de la différence des schismes et des conciles de l'Église*. 1511. Edited by Jennifer Britnell. Geneva: Droz, 1997.

Lestringant, Frank. *Cannibals: The Discovery and Representation of the Cannibal from Columbus to Jules Verne*. Translated by Rosemary Morris. Berkeley: University of California Press, 1997.

———. *Écrire le monde à la Renaissance*. Caen: Paradigme, 1993.

———. "La monarchie française au miroir ottoman: Le portrait de Soliman le Magnifique, de Charles XII à Henri III." In Veinstein, *Soliman le Magnifique et son temps*, 51–68.

Livingston, Charles. "Un disciple de Clément Marot: Bertrand de La Borderie." *Revue du Seizième Siècle* 16 (1929): 219–82.

Loicq-Berger, Marie-Paule. "Un 'Liégeois' au siège de Rhodes de 1522." *Revue Belge de Philologie et d'Histoire* 67, no. 4 (1989): 714–47.

———. "'L'Oppugnation de Rhodes' de Jacques de Bourbon: Un texte à découvrir." *Revue Belge de Philologie et d'Histoire* 69, no. 4 (1991): 905–24.

Longino, Michèle. "Imagining the Turk in Seventeenth-Century France: Grelot's Version." Working paper. http://www.duke.edu/~michelel/projects/visions/2.html.

———. *Orientalism in French Classical Drama*. Cambridge: Cambridge University Press, 2002.

Lusy, Antoine de. *Le journal d'un bourgeois de Mons, 1505–1536*. Edited by Armand Louant. Bruxelles: Palais des Académies, 1969.

Luttrell, Anthony. *The Hospitallers in Cyprus, Rhodes, Greece, and the West, 1291–1440*. London: Variorum Reprints, 1978.

———. *The Hospitallers of Rhodes and their Mediterranean World*. Burlington, VT: Ashgate, 1992.

MacLean, Gerald, ed. *Re-Orienting the Renaissance: Cultural Exchanges with the East*. Basingstoke: Palgrave Macmillan, 2005.

Majid, Anouar. *We Are All Moors: Ending Centuries of Crusades against Muslims and Other Minorities*. Minneapolis: University of Minnesota Press, 2009.

Malcolm, Noel. "Positive Views of Islam and of Ottoman Rule in the Sixteenth Century: The Case of Jean Bodin," in Contadini and Norton, *The Renaissance and the Ottoman World*, 197–217.

Mantran, Robert. *Histoire de l'empire ottoman*. Paris: Fayard, 1989.

La marche, directed by Nabil Ben Yadir (2013; Paris: Fox Pathé Europa, 2014), DVD.

Martel, Marie-Thérèse de. "La mission de Jean Yversen à la Porte du Grand Seigneur," *Revue d'Histoire Diplomatique* 12 (1983): 5–53.

Matar, Nabil. *Britain and Barbary, 1589–1689*. Gainesville: University Press of Florida, 2005.

———. *Islam in Britain, 1558–1685*. Cambridge: Cambridge University Press, 1998.

———. *Turks, Moors, and Englishmen in the Age of Discovery*. New York: Columbia University Press, 1999.

Mattingly, Garrett. *Renaissance Diplomacy*. London: Butler and Tanner, 1955.

McKinley, Mary. "An Ottoman 'Fixer' in Marguerite de Navarre's *Heptaméron*." *L'Esprit Créateur* 53, no. 4 (2013): 9–20.

Melzer. Sara E. *Colonizer or Colonized: The Hidden Stories of Early Modern French Culture*. Philadelphia: University of Pennsylvania Press, 2012.

Meserve, Margaret. *Empires of Islam in Renaissance Historical Thought*. Cambridge, MA: Harvard University Press, 2008.

Mignolo, Walter. *The Darker Side of the Renaissance: Literacy, Territoriality, and Colonization*. Ann Arbor: University of Michigan Press, 1995.

Molinet, Jean. *Les faictz et dictz de Jean Molinet*. 3 vols. Edited by Noël Dupire. Paris: Société des anciens textes français, 1936–1939.

Montaigne, Michel de. *Les essais*. 1580. Edited by Pierre Villey. 3 vols. 2nd ed. Paris: Presses universitaires de France, 1992.

Monter, William. *Judging the French Reformation: Heresy Trials by Sixteenth-Century Parlements*. Cambridge, MA: Harvard University Press, 1999.

Moore, R. I. *The Formation of a Persecuting Society: Authority and Deviance in Western Europe, 950–1250*. Oxford: Blackwell, 1987.

Muchembled, Robert. *Une histoire de la violence: De la fin du Moyen-Âge à nos jours*. Paris: Seuil, 2008.

Navarre, Marguerite de. *Heptaméron*. 1558. Edited by Renja Salminen. Geneva: Droz: 1999.

Necipoğlu, Gülru. *The Age of Sinan: Architectural Culture in the Ottoman Empire*. Princeton, NJ: Princeton University Press, 2005.

———. *Architecture, Ceremonial, and Power: The Topkapi Palace in the Fifteenth and Sixteenth Centuries*. Cambridge, MA: MIT Press, 1991.

———. "The Life of an Imperial Monument: Hagia Sophia after Byzantium." In *Hagia Sophia from the Age of Justinian to the Present*, edited by Robert Mark and A. S. Cakmak, 195–225. Cambridge: Cambridge University Press, 1992.

Nègre, Ernest. *Les troubles à Gaillac*. Toulouse: Collège d'Occitanie, 1976.

Nicolay, Nicolas de. *Les navigations, pérégrinations et voyages faicts en la Turquie*. 1576. Edited by Marie-Christine Gomez-Géraud and Stéphane Yérasimos with the title *Dans l'empire de Soliman le Magnifique*. Paris: Presses du Centre national de la recherche scientifique, 1989.

Nostradamus. *Prophéties*. Lyon: Macé Bonhomme, 1555.

Patrides, C. A. " 'The Bloody and Cruell Turke': The Background of a Renaissance Commonplace." *Studies in the Renaissance* 10 (1963): 126–35.

Pascal, Blaise. *Pensées*. 1670. Edited by Michel Autrand. Paris: Bordas, 1965.

Pastoureau, Michel. *Black: The History of a Color*. Translated by Jody Gladding. Princeton: Princeton University Press, 2009.

Paviot, Jacques. "D'un ennemi l'autre: Des Mamelouks aux Ottomans. Voyages de renseignement au Levant, XIIIe–XVIIe siècles." In Fenoglio-Abd El Aal and Burgat, *D'un Orient l'autre*, 317–28.

Petiet, Claude. *Des Chevaliers de Rhodes aux Chevaliers de Malte: Villiers de l'Isle-Adam*. Paris: France-Empire, 1994.

Pippidi, Andrei. *Visions of the Ottoman World in Renaissance Europe*. New York: Columbia University Press, 2013.

Postel, Claude. *La France-Turquie: La Turquie vue de France au XVIe siècle*. Paris: Les Belles lettres, 2013.

Postel, Guillaume. *De la Republique des Turcs*. Poitiers: Enquibert de Marneff, 1560.

Poumarède, Géraud. *Pour en finir avec la Croisade*. Paris: Presses universitaires de France, 2004.

Rabelais, François. *Œuvres complètes*. Edited by Mireille Huchon. Paris: Gallimard, 1994.

Randall, Michael. *The Gargantuan Polity: On the Individual and the Community in the French Renaissance*. Toronto: University of Toronto Press, 2008.

Reeves, Hubert. "Cosmos et créativité." Lecture, École des mines, Albi, December 1, 2010.

Riley-Smith, Jonathan. *The Crusades: A Short History*. New Haven, CT: Yale University Press, 1987.

———. *The Knights of Saint John in Jerusalem and Cyprus*. London: Macmillan, 1967.

Rossignol, Elie. *Monographies communales: Gaillac*. Toulouse: Delboy, 1864.

Rouillard, Clarence. *The Turk in French History, Thought, and Literature (1520–1660)*. New York: AMS Press, 1973.

Said, Edward. *Orientalism*. New York: Vintage Books, 1978.

Schweitz, Arlette. *La maison tourangelle au quotidien: Façons de bâtir, manières de vivre (1850–1930)*. Paris: Publications de la Sorbonne, 1997.

Screech, Michael. *Rabelais*. Ithaca, NY: Cornell University Press, 1979.

Seguin, Jean-Pierre. *L'information en France avant le périodique, 517 canards imprimés entre 1529 et 1631*. Paris: Maisonneuve et Larose, 1964.

Silver, Larry. "East is East: Images of the Turkish Nemesis in the Habsburg World." In *The Turk and Islam in the Western Eye, 1450–1750: Visual Imagery before Orientalism*, edited by James G. Harper, 185–211. Farnham, UK: Ashgate, 2011.

Sire, H. J. A. *The Knights of Malta*. New Haven: Yale University Press, 1994.

Subrahmanyam, Sanjay. "Connected Histories: Notes towards a Reconfiguration of Early Modern Eurasia," *Modern Asian History* 31, no. 3 (1997): 735–62.

———. *Courtly Encounters: Translating Courtliness and Violence in Early Modern Eurasia*. Cambridge, MA: Harvard University Press, 2012.

———. "Par-delà l'incommensurabilité: Pour une histoire connectée des empires aux temps modernes." *Revue d'Histoire Moderne et Contemporaine* 54, no. 5 (2007): 34–53.

Tarte, Kendall. *Writing Places: Sixteenth-Century City Culture and the Des Roches Salon*. Newark: University of Delaware Press, 2007.

Tezcan, Baki. *The Second Empire: Political and Social Transformation in the Early Modern World*. New York: Cambridge University Press, 2010.

Thenaud, Jean. *Le triumphe des vertuz. Premier traité: Le triumphe de prudence*. Edited by Titia J. Schuurs-Janssen. Geneva: Droz, 1997.

———. *Le voyage d'Outremer*. 1884. Edited by Charles Schefer. Geneva: Slatkine Reprints, 1971.

Thevet, André. *Cosmographie de Levant.* Lyon: Jean de Tournes et Guillaume Gazeau, 1554.

———. *Les vrais pourtraits et vies des hommes illustres* (1584). Edited by Rouben Charles Cholakian. Delmar, NY: Scholars' Facsimiles and Reprints, 1973. Delmar, NY: Scholars' Facsimiles and Reprints, 1973.

Tinguely, Frédéric. "L'*alter sensus* des turqueries de Panurge." *Études Rabelaisiennes* 42 (2003): 57–73.

———. *L'écriture du Levant à la Renaissance: Enquête sur les voyageurs français dans l'empire de Soliman le Magnifique.* Geneva: Droz, 2000.

———. "Janus en Terre Sainte: La figure du pèlerin curieux à la Renaissance." *Revue des Sciences Humaines* 245 (1997): 51–65.

———. "Une tradition réorientée: Pèlerinage et gallicanisme chez Jean Thenaud." *Versants* 38 (2000): 91–102.

———. *Le voyageur aux mille tours: Les ruses de l'écriture du monde à la Renaissance.* Paris: Champion, 2014.

Todorov, Tzvetan. *Les morales de l'histoire.* Paris: Grasset, 1991.

———. *La conquête de l'Amérique: La question de l'autre.* Paris: Seuil, 1982.

———. *Nous et les autres.* Paris: Seuil, 1989.

Tomasik, Timothy. "The World in Pantagruel's Mouth: Alimentary Aesthetics and Culinary Consciousness." In *Approaches to Teaching the Works of François Rabelais,* edited by Todd W. Reeser and Floyd Gray, 159–64. New York: The Modern Language Association of America, 2011.

Toumayan, Alain. "The Iconology and Iconography of Paris in Pierre de Grognet's 'Blason de la noble ville et cité de Paris.'" *Romanic Review* 80, no. 4 (1989): 512–20.

Ursu, J. *La politique orientale de François Ier (1515–1547).* Paris: Champion, 1908.

Usher, Phillip. *Errance et cohérence: Essai sur la littérature transfrontalière.* Paris: Classiques Garnier, 2010.

———. "Walking East in the Renaissance." In *French Global: A New Approach to Literary History,* edited by Christy McDonald and Susan Rubin Suleiman, 193–206. New York: Columbia University Press, 2010.

Valbelle, Honorat de. *Histoire journalière d'Honorat de Valbelle (1489–1539): Journal d'un bourgeois de Marseille au temps de Louis XII et de François Ier.* Edited by Victor-Louis Bourrilly and translated by Lucien Gaillard. 2 vols. Marseille: Lafitte, 1985.

Valensi, Lucette. "The Making of a Political Paradigm: The Ottoman State and Oriental Despotism." In *The Transmission of Culture in Early Modern Europe,* edited by Anthony Grafton and Ann Blair, 173–203. Philadelphia: University of Pennsylvania Press, 1990.

———. *Venise et la Sublime Porte.* Paris: Hachette, 1987.

Vatin, Nicolas. "La conquête de Rhodes." In Veinstein, *Soliman le Magnifique et son temps,* 435–54.

———. *L'Ordre de Saint-Jean-de-Jérusalem, l'empire ottoman et la Méditerranée orientale entre les deux sièges de Rhodes (1480–1522).* Paris: Peeters, 1994.

———. *Sultan Djem.* Ankara: Türk Tarih Kurumu Basimevi, 1997.

———and Gilles Veinstein, eds. *Insularités ottomanes.* Paris: Maisonneuve et Larose, 2004.

Veinstein, Gilles, ed. *Soliman le Magnifique et son temps: Actes du Colloque de Paris, galeries nationales du Grand Palais, 7–10 mars 1990.* Paris: Documentation française, 1992.

Verdon, Jean. *Information et désinformation au Moyen-Âge.* Paris: Perrin, 2010.

Vertot, abbé de. *Histoire des chevaliers hospitaliers de S. Jean de Jerusalem: Appelles depuis chevaliers de Rhodes, et aujourd'hui chevaliers de Malte.* Vol. 2. Paris: Rollin, Quillau père et fils, Desaint, 1726.

Vic, Cl. de, and J. Vaissete. *Histoire générale de Languedoc.* Vol. 11. Toulouse: Privat, 1889.

Vin, J.P.A. van der. *Travellers to Greece and Constantinople: Ancient Monuments and Old Traditions in Medieval Travellers' Tales.* 2 vols. Leiden: Nederlands Historisch-Archaelogisch Instituut te Istanbul 1980.

Virilio, Paul. *Le grand accélérateur.* Paris: Galilée, 2010.

Werner, Michael, and Bénédicte Zimmermann. "Penser l'histoire croisée: Entre empirie et réflexivité." *Annales. Histoire, Sciences Sociales* 58, no. 1 (2003): 7–36.

Williams, Wes. *Pilgrimage and Narrative in the French Renaissance.* Oxford: Clarendon, 1998.

Wittek, Paul. *The Rise of the Ottoman Empire.* London: The Royal Asiatic Society, 1938.

Wolfzettel, Friedrich. *Le discours du voyageur: Pour une histoire littéraire du récit de voyage en France, du Moyen-Âge au XVIIIe siècle.* Paris: Presses universitaires de France, 1995.

Wunder, Amanda. "Western Travelers, Eastern Antiquities, and the Image of the Turk in Early Modern Europe." *Journal of Early Modern History* 7, no. 1–2 (2003): 89–119.

Yérasimos, Stéphane. "Le turc en Occident: La connaissance de la langue turque en Europe (XVe–XVIIe siècles)." In *L'inscription des langues dans les relations de voyage (XVIe–XVIIIe siècles): Actes du Colloque de Décembre 1988*, edited by Michèle Duchet, 191–210. Fontenay-aux-Roses: Ecole Normale Supérieure Fontenay-Saint-Cloud, 1992.

———. "Les voyageurs du XVIe siècle en Égypte ottomane (1517–1600): Essai de typologie." In Fenoglio-Abd El Aal and Burgat, *D'un Orient l'autre*, 301–15.

Index

Note: Italicized page numbers indicate a figure on the corresponding page.